Dilemmas *of* Adulthood

Dilemmas *of* Adulthood

Japanese Women and the Nuances of Long-Term Resistance

NANCY ROSENBERGER

University of Hawai'i Press
Honolulu

Printed in the United States of America

18 17 16 15 14 13 6 5 4 3 2 1

Library of Congress Cataloging-in-Publication Data
Rosenberger, Nancy Ross, author.
Dilemmas of adulthood : Japanese women and the nuances of long-term resistance / Nancy Rosenberger.
pages cm
Includes bibliographical references and index.
ISBN 978-0-8248-3696-2 (cloth : alk. paper)—ISBN 978-0-8248-3887-4 (pbk. : alk. paper)
1. Women—Japan—Longitudinal studies. 2. Self-perception in women—Japan—Longitudinal studies. I. Title.
HQ1762.R677 2014
305.40952—dc23

2013012436

University of Hawai'i Press books are printed on acid-free paper and meet the guidelines for permanence and durability of the Council on Library Resources.

Designed by Publishers' Design and Production Services, Inc.

Printed by Sheridan Books, Inc.

To my parents,
Betsey and Russell Rosenberger

Contents

Acknowledgments

Inexpressible thanks go to the Japanese women who have continued to open their hearts and minds to me and have made this book possible. I am also very grateful to the people in Japan who support me beyond the call of duty in my work there; I value their friendships and insights: Ogawaguchi Teruyo, Takagi Mizue, Ota Sachiko, and Sarukawa Shinichi.

I extend my appreciation to the Japan Foundation, the Northeast Asia Council of the Association of Asian Studies, and Oregon State University's Humanities Center, Department of Anthropology, and School of Language, Culture, and Society for supplying the money and time to accomplish this endeavor. Thanks to my colleagues in anthropology for their support and to my editor at the University of Hawai'i Press, Pat Crosby, whose flexibility and patience I appreciate.

I am grateful to my children, Elise, Ted, and Laura, who always give me ideas to chew on and helped me with the title for this book. Perhaps they realize that because of my experience with these Japanese women I understand the paths of my children as emerging adults a bit better. Last, I am forever indebted to my husband, Clint Morrison, for his affection over forty years and his good-humored endurance and support of my academic pursuits.

MAJOR CHARACTERS

Chapter number	*Age in 1993*	*Age in 1994*	*Education*	*Occupation Single/ Married*	*Childhood residency*	*Singlehood residency*	*Residency in 2004*	*Father's occupation*	*Marriage age*	*Age at first child*	*Number of children*	*Husband's occupation*	*Living with parents or in-laws*
CHAPTER 2													
Ito-san	29	40	4-yr. university	Translation agency	Regions	Regions	Tokyo	Salaryman	Single in 2004				
Kawai-san	26	37	HS graduate	Retirement home	Morioka	Morioka	Morioka	Construction	Single in 2004				
CHAPTER 3													
Successful Singles													
Baba-san	34	45	4-yr. university	Translator/ interpreter	Tokyo	Tokyo	Tokyo	Salaryman	Single in 2004				
Sato-san	37	48	4-yr. university	Advertising agent/business owner	Morioka	Morioka	Morioka	Doctor (deceased)	Single in 2004				Lives with mother part-time
Struggling Singles													
Nishikawa-san	31	42	4-yr. teaching university	Teacher	Morioka	Morioka	Morioka	Salaryman	Single in 2004				
Shimizu-san	31	42	4-yr. teaching university	Teacher	Tokyo	Tokyo	Tokyo	Salaryman	Single in 2004				Living with parents

Struggling, Crashing Singles													
Shiga-san	32	43	Masters	Nurse	Regional city		Tokyo	Salaryman	Single in 2004				
Nakajima-san	31	42	4-yr. university	Medical technician	Morioka	Morioka	Morioka	Doctor (deceased)	Single in 2004				Lives with mother
Negishi-san	31	42	Jr. college	Actress/ Secretary/ Kindergarten teacher	Regional city	Tokyo	Regional city	Government worker	Single in 2004				
Hasegawa-san	**32**	43	Jr. college	Piano teacher	Village	Village	Village	Farmer	Single in 2004				Lives with parents
Horikawa-san	33	44	Nursing school	Nurse (quit)	Village	Morioka	Morioka	Poet	Single in 2004				
CHAPTER 4													
Spoiled Husbands													
Yamamura-san	32	43	Jr. college	Single secretary/ married housewife	Tokyo	Tokyo	Osaka	Salaryman	35	No kids		Salesman	
Kato-san	25	36	Jr. college	Single dorm mother, print techni-cian/Married part-time acctg.	Regional city	Morioka	Tokyo	Salaryman	35	No kids		Government worker	

MAJOR CHARACTERS, *continued*

Chapter number	*Age in 1993*	*Age in 1994*	*Education*	*Occupation Single/ Married*	*Childhood residency*	*Singlehood residency*	*Residency in 2004*	*Father's occupation*	*Marriage age*	*Age at first child*	*Number of children*	*Husband's occupation*	*Living with parents or in-laws*
Kojima-san	32	43	HS graduate	Telephone operator	Morioka	Morioka	Tokyo	Salaryman	35	No kids		Government worker	
Romantics							*Morioka*	*Salaryman*	*33*	*No kids*		*Salesman*	
Sugimura-san	32	43	4-yr. pharmacy university	Pharmacist	Village	Morioka							
Kurokawa-san	32	43	HS graduate	Telephone operator	Morioka		Village	Shop owner	37	No kids		Shop worker	
DINKS							*Village*	*Construction worker*	*41*			*Salesman*	*Lives in village with parents*
Yanagi-san	24	35	Masters	Think-tank researcher	Tokyo	Tokyo	Tokyo	Salaryman	31	No kids		Salaryman	
CHAPTER 5													
Planners													
Minami-san	33	44	4-yr. university	Translator coordinator	Regional city	Tokyo	Regional city	Salaryman	35	36	1 son	Professor	
Akai-san	31	42	Jr. college	Secretary	Tokyo	Tokyo	Tokyo	Salaryman	33	34	1 daughter	Banker	Lives with in-laws

Cocooners													
Sasaki-san	29	40	Jr. college	Single librarian/ Married doesn't work	Morioka		Tokyo	Teacher	33	34	1 son	Government worker	
Oyama-san	29	40	4-yr teaching university	Single travel agent, teacher/ married not working	Morioka	Tokyo/ Morioka	Sendai	Salaryman	31	32	2 sons	Judge	
Mori-san	35	46	HS graduate	Single resort manager/ married not working	Village	Village	Sendai	Farmer	37	38	1 son	Sushi chef	
Caretakers													
Ishii-san	29	40	2-year Jr. college/ Vocational training	Single assistant apparel dept in private school/ Married not working	Tokyo	Tokyo	Tokyo	Salaryman	31	32	1 son 1 daughter	Policeman	Living with parents since 1997
Inoue-san	31	42	Jr. college	Single secretary/ Married not working	Tokyo	Tokyo	Tokyo	Salaryman	33	34	1 daughter	Banker	

Chapter number	*Age in 1993*	*Age in 1994*	*Education*	*Occupation Single/ Married*	*Childhood residency*	*Singlehood residency*	*Residency in 2004*	*Father's occupation*	*Marriage age*	*Age at first child*	*Number of children*	*Husband's occupation*	*Living with parents or in-laws*
CHAPTER 6													
Full-Time Working Mothers: Tokyo & Morioka													
Matsui-san	34	45	Jr. college		Tokyo	Tokyo	Tokyo	Salaryman	37	40	1 son	Banker	
Yamada-san	31	42	4-yr teaching university	Teacher	Village	Morioka	Morioka	Farmer	38	39	1 daughter	Computer Salesman	
Kawahara-san	34	45	4-yr university	Teacher	Regional city	Regional city	Village	Salaryman	38	42	1 son	Teacher	
Full-Time Working Mothers: The Village													
Shimura-san	20	31	HS graduate	Local government worker	Village	Village	Village	Government wkr/ Mother worked	22	27	1 son	Local government worker	
Kawaguchi-san	30	41	HS graduate	Retirement home	Village	Village	Village	Farmer	31	32	2 sons	Local government worker	
Takahashi-san	26	37	4-yr welfare university	Retirement home	Village	Village	Village	Farmer	27 (divorced/ remarried)	27	2 sons	Farmer	
Part-Timers: Family Workers													
Hashimoto-san	25	36		Family business				Salaryman	25		3 children	Farmer/ factory worker	
Uchimura-san	22	33	HS graduate	Family business	Morioka	Morioka	Tokyo	Family Business	Late 20s	30	1 son	Family business	

Nakamura-san	28	39	4-yr university	Single museum guide/ married Family business	Morioka	Morioka	Regional city	Doctor (deceased)	34	36	2 daughters	Dentist
Part-Timers: Artists												
Murai-san	25	36	Correspondence university	Single wedding planner/married Pianist	Morioka	Morioka	Morioka	Musician/ mother musician	26	31	1 daughter	Government worker
Takagi-san	29	40	4-yr university	Piano teacher	Tokyo	Tokyo	Tokyo	Salaryman	31	33	1 daughter	Salaryman
Nakata-san	24	35	4-yr university	Dance teacher	Morioka	Tokyo	Morioka	Salaryman	28	31	1 daughter	Banker
Organic Farmer												
Tsuchiya-san	26	37	4-yr university	Organic Farmer	Regions	Morioka	Village	Christian minister	28	29	2 daughters 1 son	Organic Farmer

CHAPTER ONE

What Is Long-Term Resistance?

A CULTURAL ANTHROPOLOGIST like me talks with many people, in this case over many years. Her main aim is to give voice to these people's stories and experiences through a process of listening closely and thinking about them in relation to almost everything else she reads and does. The final result is her tale of these stories, for in their retelling the anthropologist also recounts a tale of herself, of her encounter with these people, and of the meaning that she understands in these encounters. This is truer than ever in this globalized age when these Japanese women and I are influenced by similar ideas and goods. Yet the tale is precarious in the telling. Simultaneously, we all still live in our local histories, knowledge, and behaviors. When I, U.S.-born and -raised, enter wholeheartedly into living in Japan, I feel deeply the differences, even as the similarities increase.

My tale of these stories begins with my own expectations in 1993 when I first sought out these women to interview. I expressly hunted for women between the ages of twenty-five and thirty-five who were not yet married. I asked friends and coworkers whom I had first met in the 1970s when I taught English for two years in Tohoku (northeastern Japan). I requested introductions from people I had interviewed in the 1980s during my four years of dissertation work in Tokyo and Tohoku. I started with sixty women, half from Tokyo and half from Tohoku, the northern part of the main island of Japan—now famous for the earthquake and tsunami that took place there. The women from Tohoku lived in two places: Morioka, a regional city of almost 400,000, and ten from a small village about an hour away.

I was interested in them because they were "delaying marriage" past the then normative marriage age of twenty-five. Media and government greeted them with celebration as consumers, and the 1986 Equal Employment Opportunity Law (EEOL) promised women equality in the workplace. Yet both the government and the elder generation worried about their role as future reproducers of family and nation.

This group of women also caught my eye because they seemed to indicate a trend among Japanese women toward more self-determination. In the story of national statistics, increasing singles, falling marriage age, and a decreasing fertility rate implied that women were resisting the status quo. The government was quite concerned as singleness among women increased. While in 1975, only about 10% of women were single in their thirties, the number started to climb precipitously from 1980. By 1990, 40.4% of women aged twenty-five to twenty-nine and 13.9% of women thirty to thirty-four were single. By 2000, these numbers had increased to 54% and 26.6% (Shakai Jitsujo 2005). By 2005, 32% of women thirty to thirty-four and 18.4% of women thirty-five to thirty-nine were single, with 7.3% of women single at age fifty (Naikakucho 2008, 7). In 2010, the big change was in the older groups, with 23% of women thirty-five to thirty-nine single and 17% of women forty to forty-four single (and never married; Statistical Survey Department 2012).

Ages at marriage and childbirth rose. The mean age at first marriage for women increased from 24.2 in 1970, to 25.9 in 1990, and to 28.6 by 2009. The mean age of mothers at first childbirth also rose from 25.6 in 1970 to 29.7 in 2009—with 22.5 percent of those giving birth for the first time over age thirty-five (Statistical Handbook of Japan 2011).

The government was and is most upset by the plummeting fertility rate: from 2.13 in 1970 to 1.54 in 1990 and 1.37 in 2009 (Statistical Handbook of Japan 2011).[1] The nation's population is not reproducing itself, its economic labor pool shrinking.

In 1993 I began interviewing the women I met with open-ended questions and long conversations about their lives: family, work, friends, entertainment, loves, pressures, and dreams for the future. I took everything down, trying to listen not only for what I wanted to hear but also for their "pushback"—what they wanted to tell me (Rosaldo 1989). As anthropologists do, I formed relationships, using my own self, feelings, and form of interaction as part of the path to understand people in their surroundings.

On one hand their stereotypes of overly strong American women entered into our conversations. They were always surprised, or even shocked, that my husband was caring for my three children or that I left him at home to cook for himself. Some doubted my virtue, but most just marveled at how strong American women are to get away with this.

On the other hand I brought my own stereotyped suspicions that Japanese women were stronger in determining their own lives than they had been in the past. I had been raised on popular American mythologies that idealize change toward increasing individuality as progress, and I came of age among feminist ideas that women should determine their own fates and resist patriarchal norms if necessary. I carried with me an interest in individual action, resistance, and empowerment—ideas that appeal to American scholars because of our cultural insistence on individualism and democracy (Ortner 2006).

My prejudices became clear when I asked questions such as what they saw as the advantages and disadvantages of singlehood as well as the advantages and disadvantages of marriage, or whether they felt discriminated against at work. In anthropological parlance, I was looking for agency and resistance: "agency" understood as thoughts for one's own path and actions by one's own will in a cultural context (rather like the agency given to avatars in video games); and "resistance" understood as intentional beliefs and practices meant to change the status quo of the larger society.

The Japanese women in this study have had to interact with my underlying assumptions. All the more interesting, then, that ultimately my ideas did not work as I thought they would!

My research grew into a longitudinal study based on my personal situation: I was in the midst of years dense with teaching and raising three children. I could use my research time efficiently, building relationships over time rather than constructing new ones. Longitudinal studies are valuable but relatively rare in anthropology even though we often ask questions about change in people's lives.[2] Following people over time helps us to understand the process of change in individuals' lives and in the group of which they are a part. This study would enable me to track the process of change among these young women in the context of social change in Japan and show how people have fared in the 1990s and 2000s.

In 1998 and 2004 I contacted these women again and returned to interview them. If they had moved, I followed them south to Kyushu or north to Hokkaido, but lost a few: sixty in 1993, fifty-eight in 1998, and fifty-four in 2004. By 2004, twenty-three were living in Tokyo and thirty-one in regional Japan outside of large metropolitan areas. About half were single and half married by 1998. By 2004, approximately one-third were single and two-thirds were married. Five of the nineteen singles did not work; seven lived with parents, mostly mothers. Eight of the thirty-five married women did not have children and three of them did not work. The twenty-seven mothers were all married and were just about evenly divided between stay-at-home and working mothers. They are a highly educated group, and because of that doubly interesting for the questions about self-determination that I was asking. Of the fifty-four interviewees left in 2004, four had MAs, twenty-five had four-year university degrees, eighteen had vocational or junior college degrees, and eight had high school degrees.

Finding the interpretation that fits

In fashioning my tale, however, I became concerned. To what extent could I tell this story in terms of agency and resistance and still be fair to the stories these women were telling me? I spent most of 2007–2008 in Japan leading a group of Oregon study abroad students, teaching at Waseda, a private Tokyo university, and working on my book. During this time I met and talked with two budding anthropologists, both Japanese grad students; I call them Kana and Aya.[3] Both were in their early thirties—younger than the group I was studying by about ten years—but involved with analysis of Japanese people as I was.

I remember walking with them down a narrow street in search of the best Indian restaurant around Waseda as I told them of my search for a concept that would fairly represent the experiences of the women I was studying. When I mentioned agency and resistance, Kana did not listen long before explaining: "Those words are hard to translate into Japanese, especially agency. Words exist but they are awkward." Over Singha beers, we puzzled over the best Japanese words to use for "agency" and "resistance," words that they were familiar with from studying American anthropological texts. Finally Kana said softly: "I am sorry, *sensei* (teacher), but these words just don't fit my sense of Japanese women anyway. It doesn't fit the women I am studying."

Aya, given courage by her friend, who knew me better, echoed: "I think so too. They don't fit my feeling of what it is like to be a woman in Japan now. It's too hard to resist in Japan."

Kana followed up: "And agency? The individual, me . . . I am not strong enough to act clearly on my own without always thinking of social pressures." I filled their beer glasses once again to commend them for their courage in telling me what they really felt! We laughed, but my laugh was a bit more rueful than theirs: What was I going to do now if even these younger women in grad school felt this way?

Kana reminded me about an article that we had read in class. "Remember that woman anthropologist who said Americans have a romance with resistance?"

"Abu-Lughod?"

"Yeah. It's because Americans have all these ideals about how individualistic they are. They want to see individuals as strong and free. She said resistance tells us mostly about power.[4] Like you could say that I am resisting by getting a doctorate 'cause not many women have, but it is really hard for women to get jobs and sometimes professors ask women to do secretarial type of work that they wouldn't ask men to do."

"It's dangerous to be seen as a resister or even as having too much strong will in Japan. People will pull you down," said Aya.

I saw what she meant, but I was not ready to give up. Between bites of the fried samosas we had ordered, I tried to persuade them that agency and resistance could work to analyze these Japanese women. "Okay, but there are women anthropologists who have modified these ideas of agency and resistance. They realize that women aren't entirely free to choose, but they adapt the idea of agency. Like, Mahmood who works in Egypt. She works with Muslim women who are really modest—they cover all but their faces and even become second wives. But she claims they have agency because they cultivate themselves with great effort to have spiritual humility. They get together to study and interpret the Koran themselves, which women couldn't do before. She says that freedom from patriarchal systems is not necessarily the goal of agency all over the world."[5]

They both listened politely as they sipped their beer and ate samosas. I was the *sensei* after all. Kana tried to help me out.

"Remember, we read Ortner," said Kana. I noticed that both nodded their familiarity. "She sees how ambivalent agency can be. I love that story she tells about the Indian woman who after divorce sues in court for support from her husband—even though the Muslim law says she shouldn't. So that was amazing agency, even resistance. But then, when she gets the support from the court, she doesn't take it. I guess all her neighbors and men in the Muslim community were criticizing her and the tension must have been too much for her!"[6]

"So is that agency or not?" asked Aya.

"Ortner says it's agency but agency with a lot of ambivalence in it."

Aya sighed, "People are looking in two directions. That's all we have in Japan, I think. Like have you seen those teenagers who dress up and play in bands and dance in the park? On Sundays they totally flout the norms of Japanese life, but they live with their parents and do their part-time jobs on Monday."

"A lot of Japanese women like us are like that. They live at home while they work and their mothers cook and clean for them," said Kana. "I think a woman named Dales writes about it and she thinks they are kind of replacing their fathers as the main workers in the family, but also they are dependent on their mothers, who cook and clean for them. She said they have agency, but it is kind of limited agency."[7]

Aya responded. "I still live at home with my father. My mother lives elsewhere for her job, so I cook for my father sometimes. I don't know if I have agency. I don't feel like I do. Like my relatives still ask me when I am going to get married. It's conflicted if it is agency."

Kana ran with this. "And we want to get married, but we don't want to just marry anyone and now . . . We might be too educated! We scare men off! We can't afford to have too strong an identity or like what you might call agency. We have to fit in, especially over the long term. I could rebel once and go to the U.S. to study, but I can't keep rebelling or else I won't fit in with Japanese universities." Kana laughed her big laugh. We all shook our heads and chuckled with pained expressions on our faces, glad to see the waitress coming with the hot curry and rice to cheer us up.

The heat of the curry impressed itself upon us with a vengeance, and we felt the righteous anger of having been abandoned by the academic literature. What concepts should we use? We groaned and ordered another round of beers. Staring into the amber foam, I saw that I needed to refocus and try again.

"I think Japanese prefer to have more ambiguous identities. It's safer," suggested Kana. "Like kids when they study for university exams. They have to study so hard, but it is really tough. I remember from high school that some kids would go out and fool around with friends who invited them, but then their parents would haul them in to make them study. They were kind of glad that their parents came and got them cause they actually wanted to pass the exams, but they also wanted to show that they were cool."

"Yeah, the same holds true for these kids who are dancing out in Yoyogi Park on Sundays," followed Aya. "You should go see them. Some girls dress like boys and watch boys sing, and then afterwards you can see that they are romantically involved with each other. But they like the ambiguous gender identity that this gives them, I think."

"Hmm. Okay, I have to think about this." Chin on fist, I was looking disheartened, and they laughed. "Keep trying! There must be another way!" We were quiet for a bit. I had to admit that they were right. Agency implies individuals full of will and desire, aware of themselves, and able to follow through on their actions.[8] But what they were talking about was more like people just wanting to keep a space for ambiguity or difference apart from the mainstream in their lives. Agency seemed to imply movement against people dominating you, but that wasn't always possible or desired. Even the young people cross-dressing in the park were still dominated. And resistance carried the idea of changing the status quo, or at least trying to, which Kana and Aya didn't feel that they had the power to do at all. Yet looking at these women graduate students in front of me, I realized that over the long term this very ambiguous resistance they talked of was gradually changing things.

We left the Indian restaurant and went to their favorite late-night haunt, a tiny hole-in-the-wall off the street with bar and stools. Kana mused: "There are places where you can express yourself and places where you can't in Japan. Like here at this bar people often talk about what they are really thinking. We just have to have different ways of dealing with things. You want us to talk about our real feelings, but our professors want us to think like them and our parents don't want us to say anything shocking! We have to be a bit ambiguous!"

"Right, you shift," I replied. "I like the idea that these days people have different ways of belonging in different places, especially with the changes from globalization. Like in Sri Lanka, Gunewardena writes about young factory women who in the factory can't talk or even go to the bathroom, but outside in the city they use really rough men's language. Then they go home to the village and show off their jewelry from the city. The younger girls think they are models of success. They aren't fully conforming to things, but they aren't completely going against things either."[9]

"Different ways of belonging. That fits. So what do we call that?"

"Well, these different writers use words like tensions and ambivalence, conflicted, limited. I like the word you keep using too—ambiguous," I said.[10]

"Especially because you are interviewing these people over such a long period of time, they get pulled this way and that. So what if you did something with those ideas—ambiguity, tension, ambivalence?" Kana proposed.

Gazing at the bottles lined up behind the bar, I began to see my book taking on a new pattern.

"Let's see. What are some of the words that these women I have interviewed used? There's *mayotte iru* (feeling of being confused or lost)—like when a woman is confused as to whether to have arranged meetings with prospective men like her mother wants her to or to wait to meet some guy she feels a special connection with. Or they feel *fuan* (a feeling of discomfort and insecurity) like about whether this is the right job for them or not."

Kana and Aya joined in easily. "Oh yeah, how about *nayande iru* (worried)?" Aya groaned, "That's me! And *yureugoku* (shakily moving, not sure which way to go)—that's one we use a lot." I had heard them all in the interviews.

"I also hear people say they are *aimai na tokoro ni iru* (in an ambiguous place)," I added. "Also people use the phrase *nantonaku*—like I broke up with my boyfriend *nantonaku*. What's the best way to translate that?"

Kana said, "Maybe 'somehow' or 'for whatever reason.' It's really vague."

Aya giggled uncomfortably. "Oh, these are too real!" Okay, I must be hitting on something, I thought.

"*Komatte iru* (in a fix and not sure what to do)," I said. "I hear that and that's me right now!"

We sipped our drinks for a moment. I tried to reason it out. "All of these are about tension and ambivalence, like people are puzzled, pausing, uncertain which way to go. Maybe it's about seeing several paths all at once. What do you think? Could these be central concepts for a book about women who are struggling with some kind of vague long-term resistance in their lives?"

"Why not? Long-term resistance in Japan for women will take as much conformity as change. It's definitely ambiguous." Kana and Aya were both egging me on.

"You know Foucault?" I asked suddenly.

Both of them hid their faces in their hands at the mention of the French writer, so famous for his ideas on power and resistance, but so infamous for his difficult-to-read books that they had had to slog through. "Sorry to mention him!" They grudgingly listened to me.

"Well he says there are always points of resistance but they never go anywhere."

"They never really change the system 'cause they are within the system," parroted Kana. I gave her a thumbs-up.

"That feels like Japan!" said Aya.

"Okay, so these other anthropologists took a little footnote of Foucault's in which he says that even though resistance is ineffective it leaves its mark on people and their relationships. So over the long term, people who act out their will or challenge norms . . . kind of like you two . . ."

"Ha-ha, don't say it. That feels dangerous."

"They don't change the basic premises of society . . ."

"That's for sure!"

"But just by even a short experience of resistance, they get hammered into a different shape, and so do their relationships. So even if resistance is ambiguous and doesn't make big changes, it leaves its mark of tension on people. It cuts across individuals and fractures relationships, Foucault says."[11]

"Whah!" Kana pantomimed a sword cutting across her abdomen and down between her and Aya. "Yeah, that's sort of what it feels like to resist in Japan," she laughed. "That's heavy. I've drunk too much for that! But it's like 'cause I insisted on going to the U.S., I am hammered out differently and now I get along with Aya but don't have as much in common with my sister or mother as before. And that's cool but it is also a tension."

"Or I am not sure that I want to marry a Japanese man anymore," said Aya. "That's a tension for sure!!" We all laughed.

We left the bar and came out into the cool night air, which cleared my brain. "Here's my plan," I told them. "I have to give a talk to the other professors in the International Division at Waseda. I'll use these ideas of ambiguity and tension to think about the way these Japanese women are going about changing things in Japan. They don't show a strong, intentional agency or resistance, but over the long term it is a kind of slow resistance with lots of constraints. I'll call it long-term resistance and emphasize the ambivalence in it, and see how it goes." We all started to bow good night to each other, then laughed and hugged in a non-Japanese way. I walked to my apartment along the busy street and then into the quiet back streets of Tokyo. I felt exhilarated after our conversation, because there seemed to be a way out of my conceptual morass. I couldn't wait to get back to the stories of these women themselves and see if these new concepts made better sense of the data.

I went back to reading over the interviews in my little Tokyo apartment. Between green tea and walks in the nearby parks, I found that these ideas of ambiguity, tension, and ambivalence felt quite comfortable as tools of analysis. Why not put the spotlight on these aspects of agency and resistance that others had already pointed out as part of the process? It would be an extension of others' work, a refocusing of the lens on the space in between conformity and resistance, neither all negative nor all positive, but real life with its inevitable ups and downs over time.

I set to defining terms. Tension expresses the action or the condition of being stretched to stiffness, taut like a wire between two forces of energy that can be in balance with each other or asymmetrical in strength. A person can be stretched between two balancing forces or have a sense of imbalance causing stress. Japanese have told me that stress can be good or bad, and indeed that tension can be exciting or uncomfortable.

Ambivalence is an experience of two strong forces that are contradictory to each other; people can feel both at once or in fluctuation. Ambivalence allows people the important ability to see in at least two directions at once. It is a dynamic state of thinking or seeing doubly, of acting from two or more different perspectives. But ambivalence can also result in mixed-up feelings of uncertainty and indecision. "Ambivalence confounds calculation of events and confuses the relevance of memorized action patterns," yet it gives us a vantage point to "take a cool and critical view of modernity" and question the effects of an order so strong that it is intolerant of difference (Bauman 1991, 2, 271).

That brings us back to "ambiguity," a word that comes from the Latin verb *ambigere*, to wander. I thought of it as wandering in an area of doubt because the games of life are changing and yet not changing, or maybe there are two games going on simultaneously, or the same game is open to various interpretations (Bourdieu 1990).[12] At any rate, these women seemed to be "wandering" in this space between games and also "wondering" how to play in this new situation.

These ideas fit the experience of these Japanese women who often talked about searching for or trying to develop "self" (*jibun*). Cultivating or polishing self by doing tea ceremony or being a good mother, for example, had a good connotation for Japanese because it meant that you were trying to go beyond your narrow self and connect self with the larger world beyond social norms. But developing self in the new way these women used it meant to develop self according to just what you want to do or in a way that enhances your own possibilities in the world. Would others see choosing a life for self as selfish? These women had to maintain some ambiguity because they were wandering into dangerous territory when they wanted to travel just to enjoy themselves, or keep working and not marry. In a society that honored the cultivation of a larger self, would they themselves someday suffer for having chosen the self-centered way?

Along with their generation, the women I interviewed were dissatisfied with the social system available to them and found themselves dancing on the margins of the accepted norms of Japanese society in 1993 by not marrying yet, enjoying themselves, and working. Keep in mind that all of them could have married if they had been willing to have enough arranged meetings with prospective husbands and then to choose one. But this practice has been one of their generation's main points of contention—a kind of emergent feeling that was forming but had not yet become structured into a norm (Williams 1981).[13] They wanted to wait for someone with whom they felt a connection (*en*) and they wanted to use the time and space left to develop themselves by working, travelling, and taking advantage of entertainment that had been reserved for men.

Thus, in looking at these women's dissatisfaction and uncertain resistance over the long term, I see a range of acts of conformity and acts of agency or resistance but much uncertain, thoughtful puzzlement as they cast about for a different life from that of their mothers and grandmothers. Their lives unfold in the space between the perception of risk and personal insecurity (*fuan*) and the wish for peace of mind or stability (*anshin*), with powerful discourses and people as much a part of them as their own desires and insights.

This is what long-term resistance looks like, I realized. Although they have caused dismay and concern in their families and government, these women's long-term resistance is full of *ambigere*—wandering in space and time—and wondering in the ambivalent reaches of their hearts and relationships.

Between the said and unsaid

My research turned up another study of long-term resistance by anthropologists in Africa that fit my own study and gave me some apt phrases to use. It was this study that persuaded me to continue to use the concept of resistance to maintain the meaning of push against the cultural code that I found in these women, but to refer to it as long-term resistance, a term that captures the fragile ambivalence played out over time that nonetheless makes a difference in the long run. Jean and John Comaroff did not trust the term "resistance" entirely either, because it did not ring true for the "murky" thoughts and actions that they witnessed among people in Zimbabwe who were reshaping the religion brought to them by colonialists. The Comaroffs wrote about a tense "middle ground between the said and unsaid" before thoughts are organized and spoken, full of silence and unmarked actions (1991, 31). They saw much of what was happening as "tacit"—implied, unstated—expressions that only vaguely confronted the "hegemony" or power of the system that permeated this world. The phrases they suggested resonated with me as descriptors for the sense of the women in my interviews, so I excitedly sent an e-mail to Kana and Aya listing these phrases. When Kana answered, she wrote, "I don't quite understand these all, but they seem good! Keep trying, *sensei!*" So I added some definitions of this middle ground and sent them back.

- tacit accommodation (going along with things without saying much)
- partial recognition (understanding the unfairness of the system you are facing to some extent)
- ambiguous perception (sort of seeing the contradictions of your situation and yet not directly expressing it)
- festering irritation (upset inside over time, but obvious only to others who are close)
- gestures of tacit refusal (expressing dissatisfaction by just not doing something or avoiding it)
- sullen and silent contesting of hegemony (expressing dissatisfaction with the power of the system that permeates their lives by sulking and being quiet)
- creative tensions (feeling tension with the system and using it to spark imaginative thought or discussion as to how to react)
- experimental practices (actions that you try out to shift or transform objects, practices, or relations in the system) (Jean and John Comaroff 1991)

"These feel right," she answered.

These phrases capture the ambiguity, tension, and ambivalence of long-term dissatisfaction with the social system, but leave it open as to what extent dissatisfaction will become expressed as intentional agency against domination or as resistance that would change the status quo. The Comaroffs write that this long-term process is the "most critical domain of history" (1991, 31) because understanding is simmering and ideas are cooking, oh so slowly. People themselves are ambivalent about pushing for change, to say nothing of the fact that overt resistance might cause unendurable tension or danger.

Taking off from the Comaroffs, I use the general concept of long-term resistance that I understand as occurring in these vague and ambiguous ways, full of tension and ambivalence in mind, heart, and body. Long-term resistance may herald larger changes over the long run (or not) but the factor of time allows this concept to include a range of hesitant steps in the midst of pressures to conform. Because it alludes to an in-between that floats between the "no longer" and the "not yet," it is a nondirectional stance that can include a loss of hope often cited in contemporary Japan, but also implies hope for a way forward toward something new that has not yet surfaced (Miyazaki 2010).

Dissatisfied with the social system as it has been set up by elders, the women in this study struggle to work out how to live their lives. Among the women I interviewed, the "partial recognition" of their dissatisfaction as a generation coming of age was so uncomfortable for them that it resulted in "gestures of tacit refusal" not to marry just anyone by twenty-five, not to quit a job, or not to do just the research a professor wanted them to do. Their friends were their allies in this. As a result of their "festering irritation" they have experimented with actions such as living in their own apartments, living with boyfriends, or getting PhDs. They let their performances "slip" a bit at the edges of society (Butler 2004),[14] but these women are careful in a society that isolates those who do not cooperate in legitimate roles of power. Kana, for example, wanted to be a woman professor in a land of male professors,[15] but she lived at a dormitory because she has let her performance as a Japanese woman slip by becoming so educated yet can protect herself by not living alone in the city. Ultimately, it is this ambivalent, long-term resistance in individual lives, embedded in families and social groups, that is the most salient.

Not only do tension and ambivalence fit the data in these interviews better than agency or short-term resistance, they also fit better with the historical sense of self in Japan that is more ambiguous and has vaguer borders than conceptions in the West. The word for self, *jibun*, literally means "self part," the self embedded in the whole. This is self according to Confucian ethics (influential in Japan in the seventeenth and eighteenth centuries), wherein the private part of the person is inferior to the public self that devotes itself to society. In Shintoism and certain arenas of Japanese philosophy, the self is heart/mind that is purifed by unification with the natural world. Thus, the self is at times enveloped by, even undifferentiated from, its surroundings (Berque 1992). Japanese self, shifting appropriately within contexts and different groups of people, links with various universal energies understood in Shintoism as outer energies of authority and differentiation and inner energies of generative harmony and centralization (Rosenberger 1992). An early twentieth-century philosopher, Watsuji Tetsuro, cited relationality (*aidagara*, literally, personality of in-betweenness) as the dominant characteristic of Japanese (Borovoy 2005, 71).

The Buddhist sense of maturity that continues in Japanese life in the practice of more traditional hobbies also posits self in a dialectic between the manifestation of separateness in life and the eternal reality of oneness. The Japanese sense of self is one that moves fluidly between positions of outer and inner, front stage and backstage, that are well taught and practiced within Japanese life (Rosenberger 1992, 2001). Despite ideological uses of these ideas in the twentieth century, and keeping in mind that the Japanese self also has arenas in which it withdraws into itself (Lebra 1992), these are strong historical ideas that still work in Japanese life. They convey a sense of approval for ambiguous identity and the ability to bear a double consciousness and live in-between.

But ambiguity, tension, and ambivalence are not limited to usefulness in Japan. These terms also work better for us Western social scientists who historically have worried about the question of to what extent people are free to determine their lives as individuals and to what extent people are determined by the social, economic, and political structures around them—agency versus structure. Scholars have challenged this dualistic division as inadequate to lived experience and emphasized their interaction (Giddens 1984; Bourdieu 1990), but it remains easy to damn people for conformity and praise them for brave attempts to rebel against the dominant status quo. Focus on the ambivalence and tension found in long-term resistance helps us to pay attention to subtle complexities as we place the people we talk to at the crossroads of their lives, with various pathways beckoning them to go this way or that and many unclear feelings within themselves.

My own experience of tension and ambivalence

The terms "tension" and "ambivalence" make sense of my own experience. In those formative years of the late 1960s and 1970s, my own raggedy bell-bottoms, antiwar protests, boyfriends, insistence on a career, and adventures in Japan all had appeared as forms of resistance to my parents and more conservative American society. Inside myself, what did I feel? Like the women I had talked with in Japan, I felt more tension between how I had been raised and where I was headed than I experienced a feeling of simple resistance or pure ability to maneuver my actions freely.

Even though my thinking had shifted from past ideals and expectations, I never lost affection for my parents, the church they took me to, the small conservative town of Gettysburg, Pennsylvania, where I was raised, or even, deep down, the flag that used to lead our high school band, me on the trumpet, across the cemetery on Memorial Day.

My ambivalence about career and children has been a constant throughout my life, as it has for many women in my era. My father had urged me to be a doctor, but the young me argued with him, "No, it would be too hard to do that and have children."

After meeting the first wave of feminism head-on in college, I was imagining graduate school when my boyfriend asked, "Do you want to go to Japan with me?" I was in. It was the perfect solution to my ambivalence—what seemed like daring adventure in northeastern Japan and gradual entry into the institution of marriage. I remember the first summer I was in Japan writing in my journal, "I'll get married, but I won't have children." I was trying to hedge my bets, adjust my internalized norms to a new set of ideas that I was internalizing as a young adult. When we did marry, we did it quickly and without much ceremony in the living room of some missionaries in the northern city where we taught English in Japan (Rosenberger 2001). It was as if we had avoided the tension around our decision by slipping into marriage without admitting we were doing so, claiming we were forced by the circumstances of living in strict Japanese rural society.

After three years in Japan, we returned to University of Michigan for graduate study. When I got pregnant in my third year of classes, having just gained admittance into the anthropology department after a stint in Japanese studies, I wasn't sure what to do. But I didn't want to say no to anything—the baby or the career. I was determined to live what seemed like a hard-to-integrate life and sustain both directions. It's a game that many of us play: trying to stay honest to our desire to mother that stems heavily from our upbringing and to our desires as an adult woman for individual growth and a career. I remember lugging a large pile of books through the library for checkout when I was about six months pregnant and laughing at my junior high dreams of knitting little things for my baby while sitting at home with my big belly.

An explanation that worked

Many years later, while teaching a class at Waseda University in Tokyo, I felt tension and ambivalence as I read the essays of the Japanese students I was teaching. The young men wanted a life for themselves as well as work, and the young women, interviewing for high-flying jobs, wanted enjoyment and children someday, but neither knew what the future would hold. The men and women would arrive one day in class with spiked hair, baby-doll top over tights, a chain in the belt, and another day dressed in black suits, white blouses, and shiny black dress shoes.

Most important, these ideas fit the feelings, thoughts, and even bodily ways of presenting themselves that I perceived among the women I interviewed for this study. Contradictory forces pulled them in various directions, sometimes coming together into a temporary equilibrium, sometimes pulling them off-balance and causing stress. I wanted to capture this space in which they floated, saying yes to some things and no to others.

I finally gave my talk to my fellow faculty members at Waseda University. What about this new idea? It seemed to resonate with them in an evening seminar followed by drink, in good Japanese work fashion. Afterwards Japanese and non-Japanese alike avowed: "Ambivalence? Tension? That sounded like me up there!" I laughed and poured them some beer. "What about Japanese women you know?" As they grabbed the bottle to pour for me, they assured me, "Oh, it definitely fits." Later when I gave the talk in Hong Kong, American and Chinese teachers and grad students again echoed these thoughts: "That's not just them. That's just how *I* feel." I had struck on a set of feelings that hit a nerve with people in this era of late modernity.

Contradictions

My analytical framework adjusted, I still needed one more building block. How was I going to describe the social context of these ambiguous feelings? That was part of my responsibility as an anthropologist. Again, John and Jean Comaroff's ideas came to my aid as a framework. The Comaroffs perceived that contradictions permeated the world of these dissatisfied people with their murky tensions. They wrote: "Contradictions . . . between the world as represented and the world as experienced become ever more palpable, ever more insupportable" (1991, 26). In the case of the Comaroffs' study in Africa, contradictions existed between the world that the colonial masters constructed and the world that the native people experienced.

In the case of postwar Japan, contradictions for women were built into modern institutions such as schools, and then contradictions intensified when the ideas, objects, and practices brought in by globalization permeated women's worlds as they came of age. In addition, the promises of Japanese postwar institutions fell short with the economic decline of the 1990s. The contradictions became "ever more insupportable" as the benefits of modernity came into question.

The women I interviewed, born between 1958 and 1968, grew up in the heyday of postwar economic growth in the 1960s and 1970s with all its promise of modern progress, rationality, and individuation (Touraine 1995), but with contradictions and ambivalence at its heart (Bauman 1991; Ratansi 1995). Individuation got put on hold as citizens fulfilled prescribed roles for economic growth in schools, companies, and families. Inequalities lurked as rural people, the less educated, and especially women felt "acute discomfort" (Bauman 1991) at being limited by their roles as mothers and homemakers in the modern order.

These women came of age during the growth of consumer society in the late 1970s and 1980s. A Tokyo woman recounted, "I was so excited when MacDonald's came to Tokyo while I was in high school." In Japan, the press called them the "new breed" (*shinjinrui*) that wished to place lifestyle above work and, for women, lifestyle above home (*katei*) (Sand 2006, 87). How to belong and where to belong became a question (Gunewardena 2007, 41). To further confound their experience, these women were single working women in their late twenties to late thirties when the economic bubble broke in the early 1990s and the long recession set in.

Chizuko Ueno, a Japanese woman scholar a bit older than these women, who has lived a highly successful single life, thinks that Japanese women of this age are caught forever in contradictions (Ueno and Nobuta 2004). They speak from the role-ordered world of their mothers who nurtured them, but they act from the world of fragmented identities that they must nurture for their own survival. This is a classic double bind in which the embodied habits and dispositions people have learned from family and education no longer work well (Bourdieu 1990).[16] The dispositions that these women acquired as they grew up did not prepare them to play the globalized game of various lifestyles and choices in the 1990s and 2000s. Emerging as adults, they have learned new ways of being, acting, and desiring in this more global world, yet they have never entirely lost the old dispositions, nor the desires of the old ways. For readers with little background on Japan, it is helpful to imagine the contradictory dispositions that these women integrated into their bodies and internalized in their psyches through the disparate socioeconomic contexts that nurtured their growth.

Growing up in modern, postwar institutions

When young, these women grew as girls into a strong sense of belonging to family and school groups and responsibility to exert individual efforts for the group. This was postwar Japan at its height, in which "unique" Japanese psychosocial traits made Japan spiritually superior to the West (Befu 2001, 102) in the forms of cooperation, empathy, and harmony resulting from devoted effort (*gambaru*), perseverance or endurance (*gaman*), and mutual psychological dependency (*amae*). Devoted mothers and sometimes grandmothers nurtured these traits in girls, and schoolteachers softly insisted upon, and later strictly enforced, the skills and responsibilities of being part of the group, whether working hard or playing (Fukuzawa 1994; Tobin 1992).

The bodies and minds of girls, however, usually received different disciplining than boys did at home or at school. Helping their mothers serve brothers, standing in line after the boys at school, caring for younger children, taking tea ceremony or flower arranging, girls received a certain kind of power as individuals who would cultivate selflessness and be patient, caring wives and mothers. Girls' bodies were well watched, and their minds, bodies, and spirits well disciplined from the Panopticon tower of modernity—a metaphorical tower in the middle of a prison where each individual could be watched and reformed into the preferred kind of individual for society (Foucault 1979).

Parents gave stronger encouragement and more money to boys than to girls to study hard individually and compete their way into excellent high schools and four-year universities that would pave the way to upper mobility. Vocational training for short-term jobs before marriage was enough for middle-class girls who would work only briefly, then quit and marry, or for rural and lower-class women who would continue to work at low-level or family jobs (Roberts 1994).

The conundrum of mothers

The young women in this study also inherited the sadness and ambivalence of their mothers, often passed on in private emotional moments. Mothers, caught in the contradictions of postwar modernity, exhibited tacit accommodation with almost-silent suffering,[17] but their daughters heard. Out of the interviews emerged daughters' tales of their mothers' complaints about fathers who were absent most of the week but were also trouble to take care of when home. Several women knew that their fathers hit their mothers. In the country, housewives suffered under husbands' constant authority. The daughters characterized their mothers as "old-fashioned . . . just obeying my father"; as "always sacrificing herself and not thinking about her own needs"; or as simply "resigned" (*akiramete iru*) to loveless marriages.[18] Only a few commented that they would like to have a relationship like their parents.

A past interviewee raising children in the 1970s told how she would go with her children into a closet and cry when things got too bad with her mother-in-law, who lived with them and always expected to be waited on (Rosenberger 2001). Remembering this, I knew that these daughters I was now studying understood the suffering of their mothers in the marrow of their bones. They witnessed the self-sacrifice expected of mothers and did not want it for themselves, nor did their mothers want it for them to this extent.

However, daughters also received the attention, affection, and hope of their mothers. In the interviews, the mother–daughter relationship of childhood for most was a warm memory—an intimacy that they often wanted to reproduce in their own lives. Relationships with children became a place where these daughters saw the chance to be themselves and the challenge to be their best selves (Ezawa 2002).

Mothers gave mixed messages. Mothers sympathized with their daughters' wishes to enjoy life before marriage and to wait for a person who understood and loved them (Nakano and Wagatsuma 2004), and they warned their daughters of living with mothers-in-law and the trials of elder care. However, in the long run these same mothers enforced the status quo of the modern family—the need to marry and have children in order to find "women's happiness." Otherwise, mothers would be denying their own paths in life (Ueno and Nobuta 2004). Raw resistance was tantamount to going against the emotional interdependence of the mother–daughter relationship, so ambiguous reactions such as refusing without saying much about it and seeming to slide unwittingly into decisions were the safest course.

Coming of age in late-modern Japan

In contrast to their upbringing in home and school, these women later came of age surrounded by consumption, entertainment, and the spread of global ideas about individuality and women's freedom. I call this the era of late modernity, but it is also referred to as the era of neoliberalism, late capitalism, or postmodernism.[19] The global media market of TV, movies, and magazines has been vital in the disruption of embodied ways of being, feeling, and thinking learned early in life (Winant 1995). A dream for self was born in their generation, revved up with media rhetoric that promised the individuality that modernization had not given their mothers.

As these women grew up in the 1960s and 1970s in Japan, individualized possessions, from beds and desks to Ricah dolls and Power Rangers, captivated the imaginations of children. One interviewee from Morioka tells how she poured over cartoons (*manga*), both hers and her brother's, whenever she could. Cartoons in the 1970s and 1980s offered girls heroines who were strong and facing complex questions in their lives. By the eighties, cartoons for both boys and girls offered visions of sex that were sometimes violent—boys and girls, boys and boys; perhaps girls learned to imagine being both the violated and the violator (Thorn 2004).

Media invited this generation of girls to be "Hanako," the emblematic Tokyo consumers of the marketing world in the 1980s—the working woman with money and the cosmopolitan sophisticate gathering knowledge about stores, restaurants, foreign cities, dating, and sex (Rosenberger 2001). Instead of navy-blue uniforms worn to and from school, now fashion magazines encouraged girls to do the forbidden: wear mini-skirts; go to bars with other women; and enjoy romance in a love hotel on Christmas Eve.

The advertising copy set imaginations afire (Appadurai 1996) with vague messages to express "self," "individuality," and "freedom." Sexual intimacy increasingly became part of the public arena (Ho 2008; Farrer 2010) and thinking about enjoyment and development of self seemed not only okay but was almost mandatory in these "technologies of self" that gave advice on how to be cool (Martin et al. 1988; Rosenberger 2001). Television dramas about single women, love, and work have continued to give media guidance on practices of self (Lukacs 2010).

To go back to the metaphor of the Panopticon tower, marketers were watching from the tower to make new kinds of individuals, but now they encouraged people to climb the tower themselves, watch, compare themselves with others, and learn about new appearances and experiences (Morrison 2010). The ability to desire and choose is central to individuality, but this freedom to choose carried its own contradictions. People in this so-called neoliberal era were nurtured to be individual entrepreneurs and consumers, but choices were defined by the marketers, who discarded those who did not fit or could not participate economically or culturally (Harvey 2005). In fact, it was a kind of "Panopticon sort" (Gandy 1993) of winners and losers, as the Japanese say.

The recession of the 1990s accelerated these divisions in Japanese society. Despite the Equal Employment Opportunity Law of 1986, men were hired over women and women found their best possibilities for promotion in foreign companies or freelance work (Rebick 2005). Since the late 1970s, the wage gap between Japanese women and men has widened (Osawa 2002). Neither men nor women could get jobs that fit them, and many quit after several years, becoming the lost generation, sacrificed to maintaining the expensive older men in the company (Genda 2005). Middle-class men's economic attractiveness as potential husbands decreased, because even qualified men did not get the jobs in large and medium companies that they wanted. As men joined women in their sense of dissatisfaction with postwar roles for men and their economic possibilities decreased, marriage became an increasingly troubled institution, less appealing both socially and economically (Shimodaira 2004).[20]

Whether married or single, women struggled to make ends meet in an unstable economy. A third of workers were now irregular workers (Honda 2006), some preferring irregular work (Lunsing 2006); from single mothers to homeless people, Japan's poverty rate was swelling to place Japan third among advanced nations. More than ever, parental social and economic status made a difference in unequal opportunities for education and jobs (Tachibanaki 2006, Aoki and Aoki 2005, Okano 1995). Middle-class women felt more pressures than ever if they wanted to escort themselves or their children to the front of the line and could count on less guaranteed help from elder generations to do so.

With the economic decline, governance through individual responsibility increased in Japan with retraction of assurances of ordered progress and central aid. Responding to the national situation, global trends, and these young women themselves, the government turned to a more neoliberal style that governs through monitoring a myriad of experts and demands individualized citizens who must face new risks on their own, as evidenced by the emphasis on lifelong learning, educational reform to nurture independence, and vocational retraining in the 1990s and 2000s (Dean 1999; Ogawa 2009; Miyazaki 2010). In Japan this call for self-responsibility is still coupled, however, with a moral discourse emphasizing "charity, community, moral striving, and the benevolence of the family" (Borovoy 2010:60). Such governance interacts with the evidence in this ethnography. Learning to live with increased uncertainty and disorder, these women must become more independent yet more dependent on experts; in their loneliness they reach out to friends (Bauman 1991). Simultaneously, they are beckoned to become morally mature in their gendered role of caring for others and struggle to translate the older ideal of self-cultivation (Mahmood 2001) and meld it with the new goal of self-actualization. In essence, the ground of long-term power and resistance has shifted under women's feet as the promise of emancipation and progress through strong institutions has been displaced by a weaker authority that focuses on, indeed requires, certain forms of self-actualization (Dean 2007).

The government blamed women for the decrease in the birthrate that seemed to further threaten Japan's postwar order, yet the government made some policy changes to seduce women into marriage and mothering if they could continue to work. Although they were dubbed "single aristocrats" and "parasite singles" (Yamada 1999), these women were, after all, part of the purported middle class, and the government had to respond with some flexibility to keep them in the fold (Hall and Jefferson 1976). Policy adjustments were meant to encourage women to have more babies voluntarily: increase in daycare centers for working mothers, local and national payments to families with children (with exponential increase for more children), a system of home health-care workers to help in cases where women are caring for elderly or disabled family members; encouragement for companies to not fire women upon marriage or childbirth; family leave for both men and women; and increased maternity leave (Roberts 2002).

All of these measures do help women, but women still find it easiest to quit work when raising children, because the requirements for long hours of work for men and women have not changed, and because the education competition for children is more demanding than ever. The women in this study felt that the government had not done nearly enough to make policy changes that would make having children in Japanese society easy. To a large extent, the model of the male breadwinner with the woman labeled as housewife (though sometimes working in service employment) has not changed in Japan (Rosenbluth 2007, 10). In international comparisons, Japanese mothers earn a proportionately small percentage of the household income (Shirahase 2007, 39).[21]

Gender differences are the largest and most resilient inequality in Japanese society (Hashimoto 2003). Even in 2010, Japan ranked ninety-fourth in gender equality, particularly because it lacks women at the higher levels of business and government (*Japan Times* 2010).

Thus, these women that I have interviewed have grown up with ambivalent dispositions toward the world in a context of contradictory forces. Through family and education, they have a disposition toward selflessness, interdependence with the group, sensitivity to others, and faithfulness to roles. Through the experiences of their generation in this globalized, neoliberal era, they have a more self-centered disposition that has been both encouraged and damned. This has created a double bind within them because they are riven at the center, split between two ways of being, their training for one set of social games not completely preparing them for the next set of games, yet they are fascinated by them and must play them. They struggle, bedeviled by old and new desires; but simultaneously they are learning to live in a contradictory world where they can maintain both these ways of being. Living under the watchful eye of two worlds, they have developed a kind of double consciousness and the ability to enact double identities (DuBois 1994). Difficult as it is, they vaguely recognize that in the Japan of this era they must play the game in this way in order to be tolerated as self-actualizing "humans, not just as women."

The experience of "self" itself gives evidence of this struggle. Positive feelings of new possibilities emerge when women say they are doing things "in the way of self" or "fulfilling self" (*jibun nari ni, jibun o jitsugen suru*). In the media, among friends, and with me, these work. Ambiguous feelings about themselves in relation to others surface, however, when in the same breath, they say—half-seriously, half-jokingly—that they are doing things selfishly, "as I want to" or "pushing my will" (*katte ni, ishi o toosu*). The implication is that these same acts are negative for the workings of social groups, and indeed may even put the Japan they were raised in at risk.

One interviewee from a Tohoku (northeastern) village experienced both the costs and benefits of these contradictions. She grew up on a farm and worked locally after school, but broke up with her local boyfriend in 1998 and moved into an apartment in the village. She commented, "I want my own time. I don't have to always be worrying about others (*ki o tsukau*). I can live by my own money. I can go to the hot baths or shopping whenever I want. It is comfortable." Then she added, "But I can't get too comfortable or I might not get married. I still want the warmth of a family." She was changed for good, yet still harbored sympathy for aspects of the old ways and felt the danger of her flirtation with her more globally oriented self if she were to maintain her happiness as conceived of in the village. As it turned out, she found a local husband who was the male breadwinner while she raised her small children but he helped out when he could and dreamed with her of a more enjoyable future.

In this way, these women make experimental choices and then amalgamate their psychosocial shifts with older institutions. What start as "projects" intended to solve personal struggles accumulate and set off unintended consequences as they become intertwined with relationships and institutions that affect the marrow of how power works (Ortner 2006).

What kind of self?

Given these contradictions that Japanese women of this generation cope with externally and internally, Japanese scholars have engaged in a debate over whether the idea of self that is so important in their generational discourse can stand the test of time and what form it will take. In one corner stands Miura, a male academic, who presents the idea that these women cannot succeed because they have simply taken ad copy from magazines about self (*jibun, jibunrashisa*) and innocently concocted an impossible generational vision of self as free choice, separate from the norms of being a woman in Japan (*onna, onnarashii*) (Miura 2005, 108). Miura claims that women imagine self with all the possibilities of being human, including a marriage that fits with self and a job that enhances self.

But they will surely fail, argues Miura, because this media-born view of self is saturated with self-satisfaction and self-love, and is actually shot through with the needs of this fast-changing consumer society (Harvey 1990). Women cannot actualize self because the media have made them imagine life outside the identities or subject positions that Japanese society offers to women. Women want good jobs and promotions, but they are not generally available. Miura argues that free-choice marriage has left women with the main responsibility for home and childcare, dependent on men who are either overworked or underemployed. Divorce is rising but still economically difficult for most.

Miura claims that these women have simply accrued unsatisfied selves and gotten stuck in a place of "many-layered indecision" (2005, 123).

In the other corner stands Ueno, who has a positive perspective, arguing that Japanese women can live in a "multilayered" way of being that skips among identities. She thinks that women no longer need to concern themselves with maintaining consistent societal identities (Ueno 2005, 29, 35). For her, identities exist as subject positions in the structure of society, but they "flow and twist" over time and space. Women anchor at these locations of identity with "temporary consciousness" (*karisome ishiki*), suturing and unsuturing over time and space (Ueno 2005, 29; Hall 1996). Ueno actually prefers that no one identity fully define or neatly fit her, and thus thinks that women can have selves apart from certain confining identities.

According to Ueno, one shares part of one's being with parents, part with husband or boyfriend, part with friends, part with no one else. Identity becomes hybrid and complicated, "crossing the in-between (*aida*) of fragmented identity" (Ueno 2005, 35). She thinks that this is appropriate to the increasingly multidimensional reality of Japan and does not mourn the loss of integrated identity. Because identities as daughters require feelings and actions at variance with identities with friends in evening entertainment, for example, they are kept separate externally, and even internally. What is required is management of a multiple, compartmentalized, and fluid self-narrative (Asano 2005) in order to escape the suffering associated with the contradictions of globalized, late modern Japan.

Kirishima, a popular writer and model of alternative life for women, gives similar advice, telling women that they should "ride the waves." Identities, even marriage and motherhood, can be taken on, but always with self-awareness and flexibility so as not to be caged in. Women should not resist gender inequalities and be crushed by them, but enter into identities and relationships such as marriage maintaining the ability to extract themselves. She urges independence in all ways (emotionally, financially, in daily life) so that women can survive as individual human beings who center their lives, not on marriage, but on the part of life they wish (Hirota 2004, 403). As a career woman in my study still living in the rural north said, "I want to marry at least once, even if I get divorced."

This debate about a generation of women enthralled with the search for self, as either slogging through a swamp of many-layered indecision or nimbly leaping among multiple layers of identities, sets up negative and positive extremes. The academic opinions of Miura and Ueno represent the range of powerful discourses concerning the whole question of self for women in recent eras in Japan: Over the long term does the search for self end up in a dead end of either accommodation or meaningless self-love? Or does it open up new possibilities for a multilayered perception of life that lets women ride the waves of identities? Kana and Aya, the graduate students from the beginning of this chapter, would not want to be typified as standing in either corner of the debate; nor can I pigeonhole the women I interviewed in one corner or another. What I want to look at more closely in this book is the many-layered indecision and multilayered flowing and twisting that each of them talks about. The sharp edges of their debate call for a more flexible analytical framework when looking at real lives unfolding over time and space.

Conclusion

My main questions are these: What are the nuances of ambiguous long-term resistance in the transition from modernity to late modernity? More particularly, what are the nuances of long-term resistance in the lives of Japanese women experiencing ambivalent dissatisfaction from their upbringing in postwar Japan and fashioning adult lives in the globalized and destabilized Japan of the 1990s and 2000s. Not all women are equal or alike in Japan or elsewhere, as feminist scholars have noted (McCall 2005, Collins, 1998). In this group women vary by class (income and education) and by urban/rural differences. Thus, I also ask: How do different kinds of Japanese women experience long-term resistance, especially across urban/rural and class differences?

My decision to focus on ambivalence, tension, ambiguity, and contradiction as the core concepts of long-term resistance forms the framework for the book's analysis. I have expressed this general analytic focus in diagrams that can be found in the Appendix. Set between the extremes of a set structure of norms and limitless agency/resistance, the diagram indicates that people can move along lines or continue toward risk or stability; search for self or institutional conformity; seek difference or homogeneity—or a combination of all of these—over their lives. Important in this case is that this vision of the world implies movement and process over time for people and for social groups, and indicates the struggle between the tight order of modernity and the more chaotic, albeit more tolerant, disorder of late modernity.

To give a map of the book, in Chapter 2, I develop the notions of tension and ambivalence within contradictions, letting the voices and experiences of two single women intervene. I explore how these concepts work psychologically and socially, and make regional contrasts. In Chapters 3 through 6, I hone in on the lives of women I have interviewed, grouping them according to themes that have emerged from my study of the data and analyzing their experiences of long-term dissatisfaction through the various ways of talking about personal ambiguity among societal contradictions. I discuss single women in Chapter 3, married women without children in Chapter 4, married women without work in Chapter 5, and married women with work in Chapter 6. The Conclusion returns to the question of what this study has taught us about ambiguous long-term resistance in this era with reflections on Japan in the 1990s and 2000s. In an epilogue, I present a preliminary analysis of the experiences of some of these women in relation to the 2011 earthquake/tsunami/radiation, with particular attention to their reactions to this age of increased risks.

Throughout the book I tell these women's stories in a fashion that employs the words they used when we talked to each other, giving the reader a sense of what it feels like to talk to them. I keep myself in the picture, for I am part of the story.

My anthropological goals are twofold: to make inductive generalizations about this group from the details of their stories and to understand the processes of thinking and acting through individual case studies, the ethnography of the particular. The first is an attempt to bring order where there is endless variety, change, and uncertainty. The second is an attempt to maintain the nitty-gritty experiences of particular people, living, strategizing, and feeling pain at the nexus of historical, economic, political, social, and cultural forces (Abu-Lughod 2006, 476). This is the middle ground where, very gradually, "new norms emerge in experiments with life" (Das 2007, 63).

Although our meetings have not been frequent, these women have opened themselves to me over the years, perhaps more so because I am outside of their social circles. In this book I hope to convey the richness I feel in each of their lives. They have not told me everything and that is their prerogative. Those with too much to hide have dropped out or simply remain difficult to talk to. I thank them for sharing what they have been able to share. As an anthropologist, my job is to combine their individual stories and convey the tale they are telling as humans in their time and place, while I play the role of mediator between them and the audience for whom I write. As a person, my aim is to communicate their beauty as human beings struggling to live life as best they can.

CHAPTER TWO

Ambivalence and Tension

Data Meets Theory

I FINISHED SCRIBBLING down blurbs from the ads for women's magazines hanging in the center of the subway car and ran for the door. As I made my way through the surge of bodies in the downtown Tokyo station, passing shops and restaurants in the underground mall, my eye was caught momentarily by a young woman in a deep-purple jacket, not a common color in 1993. Wouldn't it be interesting if she were my next interviewee, I thought. A glance at my watch told me that I needed to rush through the back streets to my small business hotel in time to meet the actual next interviewee whom a mutual friend, a Japanese student of mine from Oregon, had introduced me to. I hardly had time to get out my notebook when in walked the girl in the purple coat. I stood up and introduced myself to Ito-san who, despite her quiet demeanor, would have plenty to say if her purple coat was any indication.

Single in Tokyo

Ordering coffee as we sat in the lime-green plastic chairs of the coffee shop, we were several miles from the place and over a decade before the time when I would conclude that a straightforward analysis in terms of "agency" and "resistance" was not going to work in this study. I relate Ito-san's narrative at this point because my 1993 vision of her was not mistaken. She was a relatively self-directed agent, even a self-admitted rebel against the status quo. So I have set myself a challenge. If the tension and ambivalence I felt throughout the whole group of women's narratives also emerge from and enhance the understanding of Ito-san's interview, then this is one proof of their efficacy.

I pair the analysis of Ito-san's narrative set in Tokyo with that of a woman named Kawai-san who lives in Morioka, a city in the northeast. Kawai-san wore bland colors and played down, even hid, the changes she brought to her life. Their geographical contrast gives me the opportunity to discuss differences between urban and regional Japan that intersect with gender change in this book. They both serve as concrete examples through which to link concepts of tension, ambivalence, and contradiction with ideas about psychosocial development and social movements that aid my analytical eye and help the reader to understand these narratives in a broader way.

Ito-san

1993, AGE TWENTY-NINE

After we exchanged greetings, I blurted out, "Your jacket is a great color!"

"Oh, this. I went to Hong Kong with my mother. We were shopping and I saw this long purple jacket. I said, 'I want to buy it.' 'Please don't buy that,' she pleaded, 'at least not that. It's too loud. You shouldn't walk outside in such loud (*hade*) stuff.' But I bought it because I really like purple. I do get looked at, though, when I wear it. Japanese don't wear such colors much. In Japan when people stand out, people above push them down or people below pull their legs back."

"Do you look at magazines and find clothes you like usually or what?"

"No. As I walk around town, I see people who look cool, and then I find those kinds of clothes. In the magazines everything has the same look, like uniforms. I like to find things that are like me (*jibun nari ni*)."

While the coffee was still hot, Ito-san said: "I'm a bit rebellious. My father treated me like a boy. I played with my brother like a boy. I was given discipline, but my parents didn't say 'because you are a girl.' " In contrast, she described her mother as a "full-time housewife who could have worked. It was a shame but there wasn't much work in the country. I always thought I wanted to work, looking at my mother. It's scary to think of always being in the house and not knowing the movements of society."

Ito-san's hands lay in her lap, but her brown eyes danced. "I am just doing as I wish, as if I will be allowed to do things." She looked down. "But my consciousness is weak and I can't just make strong decisions like Mari." Mari was her university classmate, my master's student, and a symbol of daring to Ito-san. Ito-san's laments were poetic: "Self, what is it? Sometimes I feel lost. I try this and that. I don't go in a straight line."

Ito-san had studied in a good Tokyo university that landed her a job with promotions in a top-notch company in the aftermath of the Equal Employment Opportunity Law (EEOL). "I got a job at Fujitsu as a computer systems engineer. The EEOL had just gone into effect and women, too, worked until midnight. The surface truth was that women could go up, but there were no women on top then. You were just one gear in a big machine. You were just told to do something and didn't understand where it was going."

"So you just quit?"

"Yes, after two years. I went to work in a small company where I could see the whole picture. I was in charge of the office. I wouldn't say I felt a sense of worth (*yarigai*) in it, but it was enjoyable because it was small. I liked the people and I knew what was going on. I quit last year in September."

"Mari said that you are studying English now."

"Yes. I want to do things that enter in between people and machines so people can understand machines easily. I want work that I would like to continue for my whole life. My mother wants me to come home to the country, but there would be no work there. Anyway, when I go home, we argue. She says, 'You are uncouth (*darashi ga nai*).' "

"What do you mean? Does she think you should marry?"

"She would always send pictures—won't you meet this person? In Tokyo, if you don't marry, no one asks why you aren't married at twenty-nine, but in the country, they ask, 'Was she not able to marry?' So I don't want to return there. My mother is an old human being . . . but she has changed somewhat. Now she says, 'Do what you want to do.' "

Ito-san ran her well-shaped fingernails along the edge of the low coffee table between us. "Actually, I lived together with a guy for four years. We didn't talk of marriage to each other. We were just good friends. It wasn't that period of time to think of marriage. We just lived together—not really in love (*suki ga nai*)."

She said little more and we ended with pleasantries.

I had a note from Ito-san in 1994 that she was still unemployed and wished "there were a way to live legally with a close friend and partner." She told me that I would understand young women better if I read *Kitchen*, a novel by Yoshi Banana about the loneliness of young people and their search for relationships. Its characters felt emptiness but found friends with whom to build a new kind of family that accepted them just as they were.

1998, AGE THIRTY-FOUR

In 1998, we met in the same plastic chairs in the mezzanine lobby of the business hotel. This time Ito-san wore a long, sleeveless knit dress with horizontal wide black-and-white stripes. She launched quickly into an explanation about the question that her narrative had harbored for five years. Why did her mother call her "uncouth"?

"Before I lived with a guy—I told you, didn't I? It was a half-marriage life. But I felt that I didn't need that guy. I thought I would just go according to myself (*jibun nari ni*). I think now it was good that I did as I wanted and didn't go into his family's register (*koseki*). There is a power difference between just living together and legally entering the family registry." The latter was the legal process of marriage.

"Yeah, you'd have to get divorced to get out."

"Right. At that time, my parents couldn't understand. They were surprised like it was a crime. They said, 'You're uncouth!' But in the end, they said, 'Okay, if you want. It can't be helped.' "

"Wow—that must have been difficult to tell them."

"It was hard. But I didn't like hiding it. I thought it [living together] was right. It wasn't hurting anyone. I wanted them to understand. Now when there is something, I usually talk with my brother first by e-mail. And then I try saying it to my parents. Sometimes he acts as a go-between."

"Hmm," she mused to herself. "Am I overly dependent?"

Ito-san used the word *amaeru*—to be dependent on or indulge oneself in accepting the goodwill of intimate others (Doi 1973). It was both seductive because it was comfortable, and alarming because it threatened her search for "self." Complex in its meanings, "dependence" is a term of debate among women in this study to which we will return.

Despite the 1990s recession, Ito-san had managed to find a job at a translation agency, a new-style company that was a subsidiary of a large electronics firm. Luckily, her age still fell within the "age limit" applied to women in the employment market, which had moved from thirty to thirty-five.

"We have flex time! I couldn't live without it!" She exclaimed. "I go ten to eight because I don't like to work early. The superiors are not strict. They leave the work to each person. And we can wear jeans unless you have to meet a customer."

"And it's so nice to be in charge of your time," I said. "I like that about my job, too. What about promotion for women?"

"There is a wall. Of the assistant managers, only one is a woman. I am not a full company member. I'm a contract worker. My job is the same for salary and vacation but I wouldn't get maternity leave or retirement payments and there is no promotion. Now people are just glad to have work. People think of getting experience and skill and then they can go elsewhere. It is like America."

"Yeah, the same thing is happening in America—a lot more contract workers." I said it with a touch of critique in my voice, but Ito-san saw it as proof of a new individuality.

"We used to depend on the company but now we depend on our own skill," she observed. "But I am applying for other jobs. I really don't feel a sense of accomplishment or, what do they say, self-actualization (*jibun jitsugen*). I feel a feeling of fatigue."

"I can't live without my cable TV. I watch American movies, American sitcoms, dramas—*Sex and the City*, *Friends*, *Buffy*, *ER*, *Chicago* . . . I never watch Japanese TV." She laughed. "It's embarrassing, but I love the computer and cable TV. I like to do the internet and play games. I'm a kind of geek. But I have accepted myself."

It seemed to me that she was doing a good job of approximating her life to these shows: she had a close group of friends and another long-term boyfriend in 1998 whom she didn't live with but whose idea of fun fit with hers. She enjoyed driving to the beach to watch him parasail.

"My apartment is big and also has a parking place. I pay 129,000 yen [around $1,300]. It's on the high side for a person my age. It has one big room with a loft room. I like doing the computer on the internet on vacation days. I like the give-and-take of e-mail. And my friends will drop in suddenly to visit me in my apartment even when I am sleeping in the morning. I have cable TV and they want to watch it. I say 'I'm no coffee shop!' " Again, her quiet but open laugh. No hands over the mouth like many Japanese women.

Then, with sudden seriousness, she said, "I can really let my heart loose with my friends." She paused. "May I speak in English?"

"Sure, I think you must be quite good by now."

"It's a secret, but I have applied for a job in the Silicon Valley with an American company as a translator coordinator. I told my brother but not my parents. I will have to convince them if I get the job." Her most daring thoughts were too secret to be spoken in Japanese in Japan.

2004, AGE FORTY

By 2004, it turned out that Ito-san had not gotten the job in the United States, but another plan was brewing. We ate Italian pasta Alfredo with basil and she wore the same black-and-white-striped dress of our 1998 interview.

"I've been in the same company for ten years now so not much has changed, but I do have some big news! I am going to New York City! An American guy, my former colleague, asked me to work together to form a translation company. 'I'm in,' I said. He left yesterday. He has to get a business license and then he will support my visa. It may take half a year."

"Fantastic!" I paused with fork in midair. "Why the U.S.A.?"

Ito-san wasn't surprised by the question. "When I've traveled there, I have always felt comfortable. I can be myself. In Japan, I pretend to be a person I am not. I try to fit in. Like as a daughter, I want to make my parents proud, so I act in a certain way. It's not good for me, even though now my parents can almost accept me for being myself. I haven't lived in the U.S.A. I wonder if I will fit in. Will people be kind? If I want something there, do I have to say it clearly? Will the business be good? It is a risk."

"Have you told your parents yet?" I asked.

"I haven't told them yet," she giggled uncharacteristically. "They may worry because of 9/11. But basically they will agree and support me. Maybe they are resigned now. For them this becomes one more place to travel."

"It sounds like they don't pressure you about marriage much anymore."

"It has completely stopped. My mother takes computer classes and is in a table tennis club with her noisy friends. My grandparents are all dead now, so she doesn't have to care for them. She loves to come to Tokyo to visit my brother and his family. I see them then. I never go home."

"Things have loosened up a lot, it seems."

"Yeh, they've given up. When people ask if I am married, I just say no. It's all the same—married or not. I can take care of myself. I am comfortable being myself. I wait for the right one. I don't feel that I want children. I am forty. I am left behind—so what? Now I can be myself."

"My sister-in-law in the United States is single," I said, "and she says she feels sometimes she isn't accepted in parts of society, especially like at church."

"I have no experience of not being taken in as a single person. The only time I feel it is when I get together with my friends, who are almost all married.

Then I feel a bit behind. But mostly I don't feel this. In my department, there are quite a few women my age who are single."

I e-mailed Ito-san in 2006 only to find that she was still in Japan. The United States had not yet granted her a visa to enter the country to work. It was not until 2007 that she got permission and started her life in New York City.

Ambivalence from the beginning

Ito-san's vulnerability to internalized norms of being a daughter, sister, and achieving student vies with her ambition to be her own *jibun* (self) determined to live, love, work, and have fun in her Tokyo context. Her ambivalent tension around living with a boyfriend and working in the United States is surprisingly clear, given her self-proclaimed rebellion.

Her narrative made me ask: Why is ambivalence so deeply rooted in humans? Butler (1997) claims that, in the process of emerging, the human groundwork for ambivalence between submission to another and one's own will to power is laid down.[1]

At first a child loves being in subordination to the loved one, such as a mother, and desires only that. Through this love and recognition the child becomes a human self. As the child inevitably separates from its mother, it feels both longing and anger toward her. She/he folds the mother into her-/himself in the form of a conscience, according to Butler, that both admonishes and loves the child within.

Thus, people always carry within themselves a preconscious love of subordination to another. It makes them vulnerable to entering into and enjoying subordination to external strategies of power in the world around them. We would rather be hailed by a policeman, or as was the case with one of my interviewees, hit by an abusive father, than to not be recognized at all.[2] Ito-san is always vulnerable to the concern of her mother, or to the approval of teachers and bosses, for something in her is "passionately attached" to the approval of those who defined her early social world.

However, Butler goes on to argue that the psyche also connects with the outside world and reflects back both experiences and mental reactions to itself. This is the "fold" in the mind turning between outside and inside (Deleuze 1993). Here inner dynamics and emotions meet the ongoing dramas of life and change in relation to them. Through social and political experiences of ourselves as separate beings, a partial reversal occurs, and we take on and use the very power that we experienced as dominating us as children. We transform our sense of the power over us into a "willed effect" in the world, our own active ability to participate in the present and future world (Butler 1997, 17, 29). But the catch is that our power is always ambiguous, vacillating between the power that made us and the power that we enact—"between the already-there and yet-to-come" (1997, 15, 17–18).

In short, long-term resistance is ridden with psychological and social tension and ambivalence. As with Ito-san, even at forty she still experiences herself as a daughter and sister, not just as a "self" or subject who can do what she wants without worrying about others' eyes upon her. For this reason, she feels fatigue rather than accomplishment, and she never visits her parents in her hometown. Despite her attempts to escape by going to the United States, she, like all of us, is psychologically set up to live out both sides—vulnerability to the power of others and the will to wield power on one's own behalf in the world.

In Japanese terms, Ito-san's worry revolves around words that imply independence and dependence. She pushes her "self" to be independent and worries that she depends too much on her brother as a go-between. The word she uses is *amaeru*, meaning to play up to, indulge in the goodwill of, or depend on another person, and is often used in the mother–child relationship (Doi 1971). Such actions bind a relationship in unconditional love, but make people emotionally vulnerable to each other: the mother (or brother in this case) gains the emotional power of giving indulgence, and the child, or Ito-san, basks in that indulgence—but is also submitting emotionally (Rosenberger 2001, 49; Borovoy 2005). Not surprisingly, she calls herself out on this and pushes herself toward the United States as the dream world where she hopes her independent will to power will finally emerge. I shall return to this complex of independence and dependence.

Signals of ambivalence

Ito-san presents herself in a kaleidoscopic way: as her mother sees her, as her single friends see her, as her brother and boss see her, and as she sees herself at different points in time. The process of shaping her "self" occurs as if it were being viewed through insect eyes with many different perspectives flashing on her mind and body. Her mind/body is trying to become "a focal point of organizing space," but this is an ongoing process, and neither interior nor exterior is ever entirely stable (Grosz 1994, 39). Her lived experience pivots between inside and outside, sometimes transgressing with new relationships that open limitless opportunities yet also reaffirming past relationships that assert limits (Oksala 2005, 128). In interviews what evidence or signposts do we find for this ambivalence?

Signals of ambivalence: Mental orchestrations

I used to pay scant attention to the stories or voices of other people in analyzing interviewees' words, but Bakhtin (1981) alerted me to them as a key to understanding tension and ambivalence. Bakhtin argues that much of our inner mental life revolves around orchestrating voices speaking in various timbres and tones (heteroglossia). We hear them with emotion, take them in, replay them in conflicting cacophony, and sift through them in a kind of inner orchestration. A kind of "self-fashioning" occurs, but we are never "finished," always subject to many points of view (Holland et al. 1998, 169, 173).

The interview is a place for this orchestration to take form, as for example with Ito-san, who plays back voices of her mother, brother, and friends. Her mother's comments and opinions over the years tie her to internalized expectations from her youth, while the voice of her friend who has studied abroad counters her mother's comments, and her brother mediates between her parents' expectations and her world as a single woman in Tokyo. Self, elusive and changing, emerges out of the tension among these voices—opposition to her mother, support, envy, and some competition from her friend, and nervous alliance with her brother, on whom another voice tells her not to become too dependent!

Signals of ambivalence: Symbolic bootstrapping

Ito-san's tensions are also revealed by the concept of "symbolic bootstrapping," which turns attention to the material things that mediate struggles in people's lives. "Symbolic bootstrapping" is a process through which children interact with an object symbolically and materially to pull them into a new level in their inner thinking (Vygotsky 1966 [1933]), but it is useful for understanding adult development in a world full of symbolic consumer items. It signifies a time of tension, but also a time of potential change toward growing a psychosocial self. Through manipulating and playing with objects externally, children achieve internal control over experiences that feel overwhelming or challenging. For example, when the mother leaves, they cling to a doll that symbolizes the love of the mother, then throw it away, and find it again, but after a while will not need it at all.

These ideas help us to understand the significance of the leisure and individualized consumer goods that are a playground for creating self among this generation of women (Holland et al. 1998). Ito-san's purple coat, bought in Hong Kong against her mother's will, and her broad-striped dress that, although still flashy, Ito-san wore again six years later, make sense. The purple jacket is a symbolic bootstrap shoring up her still-forming intent to become independent from her mother and her own self within society. Later, her clothes continue to be a bit flashier than those of her peers, but obviously of lessening importance to Ito-san, who appeared in the same dress at the last two interviews. Now, computers, TVs, cars, and going to the United States have become central in this tricky, sometimes tense, sometimes painful bootstrapping operation, as she works on her self between what she has been and what she wants to be.

Signals of ambivalence: Emotions

Emotions are a last signpost of tension and ambivalence in interviews, because emotions are both inner and outer; just at the point when language arrives at its limits, they make our internal states public in laughter and tears (Lyon and Barbelet 1994, 60; Oksala 2005, 130–131). Emotions also help us to work through things, giving our bodies a way of evaluating experience as we meet it. For example, it was clear with Ito-san in 1998 that her excitement about the prospect of working abroad was linked with her sense of fear in telling her parents about it. Her voice lowered, her face tightened, and she asked to speak in English so that others in the coffee shop would not understand what she was saying. On the same subject in 2004, nervous laughter accompanied her revelations. This was an important point of ambivalence as well as change. She was going forward with her sense of long-term resistance, but her embodied experience revealed tension that could not be ignored.

Single in Tohoku, the northeast

The path to meeting Kawai-san of the northeast presents a very different picture from the stylish underground mall where I first glimpsed Ito-san in Tokyo. In 1993 I met Kawai-san at an elder-care home among the rice fields at the edge of a farming village in Tohoku, an hour from Morioka. Although she was raised and graduated from high school in the regional city of Morioka an hour away, she had come here to work as an aide five years ago. At age twenty-six, she was living several minutes away in her own apartment.

Kawai-san is interesting because she is a single woman buoyed up by neither education nor interest in a career nor big-city consumption. She is not an urban, mobile cosmopolitan consciously building a new sense of family via friends, like Ito-san. An "inadvertent cosmopolitan" whose path has unintentionally strayed from the status quo, she ends up surprised and somewhat fearful, yet takes heart in her ambiguous position as part of this emerging generational discourse.

In 1993, the village Kawai-san worked in had a new town hall and schools built with plentiful national money given to local towns in the 1980s, but they sat among a few struggling small shops. Restaurants were out by the highway, trying to survive on tourists passing through on their way to golfing and skiing in the mountains above this agricultural area. This resort and the government provided some jobs, and many people were involved in the farming economy on part-time or full-time bases. Nothing was far from the rice fields that were just now being prepared for a new planting.

In contrast to Tokyo's reputation of sporting the most contemporary styles in dress and living, this small village in the north of Honshu was pegged as "traditional" with multigenerational households ruled by strong patriarchs and mothers-in-law who demanded the work and allegiance of the elder son and his wife. But here we were in an elder-care home, evidence of the high number of elderly in the area and of the urban migration of youth that left family members stranded in this institution (Mock 2006). As in Tokyo, life was changing in this rural area, interwoven with global, national, and urban changes yet finding its own space and tempo (Traphagan and Thompson 2006).

Kawai-san

1993, AGE TWENTY-SIX

Kawai-san dashed in late to the impromptu meeting of aides gathered for my benefit. She was off for the day and had been called in. Dressed in a T-shirt and jeans, her long hair was flowing and mussed as she spoke in a relaxed, laid-back way. Sitting next to her was her friend dressed in informal sportswear, and as they talked about their work and boyfriends, Kawai-san laughed as her friend joked and jabbed at her side with her elbow.

"Yes," admitted Kawai-san, "I do have a boyfriend but no plans to marry." Her friend poked her, but she insisted. "I don't want to marry just to have children. For now, it's fun to live alone without bothering about others, even though sometimes it's lonely." She looked out of the corners of her eyes at her friend and giggled at her seriousness and at things left unsaid. For all its image of strict family-bound tradition, the village also had a historical underlay of more relaxed sexual standards than the city, and Kawai-san was living apart from her family, who resided an hour away in the regional city.

The importance of a certain form of female behavior in the northern region echoed in the voice of her mother. Kawai-san saw her often and reported her negative words: "Go quickly as a bride. At your age you should have children!" When Kawai-san argued, her mother replied, "Your attitude is not like a woman's, you are impolite!"

Kawai-san was no self-avowed rebel like Ito-san, but she had obviously thought of alternatives. "I hope to marry before age thirty and to have two or three children. But I want to pay for my own wedding and find my own husband. Not like my brother." She paused and looked impishly at her friend. "I have thought of having children even if I don't marry. My brother's children are difficult, but they are so cute." In 1993 in the northeast, this was beyond the pale of action, but showed that the global imagination had permeated these young women.

Kawai-san had tried to better her work situation within the constraints of her high school education and workplaces in the northeast. She had left an office in the regional city where the males would not listen to her and took revenge if she disagreed with them. The improvement here was slight, but at least affirmed herself as a person at work. "I can speak my opinion, but it doesn't go anywhere." She liked helping the old people, but mainly she worked "for money and because it would be boring not to work."

1998, AGE THIRTY-ONE

In 1998 Kawai-san had moved back to work at a retirement home near her home just outside Morioka. She was living in the kind of regional city where Ito-san's mother lived and Ito-san refused to visit.

The area of the city that Kawai-san lived in was the same that I had lived in when I had come to this city to teach English over twenty years before. We had lived in a new apartment where frogs croaked in the rice paddies outside our window. The trip into town on worn buses passed by farmhouses and fields that by 1998 were fast being replaced by car dealers, electronic stores, and supermarkets. I hardly recognized the place.

The city's old train station with noodle booths and wooden bridges over the tracks, no less than six hours from Tokyo when we first lived here, had been rebuilt. The bullet train now put these regional people, whom Tokyoites viewed as unsophisticated at best and hickish at worst, within three hours of Tokyo. A new elevated bullet-train station shone with an underground mini-mall of local stores for tourists, restaurants, and a department store.

Kawai-san had grown up through this transition and she suggested McDonald's, a symbol of what was new, as a good place for us to meet on her day off. To me, it was an antiseptic place to meet, but for her it held the status of Western things, and in the morning its second floor was entirely empty. Gradually our talk gave it some color. Kawai-san had changed jobs to escape difficult human relations, but things were bad at this job, too.

"They want people to quit as they age, but I am trapped. I have to cling to this job because economics are bad. The superiors don't recognize that people are working hard, doing well, and devoting themselves to other people. They only scold angrily and put us down. It's okay when I go out in the mobile truck to give baths to elders in their homes, but we have to write reports on what happens and the atmosphere in the office is bad. I avoid it."

As we sipped our coffee out of styrofoam cups, I asked, "So do you live alone now?"

"No, I live at home with my parents. The three of us." She laughed ruefully. "Every day they say 'Marry fast!' It really bothers me! I thought of getting an apartment but it would be hard to have enough money to live. Half my salary would be gone. And people might say 'Why would a girl want to live alone?' especially at this workplace. It's so close to my parents."

Many workplaces preferred single women to live with their parents to protect the reputations of both the company and the family. The female body needed to be kept safe for marriage, even when marriage might not be forthcoming.

"I'm saving up for an apartment. In the future, my older brother and his family will live with my parents. I'll have to leave the house so there is enough room. I can't depend on my brother and his wife. I must become independent."

The irony of it all, I thought. She is supposed to live with her parents, but the eldest son's position takes precedence here. Kinship structures would give her an excuse to live separately. We talked about how it felt to be single in Morioka.

"It's not great. I'm not, like, set on being single. But after all I want to choose my partner (*aite*)."

Although I knew that young women often kept boyfriends secret from their parents and even their friends, I assumed that I was far enough out of her social network to be safe when I asked, "Do you have a boyfriend?"

"Now I am going out with a person. He is not a friend, but not really a lover. He is in between. I get introductions from friends pushed at me, but they just don't hit the spot (*pinto konai*)."

At the end of our conversation, as part of her hopes for her life, she admitted, "I hope that I can marry the person I am going out with now. He is a banker."

2004, AGE THIRTY-SEVEN

By 2004, Kawai-san's tastes in coffee shops had risen. We met in the second-floor café of the poshest of the three department stores in town. She was dressed in a black sweater and skirt, her long hair in a more sophisticated mid-length style. Having lived alone in an apartment for three years now, she rented rather than buying. With a touch of humor and jealousy of richer single women, she said, "I shovel my own car out of the snow. No heated parking lots for me!"

To her dismay, she had been promoted to third in line of command at the retirement home. She was "receiving [the privilege] of putting out all her effort"—a sarcastic way of saying she had to work hard whether she liked it or not. I thought maybe it would give her the chance to express her opinions at work as she had always wanted to. She agreed that it had gotten "a bit better. I can't say and do as I want, but I talk with the person above me about things. I don't try to solve them myself. I guess I just don't think so much about people's words now."

"Are you satisfied with this work?"

She pulled on her hair and leaned back. "I don't not like it. I chose this work because I liked it. I don't have the courage or psychological power (*yūki, kiryoku*) to change work now. There's a little resignation (*akirame*) creeping in. But I don't want to go up in the world."

Kawai-san had wanted to meet here because she was going to look for a birthday gift for her nephew, whose party she was going to the next day. Our fancy cakes were done and we were just nursing the last of our tea. About that time, the boyfriend problems emerged.

"There is no talk of marriage. There was a time when I thought, if I like you so much, why don't you like me enough to talk of marriage? But now I am thinking, hmm, is it okay like this? We are both really busy. We e-mail a lot but meet only twice a month and eat together. But I am letting things go as they will. We are each into our own lives."

There was a voice of a friend inside her that she wanted to tell me about.

"My close friend from junior high school was dating a guy who was the eldest son and he was supposed to inherit the house. But his parents were against his marrying my friend, so they parted. Then they just floated back together again. But then he got laid off because of economic restructuring and he didn't tell her." Her eyes were round and serious now. "It became a neurosis and he tried to commit suicide."

"Is she okay? What about him?"

"She was devastated and couldn't work for awhile. She wondered why he couldn't talk things over with her. Even now his consciousness hasn't returned and probably won't. This is my close friend. She tells me: 'You have your own relationship. Marriage is not the only form for relationships.' "

"So what does that make you think?"

"My boyfriend's parents said to him that he is an eldest son and has to be strong (*shikkari*). They put a lot of pressure on him. So now I think, isn't it okay if I have a good relationship with him . . . he has an apartment in a town about an hour south. I could live there with him if I had to. There is no manual for this."

"Do people live together here?"

"Yes, there are people in my work who live together. Before it would have been unthinkable, but now it is okay. Anyway we are both busy and he is in a management position. Even on vacations he works sometimes . . ."

The tea was definitely gone now and the restaurant crowded, but I sipped at my cup, pretending that I still had more so the waitress wouldn't ask us to leave.

"It's true," I ventured. "You don't want to put too much pressure on him and then have something happen. But you probably get pressure from your mother to marry."

"I can't talk about it with my parents. I say it is 'a friend that I can't talk about' to my mother. I don't say I have a person I like. It's hard to talk about to my parents. I do talk with my older brother and younger sister. So when proposals come to meet a man . . . well, I don't want to go out with anyone but him. If I can't marry, I don't have to. Marrying or not, either way is fine."

"What if you said that to your mother?"

"She would start to cry. Once we argued really loudly. She shouted, 'So will you never marry for your whole life? Won't you be lonely? What will you do in old age?' I told her, 'I'll go to an old folks' home or I'll die by myself.' 'You'll be a bother to your older brother,' she yelled. When she cries, I really get a heavy feeling. My mother always obeyed. But now there are various lives. Now it is one's own life for oneself."

No manual to follow

Kawai-san seems almost startled to be in the scriptless position she finds herself in, with no manual to follow in her life of long-term resistance. She is a relaxed sort of person who just wanted to graduate from high school, work, enjoy herself for a while, and then have a family. Yet from the first interview, she was open to the generational discourse swirling around her in magazines and in the stories of girls who returned to the village from the city to extend work and enjoyment, even playfully suggesting the idea of having children outside of marriage. She doesn't delay marriage for any particular reason except to wait for the man that she wants to marry, and having found him, she becomes more steadfast in her decision to hold out for him and no other. Although she often referees tension between her mother and her sister-in-law, who live together, she is even willing to live with his parents if necessary.

The motto of her generation—to marry the man you want to marry—pushes her into a corner of having to seriously recognize that she might not marry and might be called upon to live life according to a script that is just being written, particularly around Morioka and the northeast. Because Kawai-san values the closeness of family but is not highly educated and does not value work for her self-development as many in her generation do, she strongly feels the tension of the double bind, having to change her sense of the world and to relearn how to 'be' in it (Charlesworth 2000, 62). On the one hand, the emotional warmth of the family has inscribed itself on her emotions and body and she desires to re-create it. On the other hand, new habits learned as she came of age as part of her generation—sexual freedom, her own claim on her emotions, and the reproductive use of her body, even a will to power in the workplace—have gradually become part of her. Her double bind gathers force with her devotion to the Japanese late-modern insistence on holding out for the one she loves and her boyfriend's late-modern uncertainty about his responsibility to the institution of family.

Her boyfriend's attitude points to the pressures that men began to express more openly through the 1990s and 2000s. Pressures that men of her father's generation have been willing to put up with in order to live up to their social positions in postwar families and companies feel like too much for men her age, who have grown up in a generation that expects enjoyment and latitude to express themselves (Mathews 2003). Indeed, like women, they increasingly want some semblance of a life for self. If she puts pressure on her boyfriend on top of those exerted by his parents and his workplace, he might crack.

Kawai-san's sense of living without a manual to guide her raises the specter of how hard it is for her to reorganize her inner being to accommodate an outer experience that is so unpredictable. The orderly postwar middle-class woman's life stages of school to work to motherhood to part-time work to old age under family care is not likely to be her life course now. We can almost see the orchestration of voices in her head—the voice of her close friend strengthening her resolve against the disappointed voice of her mother, toward whom Kawai-san's own voice remains silent. As with Ito-san, siblings' voices mediate the differences with mother. The boyfriend's voice is muted, reflective of his own confusion among his obligations to job, family, self, and girlfriend. Much evidently goes unsaid between Kawai-san and her boyfriend, but she risks a break with her mother to conserve the stress piling on her boyfriend. Still, she cannot be sure of his future actions even as she continues to hope for at least a declared, long-term relationship and a chance to live together or marry someday. Traversing various ways of belonging in this unpredictable world (Gunewardena 2007), she stays close to her family, enjoying her nieces and nephews and visiting her younger married sister.

Kawai-san listens and reacts in a space of risk: in the interior geography of herself that wants to marry and enjoy family; in her present actions that risk life without marriage; and in the exterior geography of Morioka, where people pressure her to marry at home and on the job. Furthermore, she must cope with the relative poverty of single women in Japan.[3] Whereas Ito-san in Tokyo receives encouragement from other single men and women and their choices of lifestyles enabling them to remain single, Kawai-san in Morioka mainly feels the pull to marry and normalize. But she follows this uncharted course because over the long years of her resistance she has been forever changed—cut, fractured, and reshaped as an individual and in her relationships with others (Gupta and Ferguson 1997). The small slippages in her normative actions are dangerous and may leave her outside forever, but she is careful, splitting with some friends but drawing closer to others, disagreeing with bosses but tolerating new ones, and turning a silent face to her mother on the subject of men while maintaining her relationship with family.

Indeed, uncertain as she appears, Kawai-san's life expands and shapes the performance of these ideas in the local area. She claims the space of her private life from her mother and her family, as well as from the local and central governments that urge young women to marry and have children, insisting in our conversation, "Having children is a private decision. Nothing the government is doing will change it." It is people like Kawai-san, an ordinary high school graduate, whose uncertain actions make people around her see that a new version of modernity is upon them. Like their fellow urban nationals, they have to accept that, as Kawai-san says, "Now it is one's own life for oneself."

Dilemma of choice

We have met Kawai-san at three different points of her life and seen her gradually become more resigned to leading her life according to unknown rules that will earn her neither full acceptance in regional society nor full contentment according to the desires and dispositions she grew up with. She is caught in a "dilemma of choice": choose one way and she loses the positions, power, and emotional rewards that Japanese women obtain through marriage and motherhood; choose the other way and she loses her ability to shape her life as she wants. Melucci (1989, 1996) writes about women like Kawai-san around the world who are dissatisfied with the modern cultural code they have inherited, with its rigid cultural categories. They are "nomads," uncomfortable in the "home" that they grew up in yet unable to find a home that fits them as they emerge into adulthood (1989, 109). Dilemmas of choice weave webs through their adulthoods, because if they become wives and mothers, they may lose the ability to escape the cultural code for women to which they object.

Women like Kawai-san find themselves in "blind spots" unable to know how their own story of self will play itself out. Should they step through "the gauntlet of choice" and marry no matter what, or will they end up with "postdecisional regret" for all they have given up (Melucci 1989; Japp and Kusche 2008)?[4] The words of a Japanese woman, long a single working woman who married late and has not been able to have children, characterizes these dilemmas: "I had lots of chances but it was hard to make decisions. I wonder now, 'Is it okay?' . . . and what about in the future?"

In Japan, Nobuta, a psychologist, indicates that for women of this generation who have experienced the feeling of dissatisfaction with the cultural code for women that they grew up with and have imagined another way of being, the dilemma of choice never quite leaves them alone. Both single and married women experience uncertainty about whether they have made the right choices and experience some post-decisional regret. (See also Goldstein-Gidoni 2012, 206.)

Single women come to counseling wondering if they have been right to hold out for the right man or value their work above marriage. They have chosen what seems to be the more "interesting" (*omoshiroi*) choice compared with marriage, as claimed in *Makeinu no Toboe* (The howl of the losing dog), a popular book that compares single and married women in Japan (Sakai 2004). Yet single people are still seen as abnormal in a society where heterosexual marriage has been mandatory and government statistics label them as "not yet married" (Maree 2004). Even dieting and exercise for single women can be seen as selfish because it may ultimately hinder their getting pregnant (Spielvogel 2003). Ueno and Nobuta note that it is very difficult for women raised in this society to reject the feeling that the preferred woman is the woman who has been chosen and is protected by a man. Neither do single women escape the authority of bosses and elder parents, who often overwork them because they are single (Ueno and Nobuta 2004).

Married women also struggle in a peer society that is newly split between single and married people far into adulthood. Nobuta sees more married than single women in her counseling practice, and the married women are also uncertain: Is it okay to have married? Is it okay to have married this man? Ueno argues that these women feel relatively deprived, because around thirty-five, the marriage they committed themselves to as a step up in status now seems like a step behind their single friends who have careers and freedom. Single women might be characterized as "howling dogs" forever in search of a man, but married women are jealous when they compare their boring, narrow lives with the imagined interesting lives of singles (Ueno and Nobuta 2004).

A social movement of ambiguous resistance over life

Melucci proposes that women participate in a new kind of social movement that features the ambiguous, uncertain resistance that I have found here. It is not an active, organized rebellion, but one that "breaks the limits of compatibility" of a system's shared rules and behavior, pushing the system beyond the range of variations it can tolerate without altering its structure" (1989, 12). Furthermore, as we see here, people dip in and out of this social movement over the course of their lives.

These single women, like Ito-san and Kawai-san and married women whom we will meet later in the book, are engaged in just such a quiet social movement that challenges the cultural code in informal, personal ways and unevenly over the life course. The social movement is common to their generation, but it has spread by desires shared and deeds explored rather than by noisy protests. These women feel a risk in committing themselves to the cultural expectations of self-sacrifice a woman must fulfill in entering her husband's household and making a family, yet they also feel the risk in not accepting the very societal role that assures women an image of maturity as well as emotional and economic security in postwar Japanese society.

Kawai-san, who continues to work and secretly consort with her chosen man in a regional city, risks never escaping from the category of "emerging adult," a category created to cover the exploratory time between high school and full adulthood. Emerging adults reach toward taking responsibility for themselves, making independent decisions, and achieving financial independence, but are not yet accepted by society and elders as full adults (Arnett 2004, 209). Of course, Kawai-san has achieved these goals and should be well past this stage, but in Japan, especially in Tohoku where pressures to marry are stronger, single women appear ambiguous and are judged as never quite having reached the maturity of wives and mothers.[5]

Given Kawai-san's dilemma with her boyfriend and her strong feeling that "there is no manual for this," she is gingerly emerging into a new field that has few models in her regional environment. She may never "emerge" as her elders expect or she had thought she would, remaining in this state of unstable liminality in relation to the society around her. Nonetheless, over the years her demeanor communicates that she sees herself as an evolving adult of a different kind, perhaps ultimately stronger than others because of the challenges she faces.

Melucci, who writes of this new kind of social movement, would agree with Kawai-san's positive evaluation. He thinks that, through dissatisfaction with the cultural code they have been raised in, young people and women develop a "growth in individual and social capacity for self-reflection" (1989, 12). Comparing themselves with media images and people throughout the world, they gain self-awareness and the ability to think about themselves and their worlds. Indeed, in a society based on information and individual risk like Japan, self-responsibility is a requirement (Hook and Takeda 2007).

Ito-san and Kawai-san both illustrate this as they participate in modern institutions with skeptical self-awareness and space for individual pursuits and talk with like-minded friends (Touraine 1995). This generation of Japan is thinking, critiquing, seeing possibilities, imagining themselves in them, and experimenting. Although they claim to be only "going at my own pace," a phrase that echoes throughout my interviews, and although many of their acts are ambiguous choices to not choose (gestures of tacit refusal), this slowing of mandated life stages gives time for thought and evaluation, and in aggregate makes a difference in national statistics.

Looking in two directions, Kawai-san and Ito-san are both bigger as people. Acts that would have been unthinkable and unacceptable before, such as living with one's boyfriend and choosing love or work over children, have become possible. As victims and perpetrators in this unstable field of love and life (Padilla et al. 2007) their way forward may be painful and risky, but living in a state of alert tension and ambivalent compliance is an engaged way to interact with the kaleidoscopic changes of the contemporary world. In fact, there may be no other way.

Urban-rural differences, class, and "tradition"

Ito-san and Kawai-san brave the tensions of their ambiguous, long-term resistance in different contexts of urban and rural Japan. In order to be even partially successful, their efforts have had to occur in what Lovell (2003) calls meaningful fields of debate. The debate over women's roles and the question of how to develop self are more clearly stated in Tokyo than up in Tohoku, but if the debate over women's lives had not already reached Morioka to some extent, Kawai-san's acts would have been unactable and unutterable. Even Rosa Parks' act of sitting in the front of the bus would not have been recognized as legitimate and worthy of widespread demonstrations had it not happened within a larger framework of national debate (Lovell 2003). Likewise, Kawai-san could not write her new manual of love, sexuality, and individual choice outside of the maelstrom of discourses and practices emanating from Japanese cities and media and passed from friend to friend in Morioka and the village.

Both geographical location and class make Kawai-san's dilemma of choice more difficult to traverse than Ito-san's. The changes that have pervaded both of them are part of a gendered generational discourse, but their gendered responses intersect with other social identities, in this case, urban-rural differences and class differences.

Although both of these women were raised in the regions, their class origins are quite different. Kawai-san is working-class—a high school graduate with high school–educated parents who always lived in the Morioka area, her father working in the building trades and her mother helping in the business when necessary. In contrast, Ito-san is middle-class—herself a four-year university graduate, her father a salaryman and university graduate, and her mother a stay-at-home junior college graduate; they moved to the regions from Tokyo for her father's job. Ito-san's father exhibits more tolerance of her single lifestyle than Kawai-san's father. While both mothers have urged their daughters to marry, Kawai-san's mother remains more family-centered on a daily basis, while Ito-san's mother follows her own middle-class hobbies with friends and allows herself to be distracted from her daughter's future.

The ambivalence and tension of this generation are less painful in Tokyo, which as a large city affords more anonymity and tolerance of various lifestyles, more spaces to walk in unwatched, more cracks to slip through—especially for women like Ito-san whose parents live in the regions (deCerteau 1984). As a single woman who moved to Tokyo from Morioka said in comparing the two: "In Tokyo, individuals are not used by others. People don't think about how others are looking at them." The easier path for women in Tokyo gains credence through women's words in this book, although it too can be overdrawn, because elder family members and bosses in Tokyo also make unfair demands of women. Nonetheless, almost across the board, whether women are single or married, with or without children, the double binds experienced by women in this study are consistently harsher in the northeast than in Tokyo.

What about the regional city of Morioka, which is in-between Tokyo and the rural village—a backwater for Tokyo-bred interviewees, but a mecca of shopping for interviewees from the village? As the Morioka woman said, people are under the eyes of others and "used by others": in family, school, and work, people are expected to watch out for each other, employ their mental alertness for each other (*ki o tsukau*), and depend on each other for favors, often with hierarchical dynamics. But the same woman pinpointed good aspects about Morioka. "Things aren't so trendy and strange there. You don't have to be fashionable. Relations with people are good. I relax when I am there and hear the accent."

I knew what she meant. I am always struck by the darker colors and plainer clothes on the streets when I come from Tokyo. Shopping cannot even be compared, although Morioka has several up-to-date department stores. People live in a narrower mold, as if the furry green mountains surrounding Morioka and Mount Iwate (6,686 ft.) to the north guard the city's inhabitants from too much change. Winters are cold and snowy, though less so here than on the side toward the Korean peninsula. The Tohoku accent known as *zuzuben* has grown on me over the years, for it is here that I learned Japanese as a young English teacher. Its lilt, pronunciation, and endings on sentences make Tohoku people stand out in Tokyo, but the accent conveys the intimate human relations of the region—warm when they enclose you, suffocating for those who are different, and cold when they ostracize you.

People are more wary of me as a foreigner than in Tokyo, but once accepted, I am embraced, with friends going out of their way to take care of me and pretension neither needed nor desired. My actions, however, reflect on the people who take care of me, and thus I hear that I have been spotted on my long walks around the city or while interviewing a woman in a downtown bar. Because I remain a guest, I do not experience "being used by others," except that people do further their contacts through me.

Another Morioka woman describes typical people from the area, including her husband: "They have patience and endurance, allow themselves little luxury, and even expect misfortune (*fukō*)." In the face of the 2011 earthquake and tsunami these traits may help, but for young women entertaining new desires and dreaming of opportunities for self, they create serious double binds. However, Morioka has variety just like Tokyo. The woman quoted here grew up in an old Morioka family, the daughter of musicians, but she does not include herself or her family in her own definition.

Women from the rural village put all of this in perspective, however. For them Morioka represents a place for a divorcee to go and drink, to meet someone anonymously. It is a place to escape village eyes and sit idly in a coffee shop or buy clothes. Moving to this regional city represents a loosening of rural family and community relations.

In contrast, the village is a conservative place of rice farmers, multigenerational households, dominant men, long-suffering women, and mothers-in-law who lord it over their daughters-in-law. Everyone knows everything about each other, which seems to make some people quite open and others quite protective of their own privacy. A place of great natural beauty, with rice fields waving below Mount Iwate's soaring slopes, the road through it leads to a national park. However, scratch the surface and this amalgamation of several hamlets has changed considerably in recent decades, with modern town halls, schools, hospitals, homes for the elderly, tourist spots, and private homes that are warm and comfortable. Although household continuity remains vital, elders far outnumber young people, and thus flexibility on how to keep households going—adult children living separately, or foreign wives for men who cannot find Japanese wives—has changed the atmosphere. If nothing else, younger people and many older people are aware of the problematic traditions they face and are often able to negotiate on how to cope with them.

For the purposes of this study, "regional" is the opposite of large urban (Tokyo or Osaka) and includes both rural villages and larger regional cities. Yet considerable differences exist within "regional," so I sometimes use the word "rural" to refer to the village and "regional" to refer to Morioka. Just what composes urban and rural/regional can be ambiguous, but in Japan the main split is between the Tokyo-Osaka corridor and the rest of Japan.

The opposition between urban and rural/regional has both symbolic and material meanings in Japan as elsewhere (Williams 1981; Comaroff and Comaroff 1992). The difference between the "modernity" of Tokyo and the "tradition" of regional/rural Japan forms a widely accepted model for explaining rapid postwar change. The modernity of Tokyo gives play to the imagination of this generation of young women, while Morioka has a dark image of lagging behind. As one Morioka woman says, "All the information you read about in magazines in Morioka is about Tokyo. It gives [you] the desire to go."

The contrast between the experiences of Kawai-san and Ito-san rides on both class and urban-rural differences that intersect with their gendered experiences. Kelly (2002) claims that the perceived modern–traditional opposition between urban and rural/regional in Japan is a symbolic disguise for material class differences. What is fondly labeled and sought after by urbanites as traditional rural Japan, close to nature and relationships, is, materially speaking, a place that has been left behind in postwar economic growth. This relationship is borne out in this book; women from the regions have fewer employment chances and lower incomes, and thus their economic ability to act on their new desires suffers.[6]

Should we discount tradition and concentrate on class differences between urban and regional? The answer is complex. If I think of "tradition" as the ideological nostalgia for what urbanites feel they have lost in modernity and they wish to dabble in from time to time, it is easy to discount it and concentrate on class differences, for this is tradition selectively imagined for urban consumption. Yet even these images have real consequences in people's lives. We shall see that this imagined idea of traditional values has led a few women to turn to rural areas for answers in their lives.

If I understand "tradition" as meaning what is thought of as a conservative emphasis on hierarchical relationships, multigenerational families, and values of cooperation, such values do make a difference for young women in the northeast and make me realize that class is not the only difference here. Their reported experiences indicate more struggle with conservative values than Tokyoites experience, more willingness to accommodate to them, and more suffering if they do not. They live intimately with the discourse of their conservative elders as well as with the discourse of their generation (Rosenberger 2006). However, these conservative values may not have lasted because of cultural devotion to tradition so much as because of the economic necessity to survive.

Urban and rural/regional in Japan are not qualitatively different in cultural terms. Regional people experience the landscape of change in Japan through television, magazines, and travel. Their sons and daughters, students and workers in Tokyo, bring big-city ideas of global modernity home, and their goals and life courses are standardized to the urban middle class (Kelly 1990). They are thoroughly modern in their sense of the world, as the women in this book show (Traphagan and Thompson 2006).

This question of the intersection of these women's gendered experiences with urban-regional differences will continue throughout the book. The indication from the experiences of Ito-san and Kawai-san is that over time negotiation of double binds and tacit refusal to run the gauntlet of choice in regards to marriage, work, and enjoyment is easier in Tokyo than it is in Morioka or the village, but not impossible in either one.

Conclusion

This chapter leaves us with nuances of long-term, ambiguous resistance to look out for: waffling between dependence and independence; signals of ambivalence such as a mental cacophony of voices, symbolic bootstrapping, and emotional expressions. Being caught in dilemmas, unable to choose with knowledge because the future is unpredictable, the past unacceptable, and the present full of double binds also characterizes this experience of the world. Kawai-san captured the feeling with her words, expressed with a certain sad determination: "There is no manual for this. . . . Now it is one's own life for oneself."

If the thoughts and actions of these women are part of a new kind of social movement by dissatisfied cultural nomads whose personal actions gradually break through the limits of compatibility of a social system's shared rules (Melucci 1989), the question of long-term resistance is: How are these women experiencing and negotiating the contradictions and double binds in which they find themselves? How do they choose or not choose within the dilemmas of choice that define their dissatisfactions with the postwar world they were born into? What are the effects of their low-level, long-term resistance on their lives, and what nature of adults emerge from these dilemmas of adulthood?

CHAPTER THREE

Living within the Dilemma of Choice

Singles

"Every corner of my house is me. It is an extension of myself." Baba-san, a freelance interpreter of forty-five, waved me into her Tokyo apartment in 2004. Only fifteen minutes from a main Tokyo station, it could not have been cheap. The apartment smelled like *oden*, a Japanese stew. "I got so much interpreting work when I came home from London that I really hit the money and paid this off! Now I am trying to have a normal life. I knew money wouldn't make me happy. I'm not trying to be a winner or loser."

A single woman friend was there to share the meal made mostly by Baba-san's mother, who lived nearby. Baba-san was an only child and had returned to Japan in 1998 after five years in London both to reconnect with "being Japanese" and to care for her parents. "There is no place to escape personal responsibilities if you live in this society," she had said, and she felt she had to come to terms with that. Her apartment had a double bed for her and a tatami mat room for her mother in the future if her father were to die first.

Both Baba-san and her friend felt pressure to be successful. "We find dissatisfaction with ourselves. We have to do everything fast. It takes energy." Referring to the book *Makeinu no Toboe* (The howl of the losing dog; Sakai 2004), which they felt criticized single women, Baba-san quipped, "But we attack ourselves like defeated dogs!"

The conversation revolved around "independence"—a media word that women tried to actualize in their lives and that was central to the contradictions and debates among which they lived. Baba-san felt that the apartment was a central expression of successful independence. "I want to say that I am completely independent now. This is advanced independence. Women friends who have bought or built houses agree with me." Because she had just been interviewed for an article in a women's magazine on single career women, Baba-san's statement fit and was shaped by the current media view, but taking the risk of buying an apartment set her apart from the risk-averse parasite singles (Borovoy 2010).

This sense of independence rooted in her apartment extended into her view of relationships. "I can have the ideal relationship with anyone now. There is not a strange desire to depend on another. It is an even playing ground." In 1998, she had felt confusion, wanting to marry after a failed love affair in England and yet feeling that her mother—unlike most mothers—thought marriage represented a loss of independence. As our dinner in 2004 wore on, her ambivalence emerged. "I go through waves of wanting and not wanting to marry. Recently I had an introduction and felt, 'Do I have to marry? I don't really need it. He would be invading my field.' But I also fear being alone. I am still hurt by the question: 'Do you have children?' So marriage may still be an issue."

Singles

In this chapter, I trace the interviewees who have remained single through 2004—about one-third of my sample. They are at the crux of contradictions in Japan and this social movement that is stretching the limits of compatibility with the societal rules. Experiencing both the chaos and the flexibility of late modernity, theirs is not an easy path, because they feel pressure to appear successful: "As long as I appear happy and successful people will be jealous of my situation," said a piano teacher, the one single woman from the village. "Otherwise, people will say that I wasn't able to marry because something is wrong with me." Even in Tokyo women sometimes confront this stereotype.

Two general groups have emerged from the data and shape this chapter: the successful singles, who are financially and emotionally stable and not suffering from huge frustrations, and the struggling singles, who vary from those who are financially independent but caught in high tension to those whose tensions have caused them to crash. The case studies in the first group are valuable for investigating the ways in which singles deal with the debate between independence and dependence, sometimes in relation to international experiences, in their evolving search for selves. The second group shows strong contradictions between singles and postwar institutions, with those who crash revealing alternative means of escape inside Japan. The regional-urban contrast, with its class and value differences, emerges in that, although all groups contain women from Tokyo and the northeast, the majority of the successful women are from Tokyo, the struggling singles are mixed, and all of the struggling and crashing singles are from the northeast.

In this sample, the singles group is the most highly educated, including three MAs, ten university graduates, six junior college or vocational graduates, and one high school graduate. Education is a valuable resource if there is any chance of becoming a successful single accepted as a full adult in society.

Successful singles

Successful singles can be seen as making "new forms of middle-class identity" as they attain financial stability outside of marriage (Muraki 2007), but what does success feel like among single women? From my observations, when it is working it feels like being the biggest winners in contemporary Japan but like running on a moving sidewalk that never slows down, always looking around for information and making comparisons with others. The way is tiring, and if the successful singles fall off, it is difficult to clamber back on. They cannot help but recognize the contradictions they face, but these women have the economic and psychological means to live in creative tension with them.

I classify eight of the nineteen single women in this study as successful, including the two women in Chapter 2 and Baba-san (Rosenberger 2001, 206, 217). I introduce one more, Sato-san, whose words contribute to the negotiation of independence brought up by Baba-san. The case studies cast light on the following question: How have these women negotiated their workshops of experience in Japan as they attempt to live the idea of independence heralded in global discourses of this era, cope with the cultural and personal meanings of dependence in their lives, have lovers, take responsibility for parents, and avoid loneliness?

These women join an ongoing debate in Japan over independence and dependence, one area of the cultural code that women push against but about which they carry some ambivalence. Dependent relations have been central to the close relationships, communication, and dedication that have underwritten Japan's economic growth in companies, schools, and homes. They depend on successful socialization in an emotionally dependent relationship between mother and child, a "maternal frame" that developed through the twentieth century (Yoda 2000). Doi (1971) brought attention to *amae* as a positive emotional security that he argued Japanese have and Americans do not, but also as something that keeps Japanese from individuating. His work was taken up as a justification for Japanese cooperation in groups and their economic success. In the 1980s Asada attacked such emotional relations of dependence as being wielded as a tool of capitalism that infantilizes Japanese and advised escape, as many of the young did, becoming irregular workers or unemployed and remaining single (Yoda 2000). Indeed, Japanese-style capitalism smacked of crony capitalism in the recession of the 1990s, and the debate has gone on in educational reform, stumbling over the problems of how to create independent children while still creating a morality of interdependence and cooperation.

Independence can easily be seen as reeking of selfishness in Japanese morality (Nakano and Wagatsuma 2004), and the emotion-laden relations of indulgence or dependence (*amae*) have multiple meanings. On the positive side, dependency is part of warm intimacy between people in close relationships—parents and children, lovers, husbands and wives who allow interdependence as an expression of fondness. Even at work, dependency can be the soft mortar in between the bricks of hierarchy through which bosses and employees care for each other over the years. The tendency is that women indulge the dependency of men and elders (*amayakasu*) so that it eases their lives and can give a certain kind of emotion-based power to women as housewives and mothers (Rosenberger 2001; Borovoy 2005). On the negative side lies the emotional power that people have over others to ask or demand that they do things for them or act in certain ways that cannot be refused. It is an extremely effective way of binding someone to one's will and echoes the painfully vulnerable yet pleasurable subordination discussed in Chapter 2 (Butler 1997). Contradictions are inherent in this era because women, in order to gain intimacy and love, can end up allowing lovers or husbands to be dependent on them to take care of the details of life (Alexy 2011). Single women trying to build their own will to power have to deal with their emotional subordination to intimate others such as parents, lovers, and even bosses. Although women criticize dependence as part of long-term resistance, for many of them it is difficult to give up, because people want to be loved as well as to be successful.

A dissatisfied "nomad" looking for a home after living on several continents, Baba-san indicated that her apartment was a symbolic bootstrap into independence in Japan because it showed high-level financial independence. Her independence focused on relationships—emotional independence from her mother and economic independence from boyfriends or future husbands. Within this expression of her "will to power," however, lurked a space of tension and ambivalence encapsulated in the fear of being alone and the hurt of having no children. Moreover, she realized that in Japan a network of relationships is expected, indeed necessary, in work, family, and friends.

Baba-san's independence thus lived with compromise: her parental responsibilities and a realization that, even in the Japanese work world, "People don't look at independence. They look at who you know and your good job." She felt that marriage was the ultimate test of maintaining independence without the "strange desire to depend on another"—an expression of the emotion-laden indulgence (*amae*) that she found in Japanese lovers as compared with British lovers—although all too often both turned out to be married men. The question for Baba-san was how to be part of the interdependence of Japan without sacrificing her personal feeling of emotional independence from a man or parents. Here the traversing of different identities felt more difficult, but she tried to digest and re-create the media message of independence while still maintaining interdependence with her parents. She implicitly asked whether she could pass through the gauntlet of marriage in Japan without risking emotional dependence, and so far the answer for her seemed to be no.

In this case, Baba-san's international experience allowed her to experience "having my own world," living alone in her London flat, interpreting, and studying opera singing. Her bid to come home was part of her quest to work out this puzzle of independence and dependence that she felt she faced "as a Japanese." Like Ito-san in Chapter 2, she idealized Western independence and used it as a path to practice separation but did not find it entirely satisfying and realized that she was in a state of ambivalent long-term resistance, trying to find a kind of independence that would work in Japan.

Several other women in this study worked both abroad and in Japan, one as a journalist and another as a manager in a department store. Their international experiences were ways to experiment away from the pressures of the cultural norms to which they objected. This was a path by which "Japanese women are getting power," said the journalist. "For our generation, seeing Japan from inside and outside is vital," said the manager, illustrating the self-reflection that life in the late-modern world required. At a personal level, relationships with men sprang out as the most important contrast: "Japanese men's consciousness has not changed yet, at least in our generation," said the journalist. The manager thought that Japanese men are "narrow, not so exciting, with no big energy compared with ladies." She preferred a man "with his own way of thinking, who doesn't have to be like everyone else." My sense is that they wanted a "contingent person" (Bauman 1991, 236) of the late-modern era who instead of wanting the solidarity of order would be, first and foremost, tolerant of difference and disorder in a normative sense, encouraging the development of self-actualization in both self and partner. Yet at the same time, they wanted someone who respected norms and accepted their obligations, especially toward parents.

Significantly, none of these women found completely satisfying answers in the idealized West, as, in their way, the men they dated abroad often seemed selfish (see Kelsky 2002). All of these single women except Ito-san had parents in Japan who would eventually need care, and they continued looking for partners in Japan. The journalist still hoped for a "darling to drink tea with." The manager looked to Japanese CEOs as potential mates who were independent-minded but understood Japanese families. She turned to aspects of Japanese culture by writing haiku and doing tea ceremony, a ritual based on serving others in a compassionate way. "Tea is so logical, calm, and beautiful" in contrast to the stress of her work life, she commented. In short, these Japanese women with long-term experience with the West found tensions abroad and tempered their original fascination, bringing the historical culture of Japan into their lives in new ways. Many of them are only children, daughters who have returned to watch out or care for parents even as they maintain their separate lives of work and enjoyment. They activate the ambivalence of their long-term resistance in a very conscious way, flowing and twisting through multilayered ways of being, both orderly and chaotic, with occasional bouts of indecision on the way. In short, they have found a way to bear the rather lonely life of sustained ambivalence and illustrate more clearly than many that individual autonomy is not the only goal in choices for self (Mahmood 2001).

Independence in Morioka

Sato-san, who runs a company with a married woman friend in Morioka, offers a more philosophical interpretation of this navigation between independence and dependence among successful singles in Japan.

In 2004, I climbed up to Sato-san's office off the main street running from the railroad station to the old castle park in Morioka. It was well-polished compared to the dingy office where she had showed me the advertisements she was preparing for clients in 1998. I smelled the lavender from the aroma therapy and massage that were now part of their business. Sato-san strode in and filled the room with her solid, husky voice, a red-flowered scarf around her neck (Rosenberger 2001, 196, 208).

"Your business looks great!" She and her friend had "gone independent" in 1994 when she was thirty-eight at the behest of another older woman friend who ran a consciousness-raising group. Although sick with cancer, the friend had challenged them: "Are you independent? Are you independent enough?" So they started their business, much to the displeasure of Sato-san's mother, who thought her salaried job with a leading advertising firm was more secure. Like Baba-san, Sato-san also had her own apartment, but she had moved from an expensive one to a city-supported one to save money. In this case the business was her main symbolic road to independence, though with strong interdependence with her business partner.

"People say that the recession is irrelevant for us. We are seen as energetic women just doing what we want (*katte ni*). But we are experts so we are accepted. I'm selling supplements to Taiwan now!" They combined aroma therapy, massage, and supplements with Sato-san's advertising and her friend's dental consultation.

The message of independence was the hidden center of their company, however, because through the introduction of the leader of the consciousness-raising group, they did counseling with Teacher Yanagida from Tokyo. "Her counseling has always been the real center of our business. We still make appointments for her and she comes up from Tokyo once a month to do counseling. Our goal is to get people to receive counseling. We receive it and require it of our employees, and my friend tries to get dentists to polish (*kitaeru*) their characters and their businesses through counseling. Now the aroma therapy makes it easier to talk about counseling a bit. Japanese people don't understand what counseling is. Counseling is about one's very personality (*jinkaku, hitogara*), so it is painful."

In 1998, Sato-san had given me a book by her teacher so I could understand this part of her business and life. The aim was to get away from "soft, spoiled, dependent places" (*amai tokoro*) and to break away from the narrow, predetermined parts of life a person clings to: family, work, hometown, sex, love, and so on. Relations out in society, and especially with friends with whom you can "share your heart," are important, because in this wider society you can grow into a mature human being (Yanagida 1991).

Sato-san continued: "The teacher advised me recently to do Zen Buddhist meditation and I went for about a year. You try to rise above the mud of everyday life like a lotus blooming above the water. You become clear about what is important. But lately I don't have time to go."

Looking back over her life, she said, "I have been given the chance to know myself. My life has been entirely different because of counseling. If I hadn't done this, I couldn't have understood my self's situation by myself (*jibun no koto o jibun de*)—what kind of human being I am. I've learned to avoid selfish human relations and look at each person well."

Stamping out dependence

Sato-san's story broadens the understanding of this struggle with independence/dependence, the key to her long-term resistance. With missionary zeal, she attacks dependence—"the soft, spoiled places" (*amai tokoro*) and *amaeru*, to indulge in the goodwill of another.

Sato-san and others in this study recognize such dependence particularly in their relations with their parents. Both Baba-san and Sato-san see it as an inner contradiction they have to rise above to be successful singles, railing against it as a negative aspect of Japanese historical values because people are bound into relationships that are too close, even "sticky," as Japanese say, with emotions so bound up that obligations are unquestionable. Reflective thinking that depends on distance is difficult and independent action impossible.

Sato-san finds an alternative via her teacher's philosophy that combines Eastern philosophies with Western counseling techniques. The answer is not individual autonomy but relinquishment of selfishness that clings to others and expectations of them. The path is to give up emotionally laden attachments that root one in the mud of the world. One becomes independent of past attachments by scouring self of soft, comfortable relationships and demanding compassionate but adult relationships. In short, this combination of Eastern philosophies with Western counseling techniques has become Sato-san's version of independence.

For Sato-san, her relationship with her mother has been key. She had fractured it with her words "Worry about yourself, not me" and the purchase of her own apartment separate from her mother. But she is putting the relationship back together, accepting the relationship as her counselor advises, but doing it self-consciously. She and her mother have bought an apartment together, and her mother goes back and forth between there and her brother's family's house, also in Morioka. She accepts her mother's dinners and ironing but aims for a future home with friends when she retires. She would not accept Ueno's criticism of single women in Japan as living with their mothers and therefore becoming dependent like their fathers before them, or Dales' idea (2005) that her independence is limited. She works her way through the double bind by contending that she provides a refuge for her mother but maintains her own independence of mind and spirit in the manner of her teacher.

Other successful singles found slightly different ways to work out the contradictions and long-term tensions they felt swirling around independence and dependence. Another successful single, a Tokyo kindergarten teacher, was less self-reflective about the need for independence, practicing it in a media-centered way as she shopped and surfed throughout the world (Rosenberger 2001, 182–183). Rooting out soft, spoiled places was not her conscious purpose, and her ongoing residence with her mother reflected her own comfort as well as her respect for her mother's sense of what was correct. She spent some evenings with her mother, but her mother also tolerated her frequent trips. Ultimately, she nursed her mother through cancer for three years before her death, an experience that affected her sense of self, making her feel that she had not only been dependent on her mother but had given the privilege of dependency to her mother. She reflected, "My friends have had the experience of marriage and children, and they can teach me. But I have had the experience of caring for my mother until death, and I have something to teach them, too." Her words indicate that, for this generation, not only independence but giving of yourself to another with emotional generosity enhances one's maturity as an adult.

Another nuance of independence for these successful singles in their long-term resistance is finding a way to contribute to the world from an inner perspective; doing something that gives their lives the feeling of worth (*yarigai* or *ikigai*). Sato-san did so by imbuing her business with her message of counseling and independent maturity to others. Another somewhat reluctant successful single in Tokyo did so in an after-school educational company that she worked her way up in, never seeking too much responsibility and always a bit sad that she had not married and had children. Although she became a supervisor of other teachers, she insisted on keeping her own class of children in order to contribute more directly to education and satisfy her desire to be in touch with children. Moving away from family in her thirties, she kept in close touch with her parents, divorced sister, and sister's child, who lived together. She used the discourse of her generation to come to terms with her situation: "My generation had to be hungry because the ones above us opened the way. . . . I have been given the chance to grow. Now I am myself."

In sum, these successful singles negotiated paths of economic independence in tandem with compassionate and reciprocal relationships with significant others, keeping their balance on the moving sidewalk as they emerged as respected adult women. They do not speak of nimbly traversing multiple identities as Ueno suggested, but rather seem to struggle to hone their independence so that it bleeds over into other identities and relationships—with mothers, friends, and bosses or employees. Over the long term, their success as singles stretches beyond independence symbolized in apartments, jobs, and international experiences, and reaches beyond the language and feelings of obligation toward mature give-and-take in a variety of relationships. As singles, they are able assess relationships, creating new ones and reinterpreting their positions within older ones in a way that fits their changing dispositions (Budgeon 2008). Thus, both within themselves and in relation to their world, they live in a creative tension that pushes away sticky, emotion-laden dependency that—ironically—society accuses them of if they live with parents but that they find so uncomfortable, and experiment with developing a version of independence that is not anomalous in Japan.

This exploration among Japanese singles rests on uncertainty as to how to live on this human continuum of independence and dependence; it is a confusing journey between global calls to emancipation and local history. One of the possible results of this is the high number of singles in this study, and in statistics, who exist without boyfriends or girlfriends or claim never to have had sex (Birmingham 2012, Buerk 2012).[1] While some may be gay, this tendency indicates a questioning of heterosexual love that in the postwar idiom was intertwined with dependency (Ryang 2006).

Struggling singles

Struggling singles are women who experience a noticeably higher pitch of anxious tension and conflicted ambivalence than successful singles, even though most are economically independent. Including both those who struggle and those who struggle and crash, eleven singles are in this group; some have collapsed and revived, but four have crashed long-term. Like a symphony in a bright major key that gradually saddens with increasing minor chords and atonal notes that hint at chaos, these women look and act like successful singles for a long while, but slowly their intonation darkens. Having wrestled with the dilemma of choice about marriage and still doing so in some cases, as well as always feeling observed in their anomalous singlehood in the northeast, they find it harder and harder to stay in tune with the operatic demands of the successful single role. By studying the tensions of the double binds and contradictions they experience over the long run, we learn much about the nuances of long-term resistance.

Although these women also have aspired to "advanced independence," societal contradictions have combined with psychosocial ambivalence to produce storms of tension that rise and fall. Their main problem is that they are enmeshed in workplaces and families that still work in the postwar manner of dependent relationships and that expect a high level of devotion and perseverance that admits little of the separation described above. These institutions and their relationships catch single women in "sticky" webs of obligation and emotion, and make the independent self of successful singlehood almost impossible to maintain internally. Enmeshed in these institutions, with only partial recognition of the overall contradictions because of their feelings of responsibility, these women experience festering irritation and contest the power of the system that permeates their lives with relative silence, tacit accommodation, and a bit of sullenness (Comaroff and Comaroff 1991).

Eight of these eleven women struggled in the regions where mutually dependent relationships in family and work, as well as opinions about the lesser place of women, continued more strongly than in Tokyo. However, living in Tokyo did not make women immune from the dangers of working in old-style institutions. These women usually worked in helping professions such as education or medicine where they could expect security and receive promotions, but nonetheless long hours and obligations backed by emotional dependence were the norm. The two singles featured here are both teachers and were both age forty-two in 2004.

Struggling teacher in Morioka

In 1993 and 1998, I interviewed Nishikawa-san in her parents' house in Morioka. We sat on *zabuton* pillows and tatami mats, her long black hair sweeping over the low table as she talked. She lived separately and taught inside the city after stints of teaching at rural schools. In the 1980s I had interviewed her mother, a housewife caring for her own father and her husband who had married into her family, rather than the reverse. As she brought us tea and cakes, I remembered watching her mother stroke Nishikawa-san's hair when she was a junior high student, saying it was important for girls to acquire a skill. Nishikawa-san got along with her mother, who often gave her food, but not well with her father: "We can't even watch TV together. We always argue. He's stubborn."

Blaming both her type of work and her location in the region, Nishikawa-san conveyed frustration over being single but not being able to live the life of singlehood that she and her generation had imagined. It was as if she felt she was enduring the double binds of singlehood without the payoff of imagined freedom. In 1993, she said: "I don't want a common life like my mother. Since I am single I want to value the life of self. But I am too busy, with no time for self. I'm jealous of my friends in Tokyo who work in travel agencies."

In 1998, she started out with words as brave as her bright-red lipstick: "I don't want to change my life like I did before. I am a public servant and I have to work with devotion." Yet later her disappointment surfaced again, "I am not using the single life positively. It is hard to use the freedom that I have here. You would think I can do as I want, but I can't. I have no latitude. I only have fatigue of the heart."

The orchestration of voices in Nishikawa-san's head pointed out the ambivalence she lived with. Voices of her single women schoolteacher-friends emerged from her narrative, encouraging her to get her own home as they ate French food together. However, they all had to wrestle with the school situation and discrimination against women. "The students don't give respect like they used to. . . . People don't see women teachers as mature. Boys act out with us. Parents say I don't understand their feelings for their kids because I've never had any children." On reflection, Nishikawa-san blamed herself for the problem. "Part of me is spoiled (*amai*). Inside myself I feel like I've not advanced."

In 2004, Nishikawa-san announced happily on the phone: "I have my own apartment now. When you come, climb up the hill behind my parents' house. I'm on the fifth floor." From her window we saw the heated parking lot and snow-covered Mount Iwate. At one end her kitchen sported red appliances and at the other a white sofa curled around the TV.

At first Nishikawa-san sounded much like Baba-san, the successful single in Tokyo: "I thought I would marry and quit my work, but I feel I can do my career with my home. I can live as I want, according to my whims (*kimama*). I want to go on living independently through my own power. A husband would be a bother now. I have my own space and rhythm. I will go to a care home when I am old." Although she seemed to have moved beyond the dilemma of choice in regard to marriage, the high tension and old feelings that she could not have a self legitimate to her generation soon reemerged. "I also feel insecure (*fuan*). I got a promotion to a model school, but I have to work hard, with little support from colleagues. It's all competition. I stay up until two a.m. making model lessons for other teachers to see. The students and parents want high test scores, but the students are tricky, and the parents ask, 'Is it okay to have women teachers? If women become the main teachers, what will we do?' It is the picture of success without real success."

So, despite her apartment and her sense that "I am living in touch with society," Nishikawa-san felt tension rather than success. "Sometimes I get so stressed, I can't eat or sleep. I don't have anyone to let my stress out with in the evenings and it goes round and round in my head." Her dream was to travel again to England, to a "different world" where she could "experience that which will widen my scope as a self."

Independence within dependence

As a schoolteacher in the regions, Nishikawa-san's story communicates the near impossibility of developing self with independence and freedom beyond consumer items like an apartment in the regions, and especially as a schoolteacher. Long-term resistance was reduced to a simmering long-term disgruntlement because the school's requirements enveloped her private individual needs and desires. Her school is what Touraine (1995) calls a rational, modern institution that aims towards reason but denies the promise of individuation, giving job security to employees, but requiring sacrifice of self to the goals of the institution in the fashion of the post-war high economic growth period. Ironically Japanese schools have reformed curriculum to produce more individualistic graduates, but superiors do not spare the teachers in creating new curriculum. Teachers must work incredibly hard for superiors to fulfill the new institutional vision, yet teachers also experience the late-modern free expression of opinion from increasingly individualistic parents and students.

In the regions, women teachers receive greater gender discrimination the higher up they go in the organization. As Nishikawa-san climbs the ranks, because her abilities are suspect as a woman, she feels added pressure to fulfill her responsibility for the institution, but she rarely has the escape hatch of drinking with superiors and coworkers, more common in the past and less accepted for women than men in the regions. Successful women in Tokyo have the chance to do more of this with other successful women.

Like the successful singles, Nishikawa-san worries about independence and dependence. But her concern about "soft, spoiled" places of dependence in herself does not lead to more transparent relationships built on compassion. Rather she worries about them because they infer to her that she is not strong enough to live up to institutional requirements. In this case, scouring out places of emotional dependence leads not to a "will to power" to develop a new way of being, but to deeper entrenchment in subservience to superiors and old ways of being. She would like to develop the new dispositions that she emerged into as she came of age, but her way is thwarted by old hierarchies and habits she was raised with both at work and in her family. Although her younger single brother lives on ancestral lands in the country, it is she who will take on responsibility for her parents in the future.

Struggling teacher in Tokyo

In the next example we see that even in Tokyo, families and educational institutions that struggle between postwar ways and the demands of survival in globalizing, neoliberal Japan can almost stymie the long-term resistance of single women. Shimizu-san, a teacher and daughter, aches with tension in her daily performance as a late-modern career woman who goes home to an environment that expects the preconscious submission and domination written of by Butler (1997). Aided by her generation's nod to maturity gained by caring for others one cares about, she reflects on her family's emotionally demanding and largely unexamined relationships, and manages, incredibly, to hang onto the discourse of choice (Rosenberger 2001, 224–225).

I met Shimizu-san at her private high school in 1993. Her words echoed the late-modern situation: "It used to be that 90 percent of the students heard the directions the first time; now 90 percent don't hear." But she had no latitude to unwind by living the imagined single life. "I'm resigned to going straight home. I'd like some free time to go to the movies or shop—just so I could free up my feelings a bit (*kimochi o kaihō dekiru*), but my mother had a stroke several years ago and, along with my father, I care for her." Marriage seemed difficult as "the conditions" to care for her parents piled up.

In 1998, Shimizu-san wanted to meet at Starbucks at Shinjuku station, emblematic of the enjoyable single's life. Perhaps symbolically, rain pelted down as we sipped our drinks. The voices in her head bespoke her partial consciousness of the contradictions in her life. She emphasized her travel to France—with her father. "It became a way to show my respect for him (*oyakōkō*, literally, filial piety). He was so happy." The story she told was heavy with implications. "Once we were sitting at a table with another man in France. My father asked him, 'Do you have children?' He answered, 'No.' 'Are you lonely?' my father asked. 'No,' he said. 'I am divorced now and have a woman I love. I divorced because there was no love anymore.' We were so amazed at this. It showed us how different the French are from the Japanese."

Later Shimizu-san painted a picture of her family mired in emotional dependencies that blocked any objective discussion of their situation. "Japanese like to stick close (*bettari*) to their families. They think of depending on their children, especially their son. I understand this feeling of wanting to depend on another. But it is difficult. . . . If you don't talk, you can't solve anything. But we don't talk. If Japanese don't agree, they don't talk. If they agree, they don't talk. They just live parallel lives, unhappy with each other."

Even her siblings' actions doomed Shimizu-san (the single woman and middle child) to this morass of dependency. She described her brother as spoiled. "He quit high school and is enjoying himself. . . . He doesn't eat with us." Her older sister is married with children in Tokyo but visits seldom. "My father thinks surely his grandchildren will come on the last weekend of summer vacation, but there is no contact."

With only her father and a once-weekly home helper from the government, Shimizu-san carried the burden. As she watched the raindrops sliding down Starbucks' big windows she said: "My life is important, too. I need to do something for my 'self' to have a life, to push my will through. Sundays pass and there is nothing for me." Thinking about her relationship with her parents, she wasn't sure she ever wanted to have a child, but she did want a husband with whom to be happy.

Our 2004 meeting was a late dinner at a Cambodian restaurant after Shimizu-san had fed her parents. Her father, now retired, had heart problems, and she herself suffered from a thyroid condition. "My favorite thing to do is eat, but the doctor says I have to lose weight!" she laughed. She had travelled to Europe with her school, but she had spent the week there sick in bed. Furthermore, schoolteaching now required her working Saturdays to recruit new students. "I'm going to retire in six years!" she said with glee.

Most significant was Shimizu-san's reflection on her life. On the one hand, she saw her life as being randomly determined: "Taking care of my parents is my fate." Yet she also credited a gain in terms of the historical values that still live in Japan: "Now I am living with my parents and I am happy that I have had a long time to be in contact with them. I am not like my older sister who has little involvement with them." But her main message in the midst of her tension was that this accommodation was a performance of choice: "If I had pushed things for my 'self' things might have changed, but I decided everything freely. I am not 100 percent satisfied, but neither am I completely dissatisfied. I have been able to do freely what I like to do even if I haven't married and had kids. I wasn't blessed with meeting a good person, but I didn't meet and marry some strange person either. This is a blessing. I am forty-two. So I think after I reach fifty, I will do something else. It is strange to say, but if my parents die, I would be free and I would like to live somewhere else. I would like to see the ways of another country."

Her dream was to go to Denmark, where "men help you with your suitcases and the beer and ice cream are delicious."

Hanging on to choice in the in-between

Shimizu-san's position exemplifies the contradictions and tensions of long-term resistance as a single woman in late-modern life in Japan. These days many married women escape the obligatory care of mothers-in-law, but single daughters often care for their mothers. Here Shimizu-san is twice trapped: first by emotions woven since childhood, and second by the more recent idea that the emotional relationship of daughters to parents is more acceptable than the obligatory in-law relationship, drawing on the notion that emotions represent individuality in late-modern logic.

Shimizu-san squarely occupies and seems aware of occupying the ambivalent space between independence and dependence, of being unable to shift the terms of her life despite her singlehood, and even being trapped because of her female singlehood. She is exceptionally clear in her depiction of the dependent relationships in opposition to which successful singles build their lives, critiquing the sticky relationships and tense silences without conscious choice. Her desire for self as imagined and witnessed in Europe and the United States when visiting a friend in Seattle haunts her, but she also attacks her siblings' lack of loyalty, praises her own, and values her relationships with her parents, hoping to give them devotion while alive and the satisfaction of good deaths at home (Long 2005). Enjoying trips with her father, she attempts to reinterpret parental relationships to the extent she can. Ultimately, she dons the central philosophy of her generation, crediting herself with free choice.

Shimizu-san's move makes sense within the ambiguous resistance of this generation (Melucci 1989). In the midst of acting in accord with the cultural code she was born into, she maintains self-reflection, filled with information and imagination of the wider world. Her period of time outside of the movement has been long but never entirely subsumed; she hopes someday to rejoin her generation's realignment of the cultural code. Like Nishikawa-san, she can only imagine it as a Western mirage, far away from Japan's postwar institutions.

Struggling and crashing singles

The two women just discussed have managed to tread water, maintaining the double consciousness of ambivalence while bearing up under internal tensions and external contradictions. Nine other singles in the study have had near-death drownings in both physical and mental ways, some reviving and some not. Most of these tragedies are attributable to overwork in institutions that expect too much. They co-opt single women's ambitious dreams of success, desire to contribute to society, and willingness to labor at lower levels under supervision in the job world. One, like Shimizu-san, crashed not because of work but because of family demands, which appropriate single women's freedom, twisting their generational version of "freedom to" pursue new endeavors into "freedom from" responsibilities, and thus availability to undertake elders' care to the grave.

The women who collapsed from overwork all ended up in the hospital with serious physical and mental symptoms of fatigue, stress, and depression. One in the regions worked into the wee hours over a period of several years writing curricula for university reforms and fell into a state of physical and mental breakdown, quitting and retreating to her sister's home. An advertising specialist in a Tokyo company with performance-based policies ended up in the hospital with exhaustion because she served an old-fashioned boss who worked her until two a.m. because "she didn't have a family to go home to." She returned to work, and later tried valiantly but unsuccessfully to pass the bar exams to become a scribe in the law system. Later, she managed to leverage a temporary job in another advertising firm, as well as time she had spent in the United States, into a full-time job in advertising and reentered the successful single classification. An only child, she lived near to but separately from her parents, who were there to catch her financially and psychologically, but for whom she would be responsible.

The woman who drowned in family demands actually withdrew from the study, evidently feeling she had failed to qualify as a single of her generation. A past insurance saleswoman in Morioka in 1993, she was proud because other singles were jealous of her—"a self who knew another world." However, she was sick in 1998, and in 2004 wrote me a letter: "I recovered my health, but my grandfather died and my grandmother slipped into complete dementia. My mother, tired out from caring for her, also got dementia. My eighty-five-year-old father has sickened and I am in the situation of caring for all three of them. I hardly have time to do the shopping, let alone meet with anyone. With about three hours of sleep per night, I myself have gotten a bit of depression. I am in no condition to talk with you. Please don't contact me."

In sum, tension in the long-term workshop of resistance for Japanese single women has the potential to be exciting, tumultuous, and in this case debilitating, as contradictions hook into vulnerabilities and block a person's will to power.

Escaping to irrational spheres of life

The other six women in this category of struggling singles bring to light a turn toward marginal or irrational spheres of life in Japan as a place to revive after double binds have fragmented into mental and physical debilitation. Rather than being areas of capitalistic efficiency or institutional bureaucracy essential to growth in postwar Japan, these are the superfluous or "enchanted" areas of life that have been discarded as a result of the "disenchantment" of modernity—namely, art and religion (Weber 1946). They present alternative possibilities for the practice of long-term resistance in late-modern Japan.

Art and religion have existed as channels for nonconformity and training grounds for spiritual strength (*seishin*) throughout the postwar period. They are not considered central parts of the rational institutional structure of schools, companies, and middle-class (urban) households that catapulted Japan into being the second largest economy in the world by the 1980s, yet they are not irrelevant, as girls and middle-class wives gain status through their accomplishment in the so-called traditional arts of tea ceremony or flower arranging (Kato 2004), and middle-class men gain maturity by participating in Zen training at the behest of their companies (Kondo 1990). Each can contribute to the building of strong Japanese spirit.

If art or religion is practiced outside of the hierarchies of accepted sects and schools, it counts against one's accomplishments in the rational institutions that spell individual and familial success. If one is participant in so-called new religions that have arisen in the last century (as the women here are), they demand active zeal and devotion, unlike older religions; often appealing to the poor and marginalized, membership in them may block entry to the highest schools and companies (Reader 1991).

Artistic endeavors are not so maligned, but it depends on the art. Among my interviewees, women who are tea ceremony practitioners earn instant status because it has the reputation for self-cultivation. Two village dwellers in this study who do countless drawings—one detailed pen drawings of bugs, flowers, and landscapes, and another of wizards—earn few social points for doing so. The nature artist said that her art and her care of the same bugs and flowers were a sublimation of her sexual tension, particularly of her love for a married man in the village where she had chosen to live. She also rides her motorcycle to the nearby city to take ballet lessons—secretly, she hopes. The wizard artist continues to hold a job and just hopes she can avoid marriage in her farm family that has no heirs to take over the land. Inside, these women feel conjunction with wider worlds of being through their art, transcending the everyday world that judges them; their art adds to their feelings of growth, and at moments to their uniqueness as interesting people. But they are seen as marginal, odd singles, outside the scope of rational life, participating in a long-term resistance that gets them nowhere.

It is telling that all six of these women grew up in the regions and all live in the northeast, although one spent much of her single life in Tokyo. Regional single women appear more liable to crash on their bumpy rides across their mountainous terrain because work, family, and community are less tolerant of them; they are seen as anomalies or misfits rather than as representatives of diverse lifestyles. Yet a narrow path is available for single women in this study through art and religion—areas that people in the regions leave open to the marginalized, perhaps because they have been left out of the profits of high economic growth, and perhaps because they feel that anomalous single women fit into these anomalous areas of life. Indeed, the northeast is known historically for shamanistic, mystical practice of religion; I have met several active practitioners in my experiences there.

Art: theater

Theater as an alternative lifestyle emerged in the lives of two women who used it as a way to experiment with new and different selves in their long-term resistance. The first, Nakajima-san, was a Morioka woman working as a medical technician throughout her life as a single. However, slowly a sense of despair set in as she broke up with her boyfriend and moved to increasingly less prestigious jobs in lower institutions as gradually her age blocked her from the best jobs. As the last straw, a colleague stole a scientific discovery she made as a technician and gave her no credit for it. Meanwhile, her mother, with whom she lived, was becoming demented, telling her not to meet with this Nanshi-san (me) whom she thought was a man. In 1998 her business card pictured her in a prison uniform behind bars. She said, "You'll find me in the bars with the actors." Over drinks, I heard about her adventures in playing an ugly old woman and her ability to coach young and old newcomers to theater in the skills of acting. In 2004 at forty-two, she was also investigating the history of public baths in the area and visiting them whenever possible.

These corners of life, irrelevant to the surface appearance of success in singles, gave her the feel of single life that she craved. She still wished for a husband, but introductions through a company resulted in only "divorced men and cowards" with whom she could not create the "meeting of equals" that she craved. She preferred men in the theater and spent time with them, but they were not interested in dating toward marriage. Theater remained an ongoing arena where she could be the self she wanted to become while maintaining her work and family responsibilities that seemed mired in old-fashioned dependency.

In the second case, Negishi-san chose theater as a way to escape kindergarten teaching and life with her parents in the regions (Rosenberger 2001, 214). In Tokyo, she sparkled as Maria in *West Side Story*, had a long affair with the man who played Tony, and dipped into poverty and uncertain, irregular work. Ultimately, her former teacher found her a job in the rational world of education. She brought her acting energy to teaching children and moved back to a teacher-training job in the regions (perilously near the Fukushima nuclear power plant). Theater was a way for her to escape the contradictions of her early life and cultivate her "self," yet it also became a pitfall of marginality from which she again had to escape to regain her sense of being a successful single. Nonetheless, she refused her "last good marriage proposal" from an arranged meeting, because, in her words, she wanted to hang on to her "self" and her vision of love. In my words, she opted for the clearer perception and less ambivalent will-to-power of single life, but in it she experienced rather keen loneliness.

Religion

Both of the single women who turned to religion had fallen victim to untenable double binds but found paths to an alternative form of long-term resistance in religious philosophies that transcended the contradictions of everyday life. Religion opened to these single women a path to understanding their relations with parents and rebirth for self in a wider cosmos of meaning that lay beyond the media-birthed self of independence to which their generation first aspired. From the village and Morioka, one was a piano teacher who had had a series of brain tumors, and the other was a nurse whose nighttime job caring for cancer patients became unbearable for her. They both followed unorthodox religious leaders popularized by the media, older women who had shaped concepts from historical religions of Shintoism and Buddhism into new forms, and who offered healing along with alternative views of power and success.

In the first case, Hasegawa-san, a village piano teacher fighting recurring tumors, went on a pilgrimage to a woman north of Morioka whom she first saw on TV. "She makes rice balls (*o-musubi*). She has a certain power. We receive the *o-musubi* and she talks and I just cry. She says to treasure every moment. I can feel that it is okay if I don't try hard [to succeed]. She thinks that God is inside you. I make *o-musubi* with her and she says, 'Don't push too hard so each grain can breathe.' I am just okay as I am." In religion Hasegawa-san found an ultimate acceptance and a reprieve from her ambition to be a successful single by which she could hold up her head in the village (Rosenberger 2001, 217, 222). At the age of forty-three, she had to accept a lesser social identity and appealed to a higher and honorable loss of identity in a universal space.

In the second case, Horikawa-san, a well-starched and chirpy nurse in 1993 and 1998, seemed like a preeminent successful single, singing French chansons and buying antiques for her apartment (Rosenberger 2001, 191). By 1998 she complained of fatigue, but streaked her graying hair purple to distract the cancer patients she served. She rarely visited her parents in the countryside, avoiding her father in particular, but she spoke with pleasure of an older married woman friend, an ally in her adventures outside of work. I finally met this woman in 2004 when forty-four-year-old Horikawa-san said, "I quit work and I want you to meet my teacher."

In the pink plastic seats of Dunkin' Donuts, I sat beside Horikawa-san, finding it difficult not to stare at how different she looked, her back curved like a shrimp, dressed in black with the gray roots of her hair showing. The teacher, gaudily dressed and speaking in a loud voice, lectured us on her powers as Horikawa-san served the tea. "I do research like you on Reiki—on the ether that wraps around the body. It is our real self. I am just finding my powers."

Horikawa-san listened. (The teacher referred to her by first name, Yumi, plus "chan," used with a very close friend or child. For adult acquaintances it is common to use the last name, as I do throughout this book, so I will continue to refer to her as Horikawa-san.)

"I speak the words of God automatically. Yumi-chan writes them down. The other day, Yumi-chan was touching me and she was thrown back from me again and again."

Horikawa-san's body seemed to wake up and she spoke. "I went close to touch the teacher and I was thrown back about four times." She arched her body and sprang back to show the physical power of her teacher's force.

"Were you healing her?" I asked.

"If I am healing, she is the healer," Horikawa-san said softly, looking at her hands in her lap.

The teacher broke in. "Yesterday I was healing a pregnant lady and she told me, 'You look two meters high!' Yumi-chan couldn't even see me!"

"The light was blinding."

"It was like gold," the teacher reminded her.

"It was like gold sand all around her top half! I couldn't see her face!" Horikawa-san waved her hands and wonder filled her face.

Only when the teacher went to the restroom did I hear about why Horikawa-san had quit her job. Quietly, she said, "It was just a half a year ago. The human relations were bad and my spirit and body were just beat, so I just decided and quit. I am without work now. I am learning from the teacher. She can teach me about the big world. This is the real thing. Now I want to give healing to other people."

"What do you mean?" I had to lean close to hear her voice.

"I was a nurse, but I didn't share my spirit with patients. It was on the surface. I want to learn Reiki and put my whole spirit into my work. I can deal with the pain of people's hearts. When I look back, I was just doing as I pleased (*kimama*). I thought I had my life together, but I was mistaken. I want to change. All has changed."

The teacher returned and chimed in. "As a nurse, she was doing hard work, all night till morning. It was terrible. The nurses all have neuroses and are taking medicine. Nursing is not a work for humans. Every day four or five people were dying of cancer. She had to clean their bodies. She would come to my house and I would say, 'Don't touch my cups because you touched dead bodies.' Terrible, dirty things happened at the hospital. She did it for twenty-three years. She took sleeping pills. Everyone did. Some wanted to commit suicide. I told her, 'Stop!' Now it's Yumi-chan's second life."

Horikawa-san spoke spontaneously, "Yes, yes. I am getting back my humanity. May I tell her about my father?"

"Of course," the teacher answered.

"He died. He was a haiku poet all his life. He won an important award, and his haiku are on the gate of the hot-springs town where I grew up."

"An American Reiki master in Tokyo got Yumi-chan in touch with her father," added the teacher. Tears welled up in Horikawa-san's eyes.

"My father said that he is writing and his haiku are important. Now I want to honor him and be devoted (*oyakōkō*) to my mother."

The teacher's cell phone rang; it was her son there to pick them up. They gave me one of the teacher's books and then sailed out the door, with the teacher in the lead. I went out into the night to wait for the bus that would take me back home, struggling inside to understand the new Horikawa-san, or as her teacher called her, Yumi-chan.

Religion as solution

Drawing on concepts common to many Japanese religions and psychological treatments, Reiki literally means "divine spirit" and uses the energy of the life force to heal by laying on hands and increasing the life-force energy in the client. Although it started in Japan, it has spread throughout the world. Believers give up self to this cosmic energy, communicate with ancestors, and heal relationships, finding gratefulness particularly toward parents. In some ways it echoes the counseling philosophy of Sato-san, the successful single already discussed, but for Horikawa-san it is not integrated with generational ideas of independence; it invites her to complete dependency, although in a unique and new way that would lead to cosmic integration. Horikawa-san's teacher turned to Reiki after several out-of-body experiences, and Horikawa-san felt its force was starting to heal her.

Horikawa-san was a successful single who crashed because of the conditions of her work in her large regional hospital, a postwar institution that was hierarchical and expected devotion from their staff. For many years, it worked for her as a financial springboard for her life as a consuming, independent self. Finally, the contradictions between her work and her spirit/body came to a head, and she was no longer able to "traverse" the various identities and ways of belonging of her life (Ueno 2005; Gundewardena 2007). Overcome by tension, she was only able to choose by whom she would be controlled (Wolf 1987).

This case and others I have examined here evoke the terrible strains of tension that can almost literally pull single women apart. In this study, more than half of the single women fall into this category of struggling singles, with more than half of those having collapsed at some point. Although a few lived in Tokyo, most were living in the regions. In the long run, the workshop of resistance, so full of festering irritation over the years, was overwhelming. Even in this study, which started with well-educated single women who held decent jobs, individual single women fell over time, losing their nimbleness and succumbing to their fractured lives.

These upstart religions make sense as one lifeline, for they forgive individual failure and redefine success in cosmic terms beyond the small world of self. It offers "nomads" a version of home that is new for them yet makes complete subservience to the universe acceptable as a kind of self-realization that is not linked with individual autonomy (Mahmood 2001, 207). In a sense, religion is a sublime subversion that puts these women beyond the reach of others' demands or judgments. A quotation from Horikawa-san's teacher's book says it best: "If God were to give you one wish, what would you wish for? I would answer: Go ahead. Make my life over" (Takahashi 2003, 62).

Conclusion

The singles interviewed here are all seeking an extended or reinterpreted version of self as the vocabulary of their quiet long-term resistance to the rules of society. Many are not opposed to enduring the complexities of marriage were the perfect man to make a connection, for the future harbors the fear of loneliness for most; but they see that, like their married friends who made the choice to marry, they themselves, often without meaning to and especially as their reproductive years wane, have already run the gauntlet of choice into singlehood. The long-term resistance that sometimes emerged in the forms of anger or panic has eased over the years as others' acceptance or resignation to the singles' often-silent contestation has increased. Their trajectory is set, but within the framework of singlehood, they continue to wrestle with the ambiguities of independence and success and, in the northeast, to fragment their anomalous identities into art and religion.

The version of self claimed by these women seeks to shift emotional dependence, not to give up relationships of the past, but to interact with them without getting bound to them or in them, and to nurture more tolerant ones with chosen allies. The successful singles, rich in confidence, material goods, and often in freelance or independent work environments, are particularly skillful at garnering such allies. Living in cities with many other singles and blessed with healthy parents, they have fate on their sides in coping with the double binds they meet.

The struggling singles in postwar institutions of schools and families must cope with others who take advantage of their singleness, trying to endure (*gaman*) and put forth effort (*gambaru*) as they are expected to by the cultural code. The modern order of these institutions is stifling, as they still experience discrimination of various sorts as single women. Yet still bearing the marks made by their points of resistance, they stay aware of the situation and evaluate its causes and effects, dreaming of a life in Europe, outside of Japan's normative requirements.

Those who struggle and crash in the workshop of long-term resistance give themselves to the ambiguities, mystery, and adventure of art and religion, opened by the dissonance of the contradictions they have experienced into a world outside of rational institutions. They attempt to create an extended version of self through still-enchanted areas of modern life, seeking, at one level, union with an alternative social and cultural milieu that gives their selves free play in this world, and at another level, union with a universe that completely reinterprets the idea of self. The latter is more common in the northeast, where pressures are harshest for long-term resistance in the guise of singlehood.

The successful singles attract praise, while the crashing singles are relegated to marginalized silence. Those struggling in less flexible institutions in the center may be the worst off; imprisoned in partial recognition, festering irritation, and tacit accommodation with smiling faces, they are the least able to hone a new version of self. In sum, all of these women wrestle with attaining their vague vision of the single life as opening new possibilities for self-actualization in an era in which the roles and norms of postwar modernity are loosening, yet in the eyes of older authority figures still seem the best bet for getting Japan back on track.

CHAPTER FOUR

No Children despite Running the Gauntlet of Choice

SERIOUS, STRAIGHT-BACKED, and dressed in dark colors, Yamamura-san held her hand on her chest as we talked in a Tokyo family restaurant in 2004. She had married quickly at thirty-five to a man she had once refused, and against the advice of her mother, sister, and superiors at the bank where she worked. Her work had lost its meaningfulness, she said, and "I think it is important to marry." She appreciated the fact that this man did not object to her discussion of art therapy or Christianity, both of which she had espoused as an adult, even travelling to the United States for a short training in Christianity. She soon had a miscarriage—"a shock in the middle of myself that I couldn't express to my husband" (Rosenberger 2001, 226).

"After the miscarriage, I no longer wanted a couple's life [sex]. We have skinship, but it doesn't come to that. He's late [coming home] anyway, drinking and playing mahjong." She wrinkled her nose. Yamamura-san had decided that having no children was best after all, because her husband was "spoiled." "He is like a child. He doesn't cooperate with things for my 'self.' He wants me to direct my feelings toward him. I can do nothing if he doesn't change his life." Furthermore, she had discovered various "dirty things" in her husband's family. His father, now dying of cancer, tore up family pictures, and his mother confessed that she had almost thrown herself and her son (Yamamura-san's husband) onto train tracks. Her husband was "strangely close to his mother," she thought, when he crawled in bed with her on a visit and invited Yamamura-san to join them.

Her body expressed her unhappiness. She got terrible head and neck aches when they visited his home, and they grew worse as transfers to new places came on a yearly basis. She still enjoyed time alone at home, but her dreams of starting an art therapy classroom had vanished and she rarely went to church.

"Is it hard to be married without children?" I asked her.

"People don't think it is strange," she said. "And I have never fit very well in Japan anyway."

Marriage without children

In this study eight women had married but remained childless in 2004. Five are from the regional city, and three from Tokyo. They have braved the challenge of choice and married, often because they felt increasingly ambivalent about the low-level nature of their work and its worth in society, but particularly because they wanted children. Marriage is a scary choice in part because it entails a commitment to children, but to sacrifice the flexibility of the single life and not to have children is worse, because women will not reap the rewards of the warmth of the mother–child relationship, a focus of hegemonic appeal in Japan that lives on in most of the women in this study.[1]

The image of shame attached to the childless woman persists from the past; even in the 1980s in the regions, I met women who had been divorced because they did not reproduce. It would seem that things have changed, yet "if the new generation feigns a certain tolerance towards childless couples, it must be recognized that in Japan marriage is still strongly synonymous with procreation" (Jolivet 1997, 40). Being a mother still endows a woman with meaning and local stature (Iwao 1993; Ezawa 2002; LeBlanc 1999). A Japanese scholar who studies infertility treatment in Japan argues that infertile women are considered "deviants," who lose their self-esteem because they cannot fully express the affection that is essential to the ideal parent–child relationship (Tsuge 2000). In short, I expected these women to be suffering from this anomalous position.

My expectations were wrong. Less than suffering from not being able to have children, half of the women suffered most from a contradiction between their ideal husband and the everyday reality. Spoiled, controlling husbands caused tension and ambivalence in their lives more than the lack of children. The vignette above makes this clear: having lost one child, Yamamura-san reasons that children would be too much in any case because her husband himself is like a spoiled child and he holds no sexual attraction for her. Like single women, she must use her experience in the sphere of resistance to be the strong, dependable one in the relationship, but unlike her single compatriots, she ends up with just what single women fear—a dependent husband. Being the dependable one can give women a kind of power in the household (Rosenberger 2001), albeit in a bargain with patriarchy (Kandyoti 1988), but without children to provide leverage, achieving such power seems hollow.

However, not all of the women in this group have to cope with a spoiled husband. The second category of case studies shows that some childless women gain satisfaction from being with their husbands and are not insisting on producing children via fertility treatment. I call them the Romantics, because they value life with "just the two of us." The last category consists of an outlier case study—the younger high-flying Tokyo career woman married to a young man with a lucrative career; they enjoy being fashionable Tokyo DINKs: Double Income No Kids. Women in this last category use the values and strategies of long-term resistance to carve out a new, if ambiguous identity, especially for women without a meaningful career.

Why is childlessness not such a problem?

In this analysis of case studies, several reasons emerged for why marriage without children did not seem like a contradiction that brought tensions to these women's lives.

First, these women were almost all older when they married, with an average age of thirty-seven and a half, ranging from the Tokyo career woman of thirty-one to two women who married at age forty-four. Their age made pregnancy more difficult, and they knew it. However, all but two (one disabled, the other career-track) had desired children at some time in their lives. The point that pregnancy is more difficult with age must be tempered with the fact that fertility treatment is available, though at the judgment of doctors and not in the form of sperm or egg donation (Tsuge 2000). These women have chosen to leave pregnancy "up to nature," in contrast with two women in this study who had fertility treatment and did become pregnant. These decisions against fertility treatment must be weighed against reports in this study that such treatment is time-consuming, painful, and inconvenient for those who live outside main regional cities.

Second, because they put off marriage for so long, expectations for marriage and children on the part of parents, friends, and colleagues lessened. Eyes turned to younger women in the nation and parents became resigned. These women were fast entering a category of women whom people feel sorry for more than get angry at: older wives who could not bear children.

Third, these women had entered the classification of housewife, which still carried cultural importance and ideological attraction, although in new forms (Goldstein-Gidoni 2007). They fit into postwar classifications of women supporting households and husbands on behalf of a productive society, yet they could still potentially express aspects of individuality while living within this older mold.

Fourth, a new aura had grown up around couples. All but two of the women had married because they felt an *en*–a special, spontaneous link between two people—that was a pillar in their generational discourse. Now they saw themselves as "older couples" who married because of a quiet attraction, usually expressed as "drinking tea together," with the implication of a companion with whom to age. Ads targeting middle-aged and older couples romanticized trips with "just the two of us"—a phrase mentioned by many as the alternative life to a family with children. In his interviews with couples seeking infertility treatment, Tsuge (2000) did find a minority of couples who perceived of childless life as happy.

Fifth, in the case of two women, the Tokyo high-flyer and the disabled Morioka worker, the high values they place on individual careers make having no children an advantage. Despite huge educational, income, and urban/rural differences between these two, they differ from others in accepting not having children because they feel they must continue their work.

For all of these reasons, marriages without children are not tragedies for anomalous women. Rather, such marriages have become a valuable laboratory for viewing marriage without the added variable of children. They spotlight the marriage relationship, and often the relationships with parents on both sides as well. There are no children to mask or reconfigure the relationships among these representatives of a generation that expected so much from marriage. Long-term resistance takes on a different hue in this subject position that on the one hand carries potential for creative experimentation and on the other redirects a woman's long-term resistance, in all its tacit accommodation and festering irritation, toward her husband and his parents.

Why the regions?

Five of the eight women in this group were raised in the regions, and four live there now. The difficulty in remaining single in the northeast, evidenced in the frustrations of singlehood in the last chapter, may account for this preponderance of regional women marrying at an age when to become pregnant is harder. To remain single in Tokyo, where single women have many like friends and no sense of anomaly in public, is more enjoyable. This study indicates that single women in Tokyo after thirty-five or forty are more likely to remain single, not compromise on partners, and enjoy friends and lovers. Indeed, overall in Japan, of all women born in 1964—age forty in 2004—22.3 percent had not given birth by age forty (*Mainichi Shimbun* 2006).

Women in the northeast are more willing to take the risk of a later marriage. They have learned endurance from their mothers and consider putting up with a husband much easier than enduring under the arm of a mother-in-law. Further, their risk matches the overall greater concern among single women in the northeast that in their old age they will be lonely and lack a caretaker.

In addition, the regions are a reservoir of unmarried men, elder sons responsible for an inherited farm or family house, graves, and care of parents. Unlike in the city, where men do not always want to marry, these men want to, and their family members work on their behalf. For example, the friend of a sister of one of these bachelors who was in the hospital with one of the interviewees introduced her to her future husband. Women partially recognize the risk, however, as the stereotype of elder or only sons as being spoiled and tied to their mothers was noted in the postwar era and continues today (Wagatsuma and DeVos 1984). During my 2004 fieldwork, a regional acquaintance had a friend who had killed her son because he refused to get a job; the blame was immediately assigned to the overly intimate and dependent relationship between mother and son.

Marriage without children after long-term construction of single self

This laboratory of case studies is particularly interesting because these women have had plenty of time to experience the excitement and pain of making new scripts for themselves as single women. Their workshops of experience have been full as they have taken on the task of building their narratives of self and challenged the makeup of their own selves and their relations with close others. How marriages and the women in them are affected by this self-construction is a question that spans all the remaining chapters. Here, the question is: How does the ambiguous, long-term resistance of these women in this globalized generation shape the ways in which they experience marriage without children, either negatively or positively?

With their skills of long-term resistance, all of these married women without children appealed to the diversity that is the emergent norm within themselves and, gradually, in society in late-modern Japan. It was their hedge against anomaly. Yet even in the performances being created by their own generation, they were in-between the single-woman world and the mother–child world. Rather than easily entering the next stage that they have acquiesced to or welcomed, they have had to use the scraps and pieces of old and new habits of mind and body to create yet another script for self in the midst of the tensions of husband's self, own self, care for parents, and work. Even if they wanted to now, they could not lose themselves in motherhood or use its power as a leverage for status. Nor had they married rich men whose wealth allowed them to lean back and enjoy life. In only one case did a woman quit her secretarial job after a year of marriage, but she was commuting several hours from a small village where the couple lived humbly in his family's old farmhouse, and her husband earned little with construction jobs.

Spoiled husbands: Kato-san

Kato-san met me at the turnstile in her station about an hour from central Tokyo in 2004. The ponytail and slim lines of her twenty-five-year-old self had given way eleven years later to a medium-length hairstyle and a new pudginess under her navy-and-white-striped shirt and red capris.

"I'm sorry for this old apartment," she said as we entered. "I want to get a new carpet and new furniture—do an interior, since I am a housewife now. But he likes old stuff—like that bookshelf—yuk! But it has memories for him. And he likes to save money. What for? I wonder! I said I would use the money I saved from my work, but he said I shouldn't use it for everyday life."

"Is this your marriage photo?" I studied the handsome couple on top of the TV: he tall in a gray tux and she dressed like a southern belle in a pink gown with a train.

"Yes." She smiled as she looked at the photo. "He's ten years older than me. He's tall but his back is rounded. We got married here and then honeymooned in Switzerland. We argued then, too!" She chuckled with chagrin and explained.

"We'd just got there and as I entered the hotel, I threw back my head and laughed—'How great it is to be here'—but he pushed me from behind and said angrily, 'Get into the room!' I know we were tired but . . . I got really mad."

"O-o-oh." My voice could only dip sympathetically. Kato-san was relaxed and open, ready to talk to me, taking my research as a chance to speak honestly to a person outside her network. She served me black tea as we settled into the old chairs.

"How did you meet him?" I knew she wasn't meeting men easily in 1998.

"It was an arranged meeting. My mother introduced us; her friend had brought his profile from his parents. His parents and mine live five minutes apart. Five years ago, the same request came, but I thought it was a joke—such an old person. Before, I absolutely wanted a love marriage, but slowly I decided I really wanted to marry and became open to introductions. My grandmother kept saying she wanted to see the face of her grandchild."

I remembered her opposition to arranged marriages from our first meeting in 1993 when she was working as a dorm mother and had a boyfriend. She wanted a husband she "could talk with about anything. If I express my opinion, he will respond in a settled way. I want a home (*katei*) where I can be free."

Kato-san explained her shift into accepting a semi-arranged marriage: "I looked into the future and all I could see was work. The printing company I worked for in Sapporo was so busy that I had no chance to meet anyone. He and I met once in December at a coffee shop and then saw each other every day for a week. I was searching for what kind of person he was. So we decided then. In March I just came here right away after I quit my job and we lived together before our wedding. I wanted to."

She hesitated, eyes cast down, and then, looking up, said: "I need to tell you he is divorced. I never thought I would marry a 'man with an X' [on his household registry].[2] You just never know about life, do you?"

She went into the kitchen and brought out a rice and chestnut dish on handsome plates.

"Well, let's see," I said after a few bites. "I remember when we talked last time you liked your work and your brother's dog . . ."

She nodded and smiled, "I miss him! I want another, but my husband doesn't like dogs much."

". . . but you felt something was lacking."

"I didn't feel a sense of accomplishment anymore, and I worried a bit, 'Is there no good person?' " Her memories of that time ripened. "When I was single I took the dog for walks late at night. I bought things I wanted like clothes, magazines, candy. I was poor but free. Now I am not sure. I want some money that I can use freely, like for Pilates."

"Do you work?"

"I wanted to work but he didn't want me to. He's an old Japanese type. He wants me home when he leaves and comes home. I worked part-time but I got tired and then I got upset when he wouldn't help take out the garbage or clear the dishes. I asked him to take up the futon and he did it, but I had to ask. I realized that if I was always angry, my face would change. I'd become unpleasant."

"Sometimes it's easier to do it yourself."

"Really, you don't have freedom. Like I get lonely and want to call up my friends at night, but I worry about his eyes. He wouldn't like it if I talked for several hours. It's his house and his telephone and his salary. So I feel constrained (*kyukutsu*)."

After a while the conversation turned to children. I remembered that even when I first met Kato-san she thought "a family would be nice." She said: "He generally doesn't like children all that much. He says he wants them but . . . I have a benign fibroid tumor and if I don't get it removed, it would hurt when I was pregnant. But if they operate, you can't get pregnant for a year. The doctors say one in six women have them now because of late marriage. So, my husband (*otto*) says that we can just enjoy life the two of us. But I say that I won't be able to have children if we keep saying 'let's enjoy life the two of us.' " She wrinkled her brow and continued. "If I had children, it would be easier to make friends. The lady next door is my age but has three children, so we don't talk."

She collected the dishes and brought Japanese tea. Several hours had passed, but she seemed in no hurry.

"So I am asking everyone what they feel as they look back over their lives." I said.

She cocked her head and thought. "I have naturally done the preferable things for each age. I thought I was individualistic and different when young, but I am a typical Japanese among Japanese. I wasn't a career woman but I lived alone, worked, and had my own money. There are places that became like a typical 'old miss.'[3] It's because Japan allowed it. I felt that I was special, but I am common now that I am married. I am a woman of now (*ima-fuu onna*)."

I nodded and took notes.

"I had lots of chances but it was hard to make decisions. I wonder now, 'Is it okay?' Maybe now it's okay when we are just married, but in the future? Sometimes I say I will divorce you or leave . . . but I don't have the courage. So enjoying things is best. I won't be hurried for children. I am trying to go slowly and get used to this life. There are various ways to live. We can take trips together."

Postdecisional regret

Kato-san's ambivalence about herself has not ended but, as an aging single who gambled on marriage, probably increased. She felt that she, along with her generation, had done something different and special, but with age she also saw the eventual emptiness and isolation of the working single woman who lived alone and worked hard without promotions. Her disillusionment overcame the risk of the blind spot that she stood in as a single facing marriage, for she realized that as a single in regional Japan working in a job in a small company, life narrowed after a point. She gave in to her grandmother's and her own wish for children, hoping that as a housewife and mother her life might broaden again.

Now in her state of marriage without children, Kato-san's description of her life hinted broadly at the ambivalence and tension of "postdecisional regret." Her narrative was sprinkled with laments for the loss of freedom centered on her depiction of her husband as old-fashioned, controlling, and overly frugal. His independence as a wage earner shifted into dependence on his wife when he walked in the door—the very postwar formula that Kato-san wanted to avoid. He took up the late-modern slogan "just the two of us" enthusiastically, as perhaps he himself perceived childlessness as a way to lighten his conventional role as a breadwinner. Her gradual understanding that he really did not want children but just wanted to be taken care of himself grew inside her like the fibrous tumor that she did not treat. In her estimation she had become "common"—a woman putting up with what she disagreed with and possibly forgoing the children that she believed would enliven her life again. The hopes of her generation were doubly dashed. Unhappy and perfectly able to perceive her predicament, but without "the courage" to divorce, she is the perfect picture of ambivalence.

However, marked by the efforts of her generation's long-term resistance, several other strategies came to Kato-san's aid. Her husband and she found ways to enjoy their childlessness by going on trips together; she could sell her work skills on the side within limits set by her husband, as she continued to do seasonally; and she had interests such as Pilates that she could pursue. Friends were a tougher strategy for her, but she communicated with old friends by e-mail and met with a nearby junior high friend.

Still, in her own evaluation, Kato-san ended up an ordinary Japanese woman of her generation. She was caught in a double bind of having learned a new disposition as a single woman but having to relearn the old disposition that her mother had displayed at home in relation to her father. This double bind was exacerbated by another—the contradiction of an inflexible, spoiled husband who blocked her from having children with whom she could shape relations that she thought she would be in control of as a mother. Her self, built with latitude for self-reflection as part of her generation's social movement, enabled her to gain insight into these dilemmas and potentially to help carve out a new role for childless married couples; but the workshop of her life mostly attested to the effects of power in her life (Abu-Lughod 1990).

Disabled with husband and cats

Disabled and with a high school education in the regions, Kojima-san presents a unique case study in this book. What has marriage, and now marriage without children, meant to her?

The answer at one level was quite positive. Because she had severe rheumatoid arthritis requiring many joint operations since childhood, she still lived with her parents in her late thirties. Unable to fully enjoy the freedom heralded by single life, her marriage to a man who promised to "be her arms and legs" opened a path out of her parents' house to greater independence. She had always said that "with this body I can't have children," so a childless life met her needs. Furthermore, she had great pride in her work as a telephone operator for the local government because she succeeded in this career despite her disabilities and high school education. Because of her lower-class status, she was determined to hang onto the economic independence that this low-level career gave her (Roberts 1994). However, her case study of childless marriage also reveals negative processes of her husband's childish ways and demands from his parents for children that did little but shift her sense of ambivalent resistance from her own parents to her husband and his parents.

At forty-four in 2004, Kojima-san still had curly, shoulder-length hair and dimples when she smiled. Her hands were bent and scarred and she walked with a limp from rheumatoid arthritis, just as when I had first met her in 1993 (Rosenberger 2001, 206). She had various questions about the United States and world politics; a Japanese man's head had just been severed by terrorists in Iraq and it greatly disturbed her. In general, Kojima-san seemed content. "I watch the news all the time. My husband got transferred several years ago, and I stay here in our apartment with the TV on and the cats. This is the best way—married but he lives apart. My time is free and I am free to do things according to my own way of thinking. I eat when I want to eat. I go at my own pace." The ambiguity of this seemed to appeal to her.

"Nice compromise between single and married life!"

"Yes. I'm busy with my cats, giving them food, cleaning their box, talking with them. I have five and now a litter of four kitties. Here, look at their pictures on my cell phone."

We bent over the cell phone to watch a small video of the kittens and another of her cat, which lifted the milk into its mouth with its paw rather than lapping it with its tongue. She laughed, enchanted. "They're so cute!" she exclaimed. "My husband thinks they're cute, too. They are my friends, because my friends from school are all busy with their children. Most are in junior high now. Maybe in ten years we can meet easily again, but for now I have the cats."

"I loved my dog, too, but she died and my husband doesn't want another. How's work for you?"

She announced, "I have been working at city hall for twenty-two years! I want to continue until I get my pension at sixty-six. There may be a problem, though. They are contracting out this service, so I may get paid less and have a different kind of pension, or maybe have to learn the computer. I don't know whether I can do it." She held up her fingers that were crippled from arthritis. "But anyway, I'll keep working. Because of my job, I can't move to be near my husband or his parents, not until I retire." She flashed a quick dimple on one cheek.

This statement was heavy with meaning. She had married a first son from Niigata, a mountainous prefecture in central Japan. His parents had built them a house to live in near them and continued to pressure her either to have a child or adopt one. She refused.

Kojima-san had realized how spoiled her husband was when he repeatedly called up his mother to defend him whenever they argued. In 2004, she said: "He finally noticed it was hard on me and doesn't do it anymore. But now he leans on me! I was surprised when he said that we are like brother and sister now. I don't think so. At least I would like an older brother who would protect me! He's like a younger brother. He doesn't even want to get together with other couples. I have the stress of worrying about the money we owe and cleaning and cooking and my health. But I have learned a lot."

"What about your parents? How are they?" I asked. Her father had not wanted to give me her phone number, and it reminded me that she had married a first and only son against their wishes; her parents didn't even go to the wedding in Niigata. They had told her, "Either marry a boy whom we can bring into the family to carry on the family name or just stay single."

Yet time was softening her relationship with her parents, just as with her husband. "My parents have given me a lot of care because of my condition, and my mother still cares for me when I need operations on my joints. I am her daughter after all. I am the oldest daughter, and I think sometimes I should go to live with them in my old age."

I could have joked that that would be a good way to get out of living with *his* parents, but I refrained. I was sure she had thought of it.

"My husband used to hardly speak to my parents, but that has gotten a little better. Now we take them to hot springs sometimes."

The agency of time

This case study is valuable for how it reveals the changes and potential in a childless marriage with a spoiled husband. However painful the process, the course of time itself became part of Kojima-san's long-term resistance (Das 2007). Her stubborn adherence to her job, the course of her disease, and her aging all were making a difference. Her husband's dependence did not diminish, but over time it shifted to his wife as an asexual sister, and their relationship was eased by pets, perhaps used like children as a common focus of attention and affection. Kojima-san was gradually coming back to her parents, bringing her husband over into their care, and building the case for never having to live with his parents. Her "lesson learned" was that marriage did not mean a place of dependency for her, but one of increased independence and responsibility. Via this childless marriage, she backed into the very independence and freedom in which her generation believed, albeit a freedom ultimately circumscribed by old-fashioned dependency. Her many cats, enjoyed by both her and her husband, can be interpreted in various ways. Like children, they are living beings to care for and afford an alternative focus within the relationship, perhaps a redirection of sexual energy. Most broadly, in the individual isolation of late modernity, pets offer an anchor of solidarity that provides intimacy without judgment or conflict.

Ironically, Kojima-san's identities as lower-class and disabled were anchors that stabilized her gender identity and gave her the determination to tough it out. However, the contradictions of the political economy might disturb the job she hung onto: Japan's growing debt diminished the resources coming to the regional cities from the national government, and jobs such as hers were outsourced. Thus, the neoliberal shift toward individual responsibility combined with the responsibility and demands thrust on her by marriage end up making the independence from her parents that she had craved more demanding than she had imagined.

Lack of sex

A lack of marital sex emerges in this section on childless wives with spoiled husbands. According to the wives, two marriages were sexless, and they seemed quite satisfied with this arrangement. Causes for such arrangements are complex, and supposedly they are widespread in Japan,[4] perhaps a bodily manifestation of neoliberal individuation and protection of self against the risks of intimacy. In these interviews, the lack of conjugal sex appeared to be related to the kind of relationship the husbands required of the wives involved—namely, more maternal or sisterly than sexual. It was also a fairly effective birth-control tool in a marriage that did not fit the mutual relationship that the women had in mind when they married.

As single women age, they marry in part to have a person to depend on. Like successful singles, they feel proud of their independence, but the effort to maintain it is continuous and exhausting, and thus they wish to ease their stress by having a person to confer with and help them out in weaker moments. The tragedy here is that these women have neither flexibility to experiment nor a person to support them psychologically and socially. In short, they have failed in extracting themselves from the "sticky" interdependent relations of the Japanese cultural code and have to use their energies of long-term resistance to keep their husbands' dependency in check and make this a tolerable situation for themselves.

The romantics

For three women in this laboratory of childless marriage, marriage has resolved much of the tension and ambivalence they experienced in their single lives. All of these women had already trod rocky paths before marriage: pressures from parents and, for the two who were high school graduates, low-level jobs with little pay or security. All of them had seen the hardships of the market self, whether as consumer or laborer, by the time I met them in their early thirties. Their expectations were already less than those of most of the women in this study, and thus their surprising marriages in the late thirties and early forties gave them a new lease on a life for self. Indeed, marriage seemed to be the "place of psychological rest" that the government ideology advertised (Rosenberger 2001), because now they have someone with whom to talk about their worries and to enjoy life. These romantics all are from the north-east and now live in villages there. They all were somewhat disappointed not to get pregnant, but did not opt for fertility treatment because of the distances to the regional city hospital and also a vague feeling that it was best to leave it to nature. Their saving grace was their belief in the marriage ideal of their generation—to be in a self-chosen relationship of mutual understanding—because they felt that by it their self-narratives were enhanced. As one said, "My husband is shy, but kind and warm. . . . I just want to be the self that I am when we are the two of us" (Rosenberger 2001, 202). Indeed, compared to an overbearing and sometimes abusive though much-loved father, her husband looked quite good.

In all of these marriages, life was bound up with care of elder parents, but each in a different way. This responsibility encouraged the young women to reach out for marriage mates who would make them feel more akin to others their age. Only one woman married and moved in with her husband's farmer-parents because her husband was the typical elder son left at home; she travelled to care for her parents in another village. The second woman married a man from Tokyo who was entranced by village life and married into her family, taking her family name and helping her parents in the shop they owned. Both of these couples had their own bedrooms and sitting rooms in the house they shared with parents, but usually ate dinner together with them. The third married a farmer whose parents had already died, but she enlisted her husband's help with her own parents in the regional city. At this point, these ancillary relationships were not an encumbrance on the marriages because the parents involved seemed to give latitude to these new relationships and the women were glad to have someone with whom to relax and share their concerns.

"Just the two of us"

The glow of marriage shone most brightly in the story of a hospital telephone operator, a high school graduate, and daughter of a construction worker–farmer. Kurokawa-san described her marriage in romantic terms, especially compared with the buffeting she had received on the regional city's irregular job market, shifting from job to job and taking up the slack with nighttime bartending over the years. Now she was married to a lower-level salaryman who worked at a local food company and lived with his parents. She continued to work evenings, but this decreased the possibility for conflict with her mother-in-law, she reasoned. Of her husband, she said: "We are enjoying life. We frequently go to hot-spring hotels in the area on weekends." Although she still had a desire for children, she counseled herself to be satisfied. "My friend tried fertility treatment for twenty years and failed. We say: 'Let's live a life of the two of us. Save money and travel.' " In looking back over her life, she skillfully combined her generational discourse of self with a Buddhist philosophy of cause and effect (karma), constant change, and acceptance: "All these things are necessary to come to the self of now. I learned from it. . . . It all comes back to you in time. . . . It all depends on your spirit. Nothing is secure."

A hint of sadness over her lack of pregnancy and children echoed in the conversation with Sugimura-san, the woman whose husband from Tokyo married into her family and her village (Rosenberger 2001, 205). She was in the city doctoring for a cold. "Well, we haven't had any children. We are for now just two (*mazu futari*)," she said. "I am forty-three, so maybe it is no use (*muri*). People, especially the older ones say: 'Keep trying! Don't give up!' But it can't be helped."

Again, it was the "awful" experience a friend had with fertility treatment that played in her mind. "I can't do it with my pharmacy work. I can't sacrifice to that point. I will leave it to nature. My parents have six grandchildren anyway. My grandmother asks, 'Who will inherit the shop?' But with a big supermarket coming in outside of town, I am not sure our small sake store will continue."

She felt that her married-without-children position allowed her to communicate with both single and married friends, but she felt that those with children had "broader worlds . . . links with people. They can learn as their children grow." She drifted off and stared out at the misty day, but then a small smile appeared. "Anyway, my husband is getting used to life in the village. At first he was annoyed by all the questions people asked him about himself. But now my parents and he are getting used to each other. As long as we get along well as a couple, all will be fine."

Embedded in family, Sugimura-san said, "I can do things without pushing my 'self' through now. Compared with my mother, I had a period of free time, and I've had choice about coming home and marrying. At work, I am the main pharmacist, equal with men. I am satisfied. But it is all I can do to keep up with my everyday existence!"

Her words reflected a combination of experiences: a renewal of habits of mind that she had been raised with in her multigenerational family, but also her own journey as a pharmacist who converted to Christianity, rebelled against her job, and volunteered to work with disabled people. Like others of her generation, she now stands at the nexus of a productive tension among the various strands of her life, all coming to bear on these women's abilities to cope with not getting pregnant and enjoying their new husbands. They continue their long-term resistance, however, for they are in a dangerous position in relation to the ideology of doctors and government pushing for pregnancy in legally married couples as well as the expectant eyes of relatives and neighbors.

Like single women who had to prove their success in career and consumption in order to escape anomaly, married women without children were challenged to maintain a meaningful couple relationship to avoid old-fashioned belittling. They maneuvered life and reported on it in such a way that their relationship fit a romantic mold, one that attained a kind of ambiguous independent responsibility in relation to a spoiled husband, or one that concentrated on parental care. They were no longer in the "free-floating" relationships of late modernity, separated from kin or economics, but they were in relationships in which, more than people married with children, the bare bones of each person were exposed, and their selves revealed to each other (Giddens 1991, 90–98, 186).

DINKs

In this last section, we meet a trendy Tokyo woman, Yanagi-san, who is by choice a self-described DINK, double-income-no-kids. A high-climber, she travelled the world—Germany, Malaysia, Denmark—studying health policy and its potential for Japan.

In 2004 I visited Yanagi-san's think tank, housed in one of Tokyo's new shiny multiuse buildings that features offices, boutiques, and restaurants. Yanagi-san was tall with short hair and wore a gray suit tailored with flattering lines. I thanked her for the New Year's card she had sent me with pictures of her and her husband in Alaska. Both had masters degrees and knowledge jobs that helped them write their own script as a young, successful married couple (Rosenberger 2001, 214–215).

"We're still DINKs!" Yanagi-san gave her high, rippling laugh. "Really this is the easiest way. We have a rich life and others are jealous of us. We worked hard to get here, so we want to enjoy it."

I remember when I first talked with Yanagi-san at the University of Tokyo in 1993. "I dream of being a bride, but I want to continue working," she had said in a loud voice. "I don't want children at all. It will be enjoyable the two of us." In 1998 at thirty, she had denied being ready to marry yet, but soon after did marry. In 2004 she characterized her marriage as a sign of her fashionable independence. "I said either no big wedding reception or no entry into the family's register (by which she would change her name and enter his family). So I entered the register but had no marriage ritual or reception. We did as we wanted, like kids."

"What did his parents think?" I asked.

"His parents were fine with it. They're cool. His father is high up in a company and his mother works at a nonprofit every day. He's the eldest son, but they don't want a *yome* [a daughter-in-law with implications of servitude]. While we went on our honeymoon, his parents went down south to visit my parents and travel. My parents don't care about the *ie* [ongoing household] either."

Yanagi-san grabbed a magic marker and drew her kin relations on the board—her husband's parents, and his older sister, still unmarried; her parents caring for her mother's parents; and her sister married with one daughter living near her parents.

She pointed at her niece: "Only one child for both families now. That feels insecure. Maybe my niece will come up here for university and I will be really nice to her and she will care for me when I get older . . . and senile." She made a face, her tongue lolling out the side of her mouth.

"Not being a mother is okay, but if I were to get sick . . . well, I need to save money. You need a person to depend on, and a blood relative is best. You need a guarantor to decide things like what to do with your bones."

I wasn't surprised that Yanagi-san, a researcher on elder policy, would think this way. But I was surprised that Yanagi-san, the swinging Tokyo-ite, would worry. The intricacies of making the choice to have children or not for both her and her husband unfolded, and it involved a great deal of ambivalence—feelings about their own lives and their trust in each other to go beyond their fashionable, self-centered selves. "I loved various people and it was enjoyable, but now I have settled down. I want kids, but he doesn't have confidence in himself so he doesn't want any. He's a perfectionist."

The second reason for Yanagi-san's chart emerged as she pointed to the stick figures representing their parents. "Our parents could raise the kids. His mother is so organized. I would be assured if she would take care of the grandchild. If not, my parents down south would. I would enlist lots of people's help. My husband says I would do that too much. Actually, I think he saw me and thought I couldn't raise kids to his level of perfection so he decided he didn't want them. But I wouldn't kill the children! He sees my plants die, and he thinks the children will too!"

We both giggled. I assured her that my plants die regularly but my children have survived.

Strolling down the broad marbled halls of her building afterwards, gazing at expensive clothes and organic foods, I felt that I had met Yanagi-san at an interesting turning point in her life. She had reached the epitome of the late-modern self, building her narrative via career, enjoyment, consumer goods, romance, and even parents and husband who respected her decisions. Yet she revealed tensions around the self-centered character that she prided herself on being—tensions that provide insight into the future of self as it evolves in this generation. Significantly, it wasn't the voices of her parents or in-laws, but the voice of her husband evaluating her—and indeed her voice evaluating him—that resonated in her interview. Skillful at developing selves that fit the globalized image of independence in career and consumption, they now looked at each other as potential parents and doubted: Is the other mature enough to raise children? Could they be the kind of people that children could depend on, and could they raise the cooperative yet competitive children that Japan now demands? Their plight represents the ultimate ambivalence of this generation.

Although Yanagi-san and her husband were financially independent in knowledge careers, they doubted each other's emotional independence to the extent that they wondered if they could care for others. They suggest that this generation, even in its highly polished and successful form, is not completely satisfied with the new cultural code that they have hammered out, and that they need some higher level of maturity to expunge the soft spoiled places.

Yet Yanagi-san did not summon herself to meet this ideal, but rather turned to their parents to raise an imaginary child, silently assuming the greater importance of her and her husband's work and lives. Disembedded from hierarchical demands of family in her single and early married life, she was still ready to be dependent on aspects of the old cultural code in the person of parents whom she assumed would be willing to step in, despite the fact that her husband's mother had her own career activities. Having married for love not children, Yanagi-san found herself in another dilemma of choice, another blind spot between past and future. The specter of her lonely aged self with "postdecisional regret" for not having children danced on her whiteboard. What she was not ambivalent about was that her "self" was actualized into her career, and in that she was different from most of the married women, and even many single women, in this book.

Conclusion

The analysis of women who are married without children resulted in somewhat surprising conclusions. These women were not without tensions, but the worst tensions did not stem from the lack of children in their lives. Families and even regional society had changed enough to soften the sharp anomaly of being a childless married woman. For those who were married with husbands to whom the wives felt emotionally close, the generational ideal of romantic love for them as a couple filled the breach of children for now, a point of view that adjusted well to the search for fulfillment on a more individual level. For the urban professional, lack of children allowed a global version of a lifestyle of urban married woman with a career, and while children presented a dilemma of choice to some extent, they were not seen as necessary, their absence only arousing worry about the far future and a cute selfishness on a personal level that further testified to Yanagi-san's devotion to work.

Spoiled, immature husbands were the main problem these women had to confront. Marrying late, they lived the reality of which many women spoke: "Women's consciousnesses have changed, but men's haven't." In short, women were going toward an independence that moved away from the confining, even cloying, dependent relationships that they identified with their upbringings and historical Japan. That several women who had wanted children did not pursue pregnancy despite probably being physically capable of achieving it indicates the measure they took of their husbands. A new double bind developed, because the very independence that these women had nurtured as they explored their options before marriage was sucked up by husbands who, also responding to the appeal of a more self-centered existence, wanted to be free of responsibility and maintain "the two of us," enjoying the indulgence of their wives.

These women's ambivalent construction of an independent self in the workshops of their long-term resistance contributed in both positive and negative ways to their experiences as married women without children. It gave all of them resources to earn money on the side and to seek out friends and activities, even when these were difficult. But it made marriage to spoiled husbands harder to bear, for they had reflected long and hard on whom they wanted to be and the trade-offs demanded in marriage. It may have led to several sexless marriages. Yet, having acquired the disposition of a single centered on self, some women's vision of romantic life as a couple was well-developed and sustained them in a long-term couple relationship. The ambivalence of this social movement made them seek some dependence, however, and women who were caring for parents welcomed having someone to depend on for even a bit of help in the emotional and physical tasks of this situation. Furthermore, becoming housewives normalized them as women in Japan, and given the decreasing marriage rate, the low birthrate, and their advanced ages, they were not ostracized. In short, these women had already inhabited the ambivalence of single life, and the ambivalence, even the tension, of a childless marriage was disappointing but hardly a new experience in their long-term resistance.

CHAPTER FIVE

Planning and Cocooning

Mothers at Home

Minami-san's husband was playing a game with his eight-year-old son on the shrine stairs as we climbed up on our sightseeing tour.

"Three times two!" her husband said.

"Six!" their son answered, and they advanced six steps.

"Minus four!" Shouted father, adjusting his heavy sunglasses.

"Two!" said the son, and he went down two. I glanced at Minami-san, who was looking on with a smile in her eyes. When we reached the top of the hill, we rang the bell and gazed out to sea while the son swung on the railing.

Minami-san had married a professor whom she met through an arranged meeting. He was older than she, and had an eye problem that turned out to worsen quickly. He still taught at a southern regional university where I was giving a talk, but she was the chauffeur for him and the family. On the way down the shrine steps she said: "My back gets tired from all the driving. I don't have much time for myself, but I manage to do some yoga and swimming while the child is at school."

I had met Minami-san when she was a working woman in Tokyo in 1993—a translation coordinator and a bass player in an all-girl band who had travelled in Mexico and the United States. At thirty-three, she had lived alone in Tokyo for fifteen years and had recently broken up with a five-year boyfriend. She described herself as "curious, soft/indulgent (*amai*), and selfish (*wagamama*)"—a negative connotation that she gave to her enthusiastic experimentation as a single. However, as a result of increasingly frequent arguments with her regional parents and her own ambivalent feelings about her late-modern self, she was having talks with prospective men. In 1994, she reported: "I want to marry fast and have children. I can do it if there is one thing about the person I respect—as long as I don't need to take care of his parents!" By age thirty-five she was married (Rosenberger 2001, 220).

In 2004 Minami-san was thinner and moved in a measured way. We returned to their two-floor house, curtains always drawn against the light that hurt the husband's eyes. "Go out and play for awhile," Minami-san told her son as she served us green tea.

"We try to encourage the child's possibilities," she said. Her husband continued, "We'd like him to be able to get into a good university and maybe study in the U.S.A. With the schools as they are," he scowled, "he has to go to cram schools for math and Japanese characters."

"My husband graduated from the University of Tokyo." That is the top of the top in Japan, and I knew the son had something to live up to, as they asked me about SATs and university ranks in the United States.

Their son returned and collapsed on the floor. "Are you going to play your violin for Nancy?" his mother asked him. He didn't move for a while but eventually entertained me. He was quite good.

Sitting around the table we discussed the trip to the airport the next morning and I saw how she manipulated the tensions of her marriage. "I think if we leave by eight thirty . . .," she ventured.

"No, we have to leave by eight or we'll be late," he said firmly.

"Shall we leave at eight? The roads are crowded then. But if I go this back way, it would be quicker. What is best, I wonder." We sipped tea for a moment and she told the son to get ready for bed and she would be up soon to say goodnight.

"When shall we leave, Papa? Would eight fifteen be good? What do you think?"

"Eight fifteen is good," he decided.

Married Women with Children

The case studies in the next two chapters represent the twenty-seven women in the study who are married with children. Passing through the various dilemmas of choice of their adult life in this late-modern age, they have taken the risk of choosing to marry and have children. Having chosen, they now meet further dilemmas associated with marriage, work, and the young children who have become their life projects for the moment (Ortner 2006).

Having lived long years as relatively self-aware singles whose choices centered on themselves, they must now live in direct interaction with discourses and structures of the family shaped by children in schools, husbands in companies, and elders' welfare.

The narratives in this chapter attest to the power of a discourse that continues to permeate the lives of Japanese women despite new discourses about working mothers: children have the best chance to become "winners" in education and jobs if their mothers stay home with them. Behind this powerful discourse lies the corporate system that still requires long hours of core salarymen with higher incomes. Statistics tell the tale: the two chief factors in women's leaving the workforce are their having husbands with higher incomes, and young children (Shirahase 2007, 50). In most countries women with higher education tend to work after marriage more than those with less education, but the situation in Japan is different. There, higher education among women is not an important factor in leading them to work after they marry. In fact, highly educated women tend to quit work more often than lower-educated women in Japan. This particular study shows only a slightly higher level of education among nonworking mothers than among working mothers; each group includes seven university graduates, but the nonworking mothers include no high school graduates, while the working mothers include two.

Even for these women who are so fluent in the language and practices of self at work and play, a postwar discourse of motherhood seeps into their experience and lurks in their psyches, showing the workings of power in their generational debate. Socially, culturally, economically, and politically, new discourses of mothering as more self-centered women raising more independent children still meet medical and educational demands for nurturing mothers raising children who are socially adept and intellectually prepared. For the most part this is an invisible process that works in terms of peaceful relationships, harmonious family life, and dreams of success for husbands and children. But the workings of power infiltrate this, because even in late-modern Japan, the state depends on mothers as resources to mold children into people with preferred psychological traits that mark Japanese-ness and make them into culturally acceptable workers and citizens. They inhabit a role that in its limited context has power, as women become decision-makers for children, financiers for family, and community participants. Middle-class urban housewives experience little gender discrimination on a daily basis within the sex-segregated home and community—less in fact than they did at work

(Borovoy 2005). The women themselves are torn, because throughout the debates on what a housewife should be in Japan since the 1950s, the housewife/mother is given ideological power as contributing to society through the successful reproduction of the next generation (Goldstein-Gidoni 2012, 46).

At some points the workings of power become visible, as when a husband demands that his wife stay at home, but more often it is the persuasive words of a well-meaning doctor, teacher, or friend who steers the mother toward better nurturance for the child (Ivry 2007, Jolivet 1997). The mechanics of power are tricky, for they can be found in the blooming of concern for morality in one's child, the warmth of interaction with family, and the fun of volunteering with other mothers at a child's school. It lies in the cultural importance placed on biological reproduction for family and nation. As one Tokyo woman said: "Raising kids is important. My DNA has been left to the next generation." All of this fits with the common sense of ideas and practices these women were raised with as middle-class girls and the common sense of the institutions of school and work in which the competition is keen for children and husbands who want to be winners in a declining economy. In late modernity these women also respond as mothers who must protect their families from such global risks as unsafe food, loss of middle-class status in an economically declining Japan, and now nuclear radiation, disciplining themselves and their children to assume self-responsibility as the neoliberal state expects (Hook and Takeda 2007; Rosenberger 2009).

As Foucault (1980) has taught us, taking on an identity such as mother within the truths of an era and a place is both pleasurable and painful. It requires endurance (*gaman*) and self-sacrifice; but it also gives singles a place to anchor their identity for the moment and redeem their societal reputation with elders and government leaders, both of which groups have wished to call an end to the era of women's singleness. What they do not anticipate is that, with the end of singleness, long-term dissatisfaction and ambivalent resistance do not end, both because the marks left by points of resistance in these women's lives still affect them and because media and government influences toward individuation continue in this neoliberal era of risk. Having passed through the fractures and cleavages of resistance as singles, these women express their desires for more fully developed selves who can live as humans rather than as women. They vaguely articulate the contradictions they face collectively as women. As a Morioka teacher now raising children in Tokyo said: "In the future it would be good if we Japanese could lightly have kids without quitting work. I worked hard and my base is work." But rather than collective action, women in this ambiguous social movement only push lightly at the rules of society, most complaints emerging as desires for their own lives: I want a meaningful job where I can work as a human being; I want to enjoy myself as my mother never could; I want a husband who understands me.

Melucci (1989) reminds us that these women are in a new kind of social movement gradually attacking the cultural code, but they dip in and out of it, often remaining in a liminal stage of partial recognition of the contradictions of their situation (Comaroff and Comaroff 1991). Having experienced acute mental suffering from inequality and reproductive expectations, they know and recognize the uncertainties deep within themselves, yet now they allow this recognition to remain ambiguous for the sake of following the course of a "normal" middle-class life as mother and wife immersed in the challenges of care and dependence. So that kin relations can continue, they "descend into the everyday" (Das 2007), a phrase that implies that they consciously remain silent about the past and try to reconcile themselves to the present as everyday life works on them and those with whom they live.

Their long-term resistance lies in their sense of making individual choices: that it is they themselves who are scripting their life dramas to delay marriage, to work, to find the ideal husband, and to have children (Giddens 1991), and that their choices are developing relationships and selves that go beyond the self-sacrifice of their mothers. They believe in the ideology of choice, but paradoxically, some feel the weight of individual choice in their decision making (for self, husband, children, and parents) in a more competitive, globalized world. Living their everyday lives, these mothers have ambiguous perceptions of the larger contradictions they live with, but their bodies and minds know the festering irritations of the psychosocial double binds associated with these contradictions. Nonetheless, they commit themselves, improvise, justify, and plan ahead as they bring senses of individual choice and emotion into the field of self-sacrificial motherhood.

In this chapter, I ask of stay-at-home mothers who have delayed marriage: What is the nature of their experience of marriage and children, given their premarriage experience of stretching cultural codes and the increasing demands for individual responsibility to deal with the risks of the era? How does their ambivalence, born in the workshop of long-term resistance, play itself out in the relations with their children and husbands that often confront them with the very contradictions they have been avoiding by staying single?

As I analyze the differences among the women who have married and had children, I am asking both how they experience the effects of power and how they enact their will to power. I am interested in how these women actively negotiate among past, present, and future within this new situation of commitment to family, husband, and children; what tensions they experience; and what advantages and power they find in this new project. I keep in mind that they are actors at key nodes of potential shifts in cultural codes affecting couple relationships, mother–child relationships, and relationships between women and elders.

I have divided the discussion of these women into two chapters: stay-at-home and working mothers. These are key categories determined by the state in their statistics and used as important differences by women themselves, but they are far from homogeneous, as will become clear in my analysis of life processes. Of the twenty-seven mothers, all are married, and one has been divorced and remarried. Fourteen are stay-at-home mothers and thirteen are working either full-time or part-time.

Have mothers gotten what they wanted?

First, have these women gotten what their hearts most desired: a husband they chose and who understands them? It is a question that is unexpectedly hard to answer. All have chosen to take the step, and most have felt an *en* or special connection with their future husbands. About ten in this group were not passionately in love but married men they had known platonically over the years, and three married men whom they "did not dislike." They were ready to stop working, marry, and have children, and thus were willing to compromise—often in ways they would not have dreamed of before—for someone to "drink tea with" and share the responsibilities of reproduction.

Second, if one of their important goals of marriage was to have children, how many have they had? Considering all the married women in this study, the rate of children per mother is 1.26, with a rate of 1.41 for women living in the regions and a rate of 1 for women living in the Tokyo area.[1] This compares with the fertility rate for Japan at 1.32 in 2006, climbing to 1.37 in 2009 (Naikakucho 2008; Statistics Bureau 2011). Statistically, the fertility rate in the Tokyo area (1.02 for Tokyo itself and 1.23 for metropolitan prefectures) is higher in Iwate (1.39), the northeast prefecture; many regional rates are over

1.5 (Naikakucho 2008, 13). Thus, the married women in this study are under the statistics except for the women living in the regions.[2] The big difference in this study hinges on work: stay-at-home mothers have had an average of 1.8 children and working mothers have had an average of 1.36 children.

Third, how many are continuing to work after marriage, another ideal of their generation's ambiguous resistance? Just over half of this group have forgone the dual identities of work and motherhood, acceding to "life away from society," one of their deepest fears. Out of twenty-seven married women with children in the study, fourteen are full-time mothers and thirteen are working mothers. These "choices" contain various personal circumstances, but overall they attest to the strong ideology that mothers need to devote time and space to nurturing successful children and to the failure of government programs to support working mothers adequately. Even if maternity leaves, day-care centers, and kindergartens support working mothers, they cannot make up for late hours in the work sphere for men and women.

Full-time mothers

The focus of this chapter is the fourteen full-time mothers. As statistics, they appear as neotraditionalists (Rudd and Descartes 2008) who have accepted the postwar status quo role for women. Here I explore more deeply: What does life look like from inside their lives, bodies, minds, and emotions?

First, this group is not just like their mothers. They all insist that they have much more responsibility for decision making within the nuclear family than their mothers had and simultaneously face more risk in relation to life opportunities for their children, safety, and future expectations.

Second, they all try to enact a shift in the cultural code away from obligation to emotion as the basis for family relations, especially in their relations with husbands and parents, but also in relation to children whom they wanted rather than having been obligated to have. Their mothers have fought the fight to live apart from in-laws, the paragon of postwar obligation for women, and these women continue it.

Third, they all have had children later in life and have reconciled themselves with the limited physical strength this entails, though it sometimes constrains their abilities to participate in activities beyond the family.

Fourth, they all live within several discourses: (1) the postwar discourse of motherhood that they have been raised with, that their mothers still represent, and that continues in Japan; (2) the more recent, globally inspired generational discourse of self-actualization and enjoyment as they develop their lives in a self-narrative; and (3) the late-modern discourse of risk perception and individual responsibility in Japan.

Three groups of full-time housewives have emerged from my analysis, which are divided according to the following criteria: level of risk perception and stress in child raising; use of the life-stage discourse for women; awareness of self as defined individually outside of the family; and level of responsibilities in the household. The first group of full-time housewives are the planners: seven women who are using their societal skills learned as singles to raise their children while maintaining future options for self-development in the next stage of life. The second group is the cocooners (Giddens 1991): five women devoting themselves to their children with little tension around their own self-development but who experience high stress about the risks their children will have to face. The third group is the caretakers: two full-time housewives with a high degree of anxiety caused by responsibilities to care for extended family members.

The planners

The women in this group are aware of multiple aspects of their lives and of their selves changing over time in the process of ambiguous but nonetheless intense long-term questioning. Though intent on navigating the challenges of current society for their families, they exhibit a high level of self-awareness—of where they have been, where they are, and where they will go. They have swum in single waters with intense curiosity and would be classified as successful singles in the sense of having attained financial and emotional stability. Although they have enjoyed active jobs, none have opted for what they consider man-like jobs, as in the management track. They are all open to taking the dominant norm of the life-stage discourse for women (the M-curve), adapting to it, banking on its shifting surface, and massaging it for their own uses. As selves, they feel they are treading water in the housewife role, yet they realize that it requires strategizing and improvisation in relation to the members of their families, the current era, and themselves. They are committed to entering into the power of their role, while bobbing up to think about the future from time to time. In short, the workshop of experience as experimenting singles has irrevocably cut across their dispositions and relationships to result in a heightened self-awareness.

I return to the ethnography of the particular with Minami-san, whom we met in the beginning of this chapter, and then describe the characteristics of this group of seven women in more detail by referring to examples of others in the group.

SLOWLY ADJUSTING SELF

The day before I left, Minami-san and I managed to have lunch by ourselves at a hotel high above the bay. As we spread the white linen napkins on our laps, I asked how she liked living there.

"I have come to really like this city. Things are slower here than in Tokyo."

"I have been so impressed with how you manage your husband!" I said honestly. "You always make it look like his decision! I always end up in an argument!" We both laughed at each other across the table and I glimpsed the old, looser Minami-san.

"Oh, I get angry, too! Ka-ka-ka!" and she held her hand in a claw. "At first when we were married, I pushed Self! Self! (*jibun, jibun*) and cried, 'Why don't you understand?' I thought it was an old Japanese idea to bolster up the husband, and I told him so. I didn't want to be like my mother who obeyed my father."

"So did you work?"

"I longed for work or something outside the house. He thought I should stay home, especially because I got pregnant almost right away. I felt very isolated."

We ordered sushi, since in this city close to the sea it would be tender and soft.

"But, you know, I have realized that my mother was not weak. I don't kill my 'self' by giving in. I am making a harmonious (*enman*) household for the child. That comes first. The woman is central. If she is energetic and bright, all goes well."

"I suppose so."

"I thought making a home was a light thing, but it is terrible. My thinking was wrong. It is difficult to accept the other person, but in a home I think it doesn't go well if both people have the right to decide. So we talk a lot, but in the end, he decides." Or at least you make it look like he decides, I thought.

"So do you feel you are very similar to your mother?"

"No, she lived with my father's parents and didn't decide by herself about things, even how to raise her children. Now there is a lot of information, but you have to decide by yourself in a nuclear family. It's a lonely feeling. That's why people use the internet or form circles with friends. People aren't necessarily free, but . . ."

After salad, soup, and sushi, I asked what she thought when she looked back over her life.

She threw up her hands—a sudden motion for this white tablecloth restaurant. She was pushing back against my question (Rosaldo 1989).

"Not yet! Not yet! I think 'from here on.' I am not looking back! I'm wondering where I will end up. When the child gets big and my husband is okay, then I can do what I want."

"Ah, you are looking ahead, not back!"

"I want to work, but now the child is small and I have lots of work in the house. When my husband said okay, I trained twice a week to be a home helper for the elderly and I learned this is terrible work. I am not able to do it—not with my husband's illness and my needing to drive him to work and the boy to lessons. For now, I have to be satisfied with volunteer work like at my son's school and in the neighborhood."

I knew Minami-san was interested in the Green Co-op, a food nonprofit that distributes organic, fair-trade food along with political messages such as antinuclear ideas. "Would you ever be able to work for the Green Co-op?"

"Maybe something small, like make organic *bentō* (lunches) and sell them at the university. A friend and I have talked about that. I also thought of getting training in breast massage for women after birth. After I gave birth, this helped so much to get my milk going. The training is in Tokyo and my husband said it would be fine, but I don't think the time is right yet."

Minami-san tasted her green-tea ice cream and stared at the blue waters below. "I'm forty-four. I don't have so much time to work in life from now on."

WOMEN WHO LOOK IN TWO DIRECTIONS

Minami-san's tensions were clear, yet what I find remarkable is her ability to stand in the midst of everyday life, look in two directions, and tolerate ambivalence as part of her long-term resistance. She does not give up long-term resistance but relinquishes a certain self-centered form of it and adopts another with ingrained capabilities learned from her own mother's ways. She keeps responsibility central, yet plans for the future that would have been impossible for her mother. She figures how best to care for her husband and son, but also how to crack open the door to the world outside the house and life as her son grows. Although intense expressions of self and its desires seem to lessen with time, Minami-san continues to make choices to do things, such as attending Green Co-op meetings, outside of home. Minami-san's story suggests several points that I see playing out in other women's narratives in this group.

First, she seems sharply aware of this as a performance that does not represent her whole person—an active pose with a voice that is different (Butler 2004; Owens 1992). All the same, the performance is a serious life project within which choices must be wisely made among various foods, various schools for her son, and various medical treatments for her husband. True to what theorists claim for the late modern era, she feels the loneliness in the freedom of the nuclear family, the lack of trusted experts, and precarious dependence on her own individualized savvy (Beck and Beck-Gernsheim 2002).

Second, Minami-san strategizes within a form of marriage that, except for the lack of in-laws, shows patriarchal control typical of the postwar era, and perhaps greater because her husband is home so much. In many ways she uses the *amae* relationship of dependence, indulging and sweetening husband and son as she oversees the household operation. Her values have broadened, from intense focus on her guitar-playing self and her willingness to wrench relationships around, to self-immersion in the goals of harmony and caregiving at present; but a key point is that she is careful not to overexploit her body and spirit.

CHARACTERISTICS OF THE PLANNERS

The planners are in the space of ambivalent "partial recognition" of life's contradictions for Japanese women, but they show continued self-awareness and even irritation, tamed but festering. Illustrating a balance of influences from the regions and the big city, all but one have experienced metropolitan Tokyo life as singles, but also all but one grew up in regional cities and villages in middle-class homes; all have some post–high school education. Three presently live in Tokyo, two in regional cities, and two in rural villages (both having been raised nearby).

As singles, the planners were strongly invested in their careers and experienced upwards movement within the bounds of their jobs, but they also knew the joys and bitterness of daily work. For example, the nurse in the northern village thought work was her purpose in life but complained that "the men on the top don't listen to me." She expressed this commitment in

1993: "Work is my meaning in life. People here thank me. Men are on top and don't listen to me, but I can work here even after I have children." In Tokyo, Akai-san, a Toyota secretary in PR, had to choose between "being part of the tea pourers or working like men and being promoted," with its heavy obligations (Rosenberger 2001, 195, 227–228).

These women had developed a sense of their own will to power. In 1993 Akai-san admitted to getting a boyfriend while living separately from her parents. "I have changed 180 degrees. My mother must be taken aback. I was such a beautiful, quiet girl. I just accepted things. Now I initiate things." Like the others, she brought to marriage an attitude of long-term dissatisfaction and an urge to push for small changes—to "stay alert (*hariai*)," and "experience society so my 'self' will grow."

The planners viewed their abandonment of cooperation with others as just temporary, avoiding acts that cut too sharply across their inner selves or their relationships. A Tokyo teacher had a three-year secret relationship with a fellow teacher in 1998, but constrained herself through the disciplined movements of the tea ceremony, where she "served others and controlled my emotions." Their mother–daughter relationships were shattered in some ways, but rebuilt in other dimensions. After moving into her own apartment, a village woman said, "Instead of arguing with my mother, now we can talk about how to take care of the apartment."

In this social movement of women seeking for personal choice within historical cultural codes, these planners had pushed the envelope yet stayed within the margins of acceptability. Having impelled their parents to give up on them, they claimed marriage as a personal decision made in a framework of choice. Although they were not ready to give up work, "When I think of children, I am getting older" was a frequently heard phrase, as if it were their own bodies and their desire for children, rather than their parents or society, that demanded their compliance. They watched friends as if surveilling them from the Panopticon tower and planned their futures. Another Tokyo teacher said: "I see that mothers being with children when they are small is good—up until kindergarten. If I work they will be lonely. So I will interrupt my work and will continue after that. A teacher can get work, though not at the same school."

Child raising was both difficult and delightful. Constraining them from one world, it opened another—a world that at least for a time gave these late-modern "nomads" a cultural and emotional home, one that they could shape in some ways as long as they accepted some temporary ironies in their life narratives. Their children were the emotional and material magnets or symbolic bootstraps that pulled them toward making positive efforts to cope with the constraints and responsibilities of motherhood in this era.

A woman who quit her village government job and left her single apartment to marry and have children captured the feeling well as her two small boys scrambled up and over the tables in the room while we talked. "Having a home (*katei*) is terrible! Enjoyable and terrible." She laughed as she rescued her younger boy from the pummeling of his brother. "To be home all day with the children. . . . My mother-in-law says, 'Be with the boys for three years, so you don't regret it.' 'Yes, it's so, for this time,' I think. I should take responsibility and raise them." Looking at her friend who still worked while raising her children, she asked, "Have I come to be doing everything in order (*junjo ni*), just as I 'should'?" She shrugged. "I can't escape. I feel I have been on a branch road for a while. I can hardly believe that I married at thirty and entered his house. I don't believe that I am raising children. I did not really want marriage yet. But for now I have the children." She dreamed of someday moving with her husband to Okinawa to open a coffee shop.

A nurse in the northern village echoed the difficulty of this shift. She had hoped to continue working but finally gave up the idea because her son had a bad heart and required extra care. In her head, friends' voices echoed the values of being an individual at work: "I was really down for two to three years after quitting. I would get phone calls from nurse friends and they would say, 'Oh, it's a waste [for you not to work]. I like to look after the kids but fulfillment I don't have. I feel like I am a fool after a while with the kids," she said in 1998. But, like others in this group, she exhibits the ability to adjust and appreciate her place in life. In 2004, now a mother of three, she looked back: "After a few years of wanting to work so badly, I began to feel that kids coming to me and yelling 'Mom, Mom!' was also enjoyable." However, she was scheming to resume regular, less vigorous nursing at the county office.

No one revealed the struggle more than Akai-san, the Toyota secretary who continued working until her daughter was two. She tried valiantly to work after a year's maternity leave, but her husband, a banker, worked long hours; when her father had a stroke and thus she lost the backup of her mother, she quit. Even though her hours were shorter than her husband's, they were too many when the child got sick, and there was no question of his quitting or limiting his hours in a managerial-level job. Watching him sleep as she got up with the baby, she realized that as a woman her long-term resistance had to become more ambiguous for a time.

In Japan, having a child younger than three significantly decreases a woman's work participation (Shirahase 2007). I thought of my Hong Kong and Thai friends who worked full-time and came home to neat homes, warm dinners, and children cared for by maids from rural Thailand, Indonesia, or the Philippines. Although that brought its own problems of global inequality, Japanese women did not have this option, either ideologically or from the point of view of immigration, which limited foreign women to certain occupations—specifically, entertainment or health care. Japanese women have only day cares and parents to turn to, and when these fail, the woman's bargaining power has to bow, at least temporarily.

Akai-san adjusted by reinterpreting the dominant postwar discourse of life stages for women. Along with several others, she pronounced the motherhood period as years of lessened stress rather than as her life's work that demanded her full attention. "Ten years ago I felt I couldn't live without work. But after a fourteen-year career, with this body and a child, I felt I couldn't work like a man. . . . Now I am laid-back (*nombiri*) with no stress. It is good to have in your life. When the child lets go of my hand, I'd like to get some work." Still, some self-discipline was required, and she took up tea ceremony again to practice "calmly serving tea to others."

Translating the first tensions of motherhood into long-term ambivalence with vague planning for their own future is a task of survival for these successful singles in this new field. The past Tokyo teacher who followed her husband to a regional city said: "I wanted to work again and I worried. My friends in Tokyo are still working. But now, inside me, the first thing is children, second husband, and third work. I am resigned (*akirameta*). I think it is only now. If I only think of the things I want to do, my stress piles up." She chose the old word used by her mother's generation, "resigned," but she interpreted it as a temporary and active position of not pushing back and turned her attention toward making friends with other mothers in a child-rearing circle.

This planning was slow and ambiguous. Akai-san thought she could find work after age forty-five and without question planned for lower-level work that was not as tied to the polishing of self, as had been her PR work before marriage. "Can I do the work, I wonder, but I want to link with society after the child is ten or so. I am thinking hazily. Maybe counseling young people worried about work and child raising. Maybe volunteering. Before, I was polishing my self (*jibun o migaku*), but now I will just give myself a boost (*jibun o takameru*). The point now is to go on living (*ikite iku*)." Her plans pitched her efforts for self a notch lower, but they fit well with the responsible individualism called for by the Japanese state in the form of volunteering to help local community and in the process actualizing self (Ogawa 2009).

True to the predictions of their generational discourse, having husbands who understood their stress and ambivalence helped these women to survive. Women reported their husbands bathing with children, taking out the garbage, and shopping on weekends. Akai-san appreciated her banker-husband's unbridled delight in their daughter: she showed me a picture sitting on their dark-wood piano of her husband hugging their daughter and laughed, "He even hugs her in public." The woman in the northeast who dreamed with her husband of running a coffee shop in Okinawa received her husband's sympathy in the form of a shopping holiday—several nights a year by herself at a hotel in the regional city.

One of the former teachers found herself in almost the same position as middle-class mothers in the high economic growth period because her husband didn't arrive home until eleven. "Father leaves early and comes home late. He only has weekends here. So I am in between. I tell the kids what papa said and I tell him what the kids are saying. But he makes evening meals on weekends, so that is nice!" The differences from their mothers' experience were few—weekends with family and a few evening meals, an understanding word from husbands—but to these stay-at home wives they spelled an important generational difference.

These women's ability to move from motherhood as a stressful double bind to motherhood as relaxed ambivalence also hinged on the degree of their freedom from in-laws and help from parents. For example, Akai-san actually lived in the same house with her mother-in-law, but they inhabited separate floors, had separate kitchens, and only visited for meals when invited. A former wedding master of ceremonies worried about this issue the most, because she would be unwillingly following her husband's job back to the regions, where his parents wanted to build a house for their son and his family next door to their own. She feared they would come in whenever they wanted to and was scheming for an apartment, and later a house at a distance away. As she fed her one-year-old daughter in Tokyo, she said she was "dying to go back to work more and more," but she wanted the help of her own parents rather than that of her in-laws.

In sum, these planners were ambivalent stay-at-home mothers juggling multiple identities over the long term. Similarly to their mothers, they used publicly accepted life stages for women, but unlike their mothers, they remained very aware of the next stage of their lives and intended to make the most of it. Overall, they gave the time and space that led to a close relationship with their children, ensuring them emotional security and the ability to manage their activities. Yet they did not seem to invest their identities and emotions completely in relations of dependence with their children as women in their mothers' generation had (Rosenberger 2001, 47). Much like their mothers, they experienced a similar work structure that kept their company-employed husbands away from the house until late at night, yet less expectations of late-night drinking and weekends off for husbands seemed to keep them in closer emotional touch than their mothers had been with their spouses.

In short, these planners exhibited a tolerance for the contradictory truths that permeated their world, quelling them into tacit accommodation with subtle attitudinal and relational changes, yet they also showed an ability, gleaned from their long-term resistance, to keep their sense of double binds alive as a motivation for the future. They gave up their experimental single lives reluctantly, reinterpreted motherhood as a time of lower stress in which to recover from the tensions of work and singlehood, and looked forward to a quiet reentry into experimentation in the larger society in the future. They brought their individuality to their motherhood, even in some cases seeing their selves expanded in the process through interactions with their children, but did not exude the sense that the household was a place to develop a self of fun and fashion that others have found among housewife-mothers (Goldstein-Gidoni 2007; Bardsley and Hirakawa 2005).[3]

Cocooners

"The world has changed in one generation. I want to raise the child in a free and easy way as I was raised in Morioka, but when you hear about the terrible things that are happening . . ."—these words of Sasaki-san, raised in the northeast and now rearing her son in the Tokyo metro area, typify the feelings of risk and devotion among this second group of singles turned housewives with children. A group of five, the cocooners shut the door to their lives of self in society more decidedly than the planners. They are on average three years older than the planners and married on average almost ten years later. Fulfilled by child raising and finding it better than work, the cocooners are not ostensibly planning ahead for another era of their lives but instead submerging themselves in their roles as mothers and housewives even at the price of isolation. They act like women of the modern, productionist era, ensconced in the status of stay-at-home middle-class housewives, yet they are full participants in late-modern risk society, fearful of the effects of crime on children, the shift to individualistic values, and the possibility that their children will be losers in this increasingly competitive educational and employment environment of the 2000s. They employ older dominant values to cope with and shield themselves from the perceived dangers of the new, building a cocoon for themselves and their children (Giddens 1991). It is not that the planners do not protect their children and arm them to compete in this society, but they do so with neither the foreboding of danger nor the focused devotion exhibited by these women.

Along with their cocooning, these women idealize the northeast, the place where all were raised, as a place where the risks can be avoided. Five grew up in the northern city, the sixth in the northern village, and only one spent part of her single life in Tokyo. All still live in the northeast except for one who married a man from the Tokyo area and moved there. Two have moved from the Morioka area to the largest regional city of Sendai. They cherish the status of the nuclear-family housewife that in the poorer northeast has represented wealth and freedom from farm drudgery as well as overbearing in-laws. None receives or gives help to family elders.

In spite of having married with at least some sense of *en* or special connection with their future husbands, they receive little cooperation from them and reflect their generational ideals as they criticize their husbands for not giving their children the time they should. They tend to be isolated from friends and consult experts or acquaintances with superior knowledge about how they should proceed, but then are directive in formulas for their child raising. With one flashy exception, their poorer upbringing in the northeast and generally antimaterialistic point of view are reflected in their plain styles of living, unlike the affluent image that characterizes more new-style housewives (Goldstein-Gidoni 2012, 138).

In short, these women hark back to values idealized during the postwar period. In a sense, they are revivalists, but they are using these older values in new ways to gain control of their environment, to feel powerful in their roles as mothers, and to engender a cultural code that will save them, their children, and indeed Japan, in a new risky period. It is not surprising, then, that they are conscious of themselves as older mothers in comparison with their children's friends' mothers.

PROTECTING HER SON

I sat in a hard wooden chair talking with Sasaki-san at a small table in her wood-floored living-dining room, which had little other furniture except for a TV and bookshelf for children's books. Small and pale from anemia, her hands folded in front of her, she spoke in a quiet but steady stream of well-articulated opinions that belied her appearance. She always welcomed my visits, perhaps because she spent so much time alone, but this time her husband was upstairs entertaining her seven-year-old son. It was Sunday, but I was surprised to see her husband, because in 1998 she had described his hobbies with friends on weekends and her long hours of vigilance over the child. Even now, she told me, he coached a girls' volleyball team on Sundays, but she was trying to get him to give up his "shallow existence" outside of the family and spend more time with their son (Rosenberger 2001, 226–227). They lived in a house built jointly for them and his widowed mother, but the mother still lived in her apartment in her old neighborhood. Sasaki-san hoped to keep it that way.

Sasaki-san's son sneaked down from upstairs every half-hour or so to have a look at me, but she didn't seem to mind. He would sidle up to the table to sample the snacks I'd brought and she had laid out. She was quietly pleasant to him: "You want to have some? Then say it. Wash your hands and have some." He did as he was told, and then scooted across the wood floor with his play truck.

"I am forty now and feel far from the younger mothers around here. I am deeply colored by the Showa era [1926–1988] and they by the Heisei era [1989–present]. The young mothers' sense of things is different from mine. I want to keep my own house and watch my own child correctly, with a sense of loyalty between parent and child (*oyakōkō*, or Confucian-based filial piety). But some mothers raise children differently. The children don't give greetings and listen to others in school. They can't put up with difficulties anymore (*gaman*). The mothers think, 'Well, kids are just like that!' and let it go. Are they coming face-to-face with their children? I wonder. Their thinking is too simple. While the children play at the park, the mothers stand around doing e-mail, talking on the telephone. At home the kids play video games while the mothers work just because they want to. I've talked to the teachers about the children's inability to endure (*gaman*) and the need to teach them. She agrees."[4]

This was a conversation where I didn't need to ask many questions. Sasaki-san had her tale to tell, and I simply nodded and sympathized as I took notes.

"Other mothers ask me 'Aren't you working?' " She raised her eyebrows meaningfully at me and held up her hands, palms out. "My hands are full raising him." She looked over at her son and said calmly, "Go upstairs now and read books with father." He scuttled up the stairs and she went on with quiet passion. "I want to tell them, 'You are parents!' You only have so long to send your child off [into adulthood]."

I remembered Sasaki-san's criticism of other young mothers in 1993 as well—as individualistic, self-centered, and immature (Rosenberger 2001, 226–227). I had thought at the time that she was simply old-fashioned, but my opinion had changed. She represented one type of late-modern reaction to living in an information-dense, globalized society: a feeling of dizzy imbalance wrought by the chaos of the global market of things and ideas and a search for stability through criticizing others.

Her role as mother and housewife took on huge meaning in the need to defend her child in this chaotic world. Sasaki-san's eyes smoldered. "Every day begins and ends with him and the days pile up. I feel that I am raising a living being. I am excited and nervous." She talked at length about the risks in the immediate environment that he might have to meet. "Pick up garbage and the can might explode. . . . Children have been taken in cars that follow them slowly on the way home. . . . Someone flashes to a kid. . . . Things get stolen at school. . . . At school even the classrooms are unlocked. I do patrol every day for the kids as they cross streets walking home." She pointed out the front window toward the school beyond the rice field that still stood at the center of her new development. "I watch and see if the kids are coming home, and if my son doesn't come, I go over. My husband does night patrol when he can."

"He's concerned too?"

"Oh, yes!"

The afternoon shadows were long on the wood floor and her son was getting restless. "What are your dreams at this point?" I asked her.

"To move back up north," she answered without hesitation. Merriment sparkled from her eyes for the first time. "I am famous among my husband's friends for being from Morioka. My husband loves Morioka now too. We dream of moving up there someday to be close to nature and among people who can trust each other. My mother is a model of child raising for me. . . . We talk on the phone often."

Afterwards, the four of us ate at a Chinese restaurant. The parents chuckled at their son's loquaciousness and glanced at each other with suppressed smiles at the overly informal approach of the waiter. Her husband ordered loudly for everyone, and then she quietly told the waiter what she wanted, changing his order to her liking.

IN PRAISE OF ENDÒURANCE?

Sasaki-san's way of discussing the contrast between Tokyo and the northeast indicates a worldview of the cocooners that turns on the symbolic values of urban versus rural. She uses the opposition between the urban and the rural/regional to symbolize the chaotic and the stable in the changing social order that scares her (Comaroff and Comaroff 1992, 159; Williams 1981).

Sasaki-san emphasizes the value of endurance (*gaman*) in the face of hardship as the exemplar of rural/regional superiority, ignoring its political-economic inferiority. Selected from samurai history and the suffering of World War II, endurance has been idealized in postwar schools and nationalist rhetoric, and is at the fore of post-tsunami efforts as well. Sasaki-san's foil is the city and its opposite value of self-centeredness that plagues young mothers and most of the children. If only city people would go back to the endurance of the northeast, the dangers of a hedonistic, selfish consumerist society in Japan could be averted.

Sasaki-san empowered herself by focusing on this residual value of endurance, her cultural weapon of attack from a historical, rural ideal. She claimed it as her high ground with other mothers and the expert, the teacher, whom she looked to for reinforcement. In the northeast and throughout Japan, historically it was considered the ideal gendered response by women to unreasonable patriarchal control expressed by mothers-in-law, fathers-in-law, and husbands. It is the counterpart of spoiled actions coming from "soft" places (the word for spoiled, *amae*, relating to the word *amai*, or soft) and is recognized for the personal effort it requires, for the enduring female is often the one who allows others above and below her to vent their emotions as they wish.

However, Sasaki-san ignored other aspects of *gaman* that earned it reprobation from others of her generation who in general differentiate their situations—which in many ways are not unlike their mothers'—by the shift away from unquestioning endurance (Goldstein-Gidoni 2012, 141).

Indeed, Sasaki-san herself suffered from the negative sides of *gaman* just like northeastern women before her. Caring for her son day and night as essentially the sole caregiver had taken a toll on her body, and she did not feel that she could have more children, "with apologies to my husband because he wanted a lot of kids." Meanwhile, she wove a tight web of emotional dependence with her son.

The endurance of the cocooners exposes the dilemmas in writing a new script for self as a late-modern mother in Japan. Interpreted as spiritual strength, endurance at its best represents the ability to "kill self" (a Buddhist ideal of becoming part of the universe) and accept one's place in life. From a spiritual and historical point of view, it can be a mark of high maturity. Mahmood (2001) would see it as an agency of cultivated, self-controlled commitment to a religio-patriarchal system, and in reference to Japan, Ivry (2007) calls it an agency of nurturance that gives women power within the national system and normalcy within the medical system. Here I am interested in the dynamics of its tensions.

The historical value of endurance is significant in Japanese women's efforts to bring global and local values together into a Japanese version of late-modern self. Endurance (*gaman*) represents the fulcrum upon which the independence of the self-centered "self" comes to ideal adulthood for women in Japan and can potentially turn into a culturally idealized independence of the other-centered "non-self," a spiritually deepened version of self-sacrifice. This shift works on social and spiritual levels for a cocooner such as Sasaki-san, who was a struggling single and has gained temporal power through motherhood and child safety. But the question for all women of this generation is how to straddle, traverse, and translate these various cultural ideals of different eras, combining the efforts of self-cultivation with self-actualization and thus create their own script for a mature woman adult of today.

CLOSING OFF CHANGE

In contrast with the planners, the cocooners show that long singlehood does not necessarily result in openness to change. After a conservative, northeastern upbringing and an unsatisfying singlehood, marriage was a step up economically and socially for them. One cocooner living in the northeast married a doctor from the medical school where she worked at a secretarial job with pay so low she could not even afford to have hobbies (Rosenberger 2001, 189). She lost her poverty and gained status, but also a life of isolation from friends and responsibility because of her husband's schedule. She stated flatly that, because of her position as a doctor's wife, "I will never work." Even in Morioka, she worried about her young children getting kidnapped and hoped fervently that her husband would not take them to live in Tokyo—even farther from her mother who lived on the northeast coast. "Scary!" she exclaimed with uncharacteristic emotion.

COCOONING WITH AN ALLERGENIC CHILD

The dangers of the present world increasingly intruded on mothers in the form of children's allergies, which have increased in Japan in the last several decades. Although all mothers turned to doctors as experts to guide them, these mothers became particularly dependent on them, their lives governed by doctors' opinions. They experienced an ironic paradox of the late-modern era: increased independence in making self-narratives and in solving problems, yet heightened dependence on experts who appeared as the bulwarks against risk (Bauman 1991). In this case, Oyama-san felt that she had no choice but to abandon the life of self because she had to give herself entirely to navigating her son through the risks of local and global pollution (Rosenberger 2001, 229).

Oyama-san welcomed me to her small apartment in Sendai, the largest northeastern city. The apartment was sparse; she had taken out curtains, rugs, and furniture and vacuumed morning and night, putting the futon bedding away immediately. At the behest of the doctor, the family existed with the allergic child on potatoes, rice, miso soup, and a bit of pork, although she said, "We do sneak a bit of fish now and then." Dangers for her child lurked in every nook and cranny, not only outside her door but in every action she took as a mother responsible for his life in a world of dust and toxins. Dressed in a saggy black top and slacks, she said, "I am chased by each day. Since kids, I just wear anything. I don't know the fashions. I just go to the park and the supermarket, though a health-food store delivers much of the food. . . . I am making no friends, none. . . . I can't even make the cookies I used to enjoy! . . . My dreams are only that the children grow up and become mature adults. I want to live peacefully as a couple. Maybe move back to Morioka if we can. They are not big things, are they? I am full up with raising kids!"

I assured her that these were very important things, although I understood the apologetic look in her eye—a glimmer of the ambivalent awareness of the life of self she had known as a travel agent in Tokyo and later as a teacher in Morioka. Her bit of rebellion against the doctor's orders indicates her trust in her own experience and expertise as a past home economics teacher. Like Sasaki-san, Oyama-san also dreamed of returning to Morioka and building a house there. The boys could have a stable high school experience there, as her husband had many transfers.

COCOONING WITH CHILD FOR SUCCESS AND UPPER MOBILITY

This description of the process of cocooning is not complete without the case of Mori-san. She could be described as an education-crazy mother of the late-modern consumerist period or as a vestige of status-climbing village people. Although she differs from the other cocooners in her flash and sociality, she adds the insight that cocooning in the mother role can appear as a high level of competition for the child and the mother (Rosenberger 2001, 207).

Mori-san knits her motherly cocoon of safety against a late capitalist world divided between winners and losers by unabashedly striving for urban middle-class status. Married to a sushi chef who is not wealthy, she has leveraged his high-rise condo overlooking Sendai as the base for wealthy friends who can advise her and whom she can watch to discover the best opportunities for her son. Although her husband wants her to work to help pay the mortgage, she refuses, despite her years spent as a low-level manager at a ski resort near her village. At forty-six, this would be a "status-down" move because many good jobs have an age limit of thirty-five. It would also expose her true age, which to friends, teachers, and son she has represented as eight years younger than it is.

In 2004, Mori-san, dressed in heels and a flounced skirt, arranged a tour of her life so that I could see the successful framework she had built. It started with her best friend, "ten years younger than I am," with whom she patrols the area for "strange people." When Mori-san noticed that everyone in kindergarten had computers, this friend advised her on what to buy. We met the principal at the Christian-run kindergarten where her now seven-year-old son had gone and which he still attends for after-school English club lessons with other alums. Mori-san sang in a mama-san's choir there. She took me to a French restaurant, where we ate in a red-velvet nook in view of other mothers, our conversation full of her son's violin, soccer, and English prizes. Later that night, after I had returned by train to Morioka, she called me up and had her son speak to me in English, intent on making sure that I knew she was making a winner.

Is Mori-san really a cocooner? She is consumer-oriented in comparison with other cocooners and comes closest of all the mothers to the picture of Japanese housewife/mothers as marrying for money, comfort, and consumption-oriented enjoyment (Goldstein-Gidoni 2007). She invests in her son's success much like Minami-san, the planner at the beginning of this chapter. However, I think she is a cocooner-mother who teaches us something about cocooning in the global world today. Giddens (1991) speaks of cocooners as withdrawing into groups that oppose individualistic change and protecting themselves from risk in such groups as fundamental religions. Mori-san cocoons in her role as a normal, middle-class mother, despite her husband's lower income and high school education, which, statistically, would make him want her to work (Shirahase 2007). Unlike other mothers in her generation who tend to be less concerned with social status than their mothers were (Nakano and Wagatsuma 2004), her village background influenced her toward status seeking. Ignoring her own self-actualization, she dives into the cultural and social capital of the consumer world to build a fortress for her and her son on the basis of her son's achievements. In short, Mori-san reveals that cocooning against risk can spring up in consumerist forms that appear to bring independence and freedom, but that actually construct the very relationships of emotional dependence to which women of this generation object. I hoped for her sake that her son would not reject this path she laid out for him as so many other young people have, and that her cocoon would stay intact.

In sum, these cocooners seem to have lost the ambivalence of their long-term resistance as singles, directing all their energies toward children and a framework for future status. However, my observation is that this strong direction is a bulwark constructed in resistance against the wolf at the door—the sense of late-modern instability and a weakened nation beset with crime and economic decline. Thus, they construct their positions with awareness that the cultural code is changing in ways they did not predict, and that the change presents contradictions for them as mothers to reflect and act on. Cocooners assume this stance in the shape-changing course of long-term resistance. The extent to which their ambiguous long-term resistance will reemerge in personal ways will become clear in future interviews.

Caretakers

"Right around the time my baby was born, my brother was killed in an accident. I am the only daughter of my parents now. Then my father died and with all the red tape to handle, we moved near my mother because she has dementia . . . I don't have any time or money. It's a life in which I am always driven, chased. So I just flow with things. I don't have energy to do anything more."

Only two of the full-time housewives with children fall into the category of caretakers who simultaneously care for their children and their parents:

Inoue-san, forty-two in 2004 (just quoted), and Ishii-san, forty in 2004. The burden is onerous and denies to them the latitude of the planners to look in several directions, or the concentration of the cocooners whose gaze wraps their children in protection. The caretakers' lives exhibit the contradictions of a welfare system that still depends on the family, particularly women, even though the system brings in part-time home helpers supported by taxes paid by all citizens over forty. Urban Tokyoites their whole lives, these women make it clear that the endurance demanded of women and evidenced here is not simply a rural/regional phenomenon but also a result of the political-economic system. This contradiction hit both these women early, in their mid-to-late thirties, just after they gave up single life and their fairly satisfying work in public schools and soon after finding partners that felt "right in my heart." They each now have two children, but parental sickness has snatched away the emerging adulthood that they were fashioning.

As is typical of the late-modern era, both care for their own parents, to whom they are emotionally attached, rather than for their in-laws. In 2004 both women told me, "I feel grateful to my parents for all they did for me now that I have my own children." Still, their relationships with their parents had been hammered out through both conflict and affection. In 1993 at twenty-nine, Ishii-san had "lots of touch with the outside world" and complained of her parents being "overprotective," though their "understanding" was increasing as she aged. At that point she was "not thinking" about her status as an only daughter who might have to care for her parents someday.

Boom. Ishii-san's father had a debilitating stroke from diabetes in 1996 when her first child was one year old. Even though Ishii-san had said "I want to be accepted not as a man or a woman, but just work and live straight as I am," societal and family expectations colluded with governmental and company policies to elect her, a stay-at-home mother with small children, as her father's caretaker. She and her husband moved in with her parents, and her mother, at sixty-eight, continued her work as a well-paid "professional secretary."

In 2004, I met Ishii-san over coffee at a metro station mall in the Tokyo suburbs. Her hair was as long as when I first met her, her teeth were crooked in just the cute way Japanese like in their pop stars, and her striped jersey looked like a relaxed housewife's costume. But costume it was, for her father had suffered a second worse stroke in 2002 that put him into a wheelchair, and her schedule rotated around him. They received some help from the government insurance program, so she could get out of the house and talk.[5]

"I am busy in the morning getting the kids off and getting my father ready for the day and heating up his food. My mother leaves at 8:30 for work and he leaves for day-care service at 9:30. I didn't even have time to eat breakfast this morning. My mother comes home from work at 8 p.m."

I responded, "My mother had a stroke and was quite agitated. Is your father?"

"No, he is quiet, though sometimes he gets depressed and wants to die. Then I get depressed. Once I put him out in the garden and some religious person came by and proselytized him." She giggled for the first time. "I really can't let him out of my sight! 'Is there no good way?' I thought." Her hand rubbed her forehead.

I realized that children had been forgotten in the father talk. "And your children?"

"I've had another since we talked the last time. She is five and her brother is eight now. I am forty, so we can't have anymore. I couldn't with my father anyway." My notes told me that she had wanted three children.

Ishii-san hesitated for a moment, glanced aside, and then dove into a story that marked her harsh awakening to where life had taken her.

> The younger one is five, but started kindergarten at three. I was busy then and I guess she was lonely, but I didn't realize it. She felt insecure. I feel very terrible about that time. I was centering myself on my father and she wanted to be hugged but she couldn't say so. I didn't have time to hug her. She couldn't express herself and just put up with it (*gaman*). She bit the inside of her cheeks very badly. Then she played with her fingertips and they bled under the fingernails. I was full up with the house and Dad. My feelings had stopped.

She looked down. I murmured empathetically, but didn't need to say much.

> Last summer, I took her to the doctor for a cold, but when he saw the bites on the inside of her cheeks, he was very harsh. "If this continues, she'll cut her wrist in the future," he said. I had no space (*yuttori*) left in me, so psychologically this was really hard on me. I just drank in those words. I thought, "I've done this to my child!" Afterwards I told my friends, and they said it would be okay and not to worry. She would be okay as an adult. I just needed to hug her more and tell her "I like you." Little by little she is getting stronger. I learned.

Using the doctor's words to legitimate herself, Ishii-san asked her mother to help more so she could put her children first, and thus they started on the day service. The words of the doctor-expert, that in this era of too-few children her attention should be on her children, were thus both a boon and a form of regulation on Ishii-san as to the kind of mother she should be. The doctor ignored her hurt feelings and dismissed the squeezing pressure she felt in her chest as "stress, don't worry," instead reinforcing the importance of the mother–child bond and implying that it was her mother, not she, who should make sacrifices for her father. Fortunately, the voices of Ishii-san's friends played a comforting cello to the doctor's alarming trumpet in the orchestra of her mind, reassuring her that her motherly affection over time would be adequate. But she felt put to the test, under the gaze of the expert in the Panopticon.

Our conversation ended with a few soft, positive notes: her policeman-husband who helped cook and bathe the children when he was on day shift; and her work of sticking Disney mascots on packages late at night while watching movies. "I do it for myself, just to relax." Her friends, sympathetic with her need for even a slender thread of self outside the family, had found her the job. She hoped to work again someday, but wondered if she would be healthy enough.

Emotionless endurance (gaman)

This case study of a caretaker expands the understanding of endurance in this era. The very value of endurance, already passed on to her daughter quite effectively, came back to bite her as a mother, even as her daughter literally bit herself. Endurance remains the psychosocial place to go for women enmeshed in the crises of family caretaking. However, Ishii-san's tale indicates that in extreme exigency endurance is neither honorable nor spiritual; it results in an emotionless independence that has closed off the "fold" between the inner psyche and the world around her. In the late-modern world, endurance followed too far becomes a mature self gone awry; the ideals of individuality expressed through emotion toward one's own parents or children are lost. Instead of forestalling risk, it invites risk.

This case study shows the process of the effects of the family's power exploding in the life of someone who has quietly challenged the status quo as a single. What is interesting here is that the family's power that (somewhat unwittingly) places parental care above childcare comes up against a societal discourse of motherhood. Ishii-san is not caught between the obligation of caring for in-laws and the emotion of caring for children as might have been the case in the past, but between two sets of emotions, grounded in her deepest psyche, toward her own parents and children. As a way out, she cuts off all emotion, largely detaching herself from her project of long-term resistance, but it is individualized emotion toward her child to which she returns in her recovery of efforts to regain self, however tension-filled it is.

This case study also reveals the strength of the discourse of mother as a necessary source of security and affection for her children in late-modern Japan and the doctor as the powerful purveyor of that truth. The doctor is the legitimatized source of pressure on young women to reach back into the dispositions of their childhoods and give of their bodies and emotions (Ivry 2007; Jolivet 1997), although we also see here the saving grace of Ishii-san's friends, who shore up her self-esteem against the doctor's harsh words. Significantly, the doctor makes the choice to support the mother–young child relationship over the parent–adult child relationship, thus clarifying another truth of late modernity: that society must bend toward nurturing the young even though elders are increasing in number proportionately. The future of Japan depends on it, and, because it is more likely to position the mother in an emotional relationship within the nuclear family where she has some control, the ambiguous long-term resistance for the mothers discussed herein also benefits from it.

Conclusion

With each chapter of this book increased depth and complexity gather around the concepts of ambivalence and tension in a field of contradictions in the late-modern era of a non-Western, globally powerful nation. Japan offers a particularly interesting example, because it is wealthy and technologically advanced yet also has a rich non-Western history. All the imaginations of the global world lie at the fingertips of these women, yet they must work out their versions of late-modern selves within the terrain of their personal and societal histories.

In this chapter this process has resulted in a heterogeneous set of ways to meet these women's dissatisfactions with the postwar cultural code. The planners focus on the contradiction of family versus self. They live with the tension but lighten it by seeing motherhood as easier than other work, assessing information through their cosmopolitan experience and by staying aware of both past and future. They strategize within marriages in which husbands are busy and wives are left to care for house and children but in which husband–wife communication continues. Less dependent on experts than the cocooners or caretakers, they activate their own responsibility to gather information and make decisions. Although they form intimate relationships with their children, their own identities do not depend on them, and they try not to push their endurance too far. They find acceptance among younger mothers in the community and worry about their ages only because their life-stage formula depends on time.

The cocooners focus on the same contradiction of family versus self, or endurance and care for others versus individuality, but they redefine it morally and frame it in the regional/urban divide. Their ages as older mothers take on meaning for them, emphasizing their capacity for devotion to their children, but also their differences from the current middle-class mold. Although they know which side they are on, their critique sharpens their vision of both sides, and the tension of fear and defense weighs heavily on them, making them more dependent on experts for guidance and reinforcement.

The caretakers are almost incapable of focusing on the family-versus-self contradiction. They experience tension and ambivalence over the contradiction in the late-modern institution of family between care of elders and care of children, a tension that is magnified because in this era both claim their emotional commitment. The data suggest that in response caretakers may withdraw their emotions from both in a destructive, emotionless version of endurance, partly because the self of their early adult script has been reduced to pasting Disney mascots on packages at one in the morning.

CHAPTER SIX

Working and Raising Moral Children

As I walked down the broad sidewalk in Tokyo, neck craned upwards to spy "Toyota" above the towering stone entrances, I felt curious, as if in by looking into the life of the woman working nineteen floors above me I would find out something about myself. Of the three Toyota secretaries whom I interviewed in 1993, only Matsui-san had remained at the company, still an "office lady" after twenty-five years of work, but now married with a son. Of all the married Tokyo interviewees in 2004, she alone was still working full-time while raising a child. What motivated and challenged her?

My curiosity was piqued because this was a drama in my life as well—the struggle to maintain a career while raising children. The click of my heels and the whir of the traffic created a rhythm for reminiscence: shifting gears from reading Bourdieu to reading Rumpelstiltskin; falling asleep with the children and then getting up at five a.m. to prepare for class; rushing home after class to care for a child with chicken pox.

No Toyota building yet. How did I do it? I lived far from parents, but my husband was part of child raising—a translator who worked at home and could pinch-hit in the late afternoons. I did not have long commutes. No boss was constantly looking over my shoulder and no coworker felt that s/he had to do more work because I was going home early. On the other hand, I had to write and publish on my own steam in all the cracks of private life. Quite a different arrangement from working as an office lady at Toyota.

I entered Toyota's marbled interior and asked for a badge to visit Matsui-san. How was she managing to negotiate this divide that fills the life of me and countless other women in late modernity and was integral to her long-term resistance? (Rudd and Descartes 2008).

Questions

Over eleven years, this group of fifty-four women has produced seven full-time working mothers and six part-time working mothers—about a quarter of the whole group and about half of the women with children. In 2006, of mothers in Japan overall 25 percent were employed six months after birth and 46.8 percent at four years after birth. Of these, 22.2 percent were part-timers (Naikakucho 2008, 43). Thus, the statistics in this small sample show a lower employment rate for mothers, but overall their children are still young.

The geographical distribution of these thirteen working women begs for explanation. I expected numbers to be higher in Tokyo, the area of lowest fertility rates and the most cosmopolitan in terms of accepting differences in lifestyles and dreaming to work equally with men. But five of the seven full-time working mothers lived in rural villages, and four of the part-time working mothers lived in northeastern cities.

This fact leads to important questions: How do the conditions in urban, regional, and rural places interact with the contradictions between work, family, and children for women in this ambiguous social movement? Simultaneously, how do questions of class intersect with women's work-family tension and these geographical differences?

The first part of this chapter delves into the nature of the experiences of six of the full-timers, and the second part the experiences of the six part-timers. Each group has a division within it of mothers working more for self and mothers working mainly for money, a division that reflects two ends of a continuum of motivations for women's work as well as class differences. I ask: What amplifies and eases tensions for these women? If tensions become particularly high, what solutions do women turn to? In the last part of the chapter my attention turns to an outlier—a mother with three children who works full-time running an organic farm with her husband. Her life on the margins mediates a number of conflicts met by her generation, but also creates others.

Tokyo: A full-time working mother

I met Matsui-san at the top of the elevator. At age forty-five, she was stout with long hair and wearing an orange jacket over a black skirt, very different from the thin-faced woman of thirty-four in blue uniform I had met in 1993. Her demeanor still serious as always, she ushered me into a conference room.

"I was switched into the environment department soon after I got pregnant and was out for a year on maternity leave. That doesn't happen with women a lot." She handed me a book she had helped to produce. "I just deal with the materials. Help the men."

A younger woman brought us tea. "I have a few younger women under me now. Everything has changed. Now all the women in our department are over thirty and single. Now people can take two years of maternity leave! The union pays 15 percent of their salary."

"Wow—we couldn't think of that in the U.S.A."

"The individual has become strong. It goes with the nuclear family. Now we couldn't think of leaving our families behind and skiing with the whole department. If people don't want to go out drinking now, they just refuse."

She got to the point without any prompting.

"I worried about going back to work, but for 'self' it is hard to be home all day with the child. I have no friends in the neighborhood. At first he was lonely and cried when I left him at day care, but he has come to enjoy it. He will ask, 'Do I go today?' He likes his mother, but he likes his friends, too. The child has his own world."

"How do you manage every day, working with a child?" I ask. "I've done it and I know it isn't easy." She nodded, her eyes softening into this question that preoccupied her even as she edited documents.

"I can't do much overtime work anymore because of the child. He's six and he is in daycare until six thirty. Then my father picks him up. He and my mother used to go travelling but now they have had to adjust to this. My father especially enjoys it."

In 1993, her father's voice had surfaced in her interview forbidding Matsui-san from living alone and chiding her for talking too much and losing her sweetness, yet here he was backing up her work.

"My husband gets home at seven thirty, so he can help too if I have overtime work to do and plan to get home late. He helps with the laundry. He lived alone a long time and can do everything."

"That's an advantage of marrying when you are older!" I quipped, and Matsui-san smiled wanly.

"I have no latitude. I usually fall asleep with the child and then awake at about two a.m. and clean up. I stay up until four or five a.m. I can't sleep. I worry. I always have to rush the child. I'm raising a child who doesn't see how to care for others (*sewa shinai*). My friend says to me: 'Think about this! Is it okay to be doing this?' "

"What do you think?" I ask her.

"I have changed. I used to get attached to things and I was disappointed if I didn't get clothes I wanted. Now I am not so interested anymore. Before the child, I was alone with my parents as my base, in their shadow. I just thought of my own things. When I married, we were two and it didn't change much, but with the child, it isn't just 'self.' You have the child and also his parents and your own parents. You come to think about family. And now that my son is ready for school, I am more worried."

"Really? I always thought if I got the children to school age, I could relax and do my work."

"It might get worse. Many women quit for elementary school because in summer vacation the child is all alone. And after-school care is only from nine to five. You begin to think it is a burden on the child."

Sleepless individuality

My surprise at Matsui-san as the only full-time working mother in Tokyo reflected my American expectations. Statistically speaking, urban Japanese women who work in large companies are especially disadvantaged "because of limited prospects for career advancement" (Shirahase 2007, 53). Furthermore, her husband's income as a banker militated against her working, so she was really working against the statistical odds. What does Matsui-san's case reveal about her ability—and her struggle—to resist these odds?

Ironically, the secret to being able to continue working while raising children rests in the very relationship that resisted the experiments with individuation run by Matsui-san and her peers in the first place: the parental generation. Five of the seven full-time working women among the interviewees had parental support. Company maternity leave policies, government day-care policies, and her banker-husband's willingness to help all supported Matsui-san's desire to work. But for this woman in a full-time job at a high-flying company in a large city in Japan, her parents and sometimes her husband's mother and aunt had to fill the gap that remained. The precariousness lay in their elders' health. A blood vessel pops, a golf cart turns over. In Matsui-san's case, her parents' ages as well as her own kept her from having more than one child.

Matsui-san's sleepless nights cried out to be heard. She was working, but with deep wells of stress that drove her both to continue working and to consider quitting. Her stress revolved around debates on child raising and mothers' lives concerned with competition and class, changing views of self, and morality.

Competition is high in large urban centers like Tokyo, particularly for salarymen households and their educated wives with high middle-class consciousness. This case study shows competition both for the woman and the child. Matsui-san's income helped her family to compete in housing and schooling, but not only that. With her working, Matsui-san and her son could also compete more successfully in the market of individuality that she saw in her Tokyo company as the wave of the present. She maintained "self," and her son developed a "world of his own." This discourse of separation between mother and child's worlds as developing her child's individuality has sustained Matsui-san's decision to keep working as part of her long-term resistance.

But a debate raged between this more global-Western idea and the ideals of intimate mother–child skinship (physical closeness) popular in the high economic era (Borovoy 2005, 149). Matsui-san's job threatened her son's ability to compete in the educational system if she did not give him adequate support at home and opportunities for extra lessons. It made life less enjoyable for her—enjoyment being a goal of women younger than she and a way of shifting the meaning of the housewife-mother role generationally (Goldstein-Gidoni 2012). On one hand, she thought it was fine that he was playing and hopefully developing in creative ways rather than going to classes five days a week as other children his age were. On the other, she wondered if age made her less capable of playing the game of middle-class mothering appropriately: "I am older than other mothers and my way of thinking is older." Was she accurately understanding the requirements of urban class status, or was she stuck in generational ideas about self and work that were becoming old-fashioned?

Indeed, surveys show that women who have married in their twenties are more likely to think that mothers should stay home than women who have delayed marrying until later (Shirahase 2007, 41). Class also makes a difference: parents of urban working-class children are not so concerned about children's progress and, while often emotionally supportive, do not push them toward academic success (Yoder 2004). Rural parents living in a rather depressed economic sphere are also more relaxed than urban middle-class parents.

A changing sense of self within and over generations also discouraged Matsui-san at work. Although the policies were good, her secretarial job was glaringly static. Although she continued because of her original dream in 1993 to "do the work to develop self . . . but not for a career," now she noticed younger women quitting work earlier. If her own sense of self started to subside in favor of family, and other middle-class mothers were giving up the goal of attaining self via work, then the meaning in her work lessened.

"Is it okay to be doing this?" The words of her friend fueled the child-raising debates simmering in Matsui-san's head. Mothers in this historical moment needed to encourage their children in individuality, but they also needed to train them in other moral values, here represented by her words "caring for others." Herein lay the contradictory demands of twenty-first-century motherhood in Japan and elsewhere: in their attempts to maintain their own flexibility as well as to raise morally acceptable, individually strong, and societally competitive children. It was a debate being waged not only with elders but within this generation as Matsui-san's friend stood in the Panopticon, judging her. Thus, long-term resistance aimed at developing opportunities for women to lead fuller lives also held risks both for their children and for relationships with friends in their generation—all of which pointed once again to the precarious ambivalence of the movement.

This case shows the ongoing debate in which a generation is working out the local meanings of child-raising, work, motherhood, and self for dissatisfied women of the middle class. The discussion implies that, to form the ideal child, day care, and perhaps even Matsui-san's parents' care, is not adequate, but rather requires the efforts of a middle-class stay-at-home mother and her ability to shape her individuality to enjoy that life—a verdict that gives Matsui-san nowhere else to turn.

Full-timers across the urban-rural divide

The three women with children in professional, full-time work present us with an opportunity to look at women across geographical areas in Japan. In addition to Matsui-san, the other two are teachers, one in the regional city and one in a small village. What does this ethnography of the particular show about differences and similarities surrounding the ways in which work and mothering are developing in the generational discourse across the urban-regional-rural continuum? How do practices and meanings of these geographical differences articulate with experiences of mothers struggling with child raising and work?

Many ideas and practices were similar across this geographical continuum. An internalized sense of self vibrated through the stories of Yamada-san in Morioka, Kawahara-san in the village, and Matsui-san in Tokyo in relation to the search for husbands in 1993 and 1998. Kawahara-san said, "For me I have a self. I would like to marry a man who meets with that." All profited from new government and company policies for maternity leaves, but this strong sense of individualized self drove them back to work. Yamada-san was in the country with her mother for one year and felt competitive: "Is it okay to be here just doing nothing in the middle of the day? I was left behind (*torinokosareta*)!"

Kawahara-san felt even more strongly. She had married at thirty-eight and undergone fertility treatment to get pregnant. "Public teachers get three years of maternity leave and my husband wanted me to take them, but it was hard for me to stay at home with only my son. After he was a year old, I felt like I couldn't breathe at night. The doctor said it was the psychological stress of child raising. So I returned to work after two years."

Kawahara-san laced her story with tales of women who had killed their children. Her saving grace was a day-care center in Morioka where she went with her child and met mothers and grandmothers of all ages who were also experiencing high stress, so she felt "normal." Indeed, the doctors have medicalized her condition into something speakable in Japan—child-raising neurosis (*ikuji noiroze*)—for which getting out of the house, though not necessarily back to work, is the treatment (Rosenberger 2001, 220–221).

Unlike Matsui-san in Toyota's Tokyo office, the teachers up north both felt motivated to continue their work because they found meaning (*yarigai*) in their work; they were raising citizens for a strong Japan, as Yamada-san said. Yamada-san taught in a private school in Morioka and experienced the stress of a shrinking school population having only six in her first-grade class, while Kawahara-san, in the village public middle school, felt the stress of boys who put down women teachers.

Particularly telling for the generational discourse on mothering and professional work across the urban-regional divide is the fact that all three accepted the idea expressed by Matsui-san: that individuation and separation were good for both parent and child. According to these teachers, parents were too protective. They should "let kids do things alone" and "see their children objectively from a distance . . . respect them in an equal relationship."

Otherwise the pressures on the children were too great. Yamada-san's conclusion speaks for all three: "So it is better for me to be out in society."

Yet the teachers also felt some ambivalence in the moral debate that Matsui-san raised between individuality and care for others. Yamada-san of Morioka said: "There is a mental/spiritual (*seishinteki*) part of me and my daughter that I want to care for. She has taught me to go slower, that a new house is not so important. My husband wanted to build a new house, but [why go into] debt?—for what? We can eat and sleep here just fine. He agrees. I am thankful."

A difference between the urban and regional points of view emerges at this point. For Matsui-san and her friend in Tokyo the answer was to return home as a middle-class, nuclear housewife. She herself would be the answer for her child, whom she wanted to be normal and well-balanced, the implication being that a mother's morality is superior to those of children's friends or of teachers in the city.

However, women in the regions faced the problem of morality for themselves and their children somewhat differently. The first answer to the moral question for these teachers resided in the trust they had in regional people and culture as being inherently moral; rather than turning to educated experts, they were willing to depend on homespun bearers of wisdom. They believed that adult carers would teach their children concern for others and correct personal habits. Second, they searched for moral answers in existing systems of thought—organized religion and rural life.

Yamada-san, the Morioka teacher who was raised on a farm, found one moral solution to child raising through the elder neighbor woman who watched her daughter during the day. "She teaches her right and wrong. We would spoil her because we aren't with her all the time. She feeds her good food and advises me on taking her to the doctor. She makes up for the parts I lack."

Likewise, Kawahara-san listened thoughtfully to the day-care teacher's advice to be stricter with her son and put him to bed early, and to her mother-in-law's advice to keep his socks on. She was grateful for the balance these stricter people brought to her child's upbringing, but she also insisted on her ability to think it through and stuck by her practices of no socks and letting the child go to bed at nine, because "He plays with us after dinner because we don't see him during the day." The balance seemed a good one as a bargain with her long-term resistance.

Kawahara-san, who grew up in a neighboring prefecture in the northeast, felt some conflict with her mother-in-law, with whom she will probably live someday. But she kept it in check, transmuting it into sympathy with her mother-in-law, who had been bullied by *her* mother-in-law when she was young. Her reference point for this was the other moral answer she brings to the stress of her life—religion. Kawahara-san had chosen to talk to me in a coffee shop in Morioka when she came from the village on the weekend, and quite spontaneously Kawahara-san leaned close toward me over her empty coffee cup and the few crumbs left on her cake plate.

> I don't know if I told you before. I am religious—Buddhism, Shinnyoen.[1] We go to a temple here in the city. My husband and his parents and I all go. We pray, and doing that everyone becomes gentle. The priest teaches us how to live and how to correct our hearts (*kokoro o tadasu*). We shouldn't struggle. For example, I am busy and my husband is busy. There is lots of housework and we have to care for our son. We know we should cooperate, but I say I am doing too much housework and we struggle. We appreciate each other when we go to Shinnyoen. The priests says to me, "I understand that you are busy but you wanted this child and you got it. You are busy with work but you wanted this work. You need to show appreciation to your husband, your work, and your child."

This priest had also contacted her dead ancestors and made offerings to them to help her get pregnant. I was cautious. Was the religion piling everything back on her? I remembered that in 1993 she had remarked on the beauty of "devoting yourself to another person," even as she wanted equal acceptance at work. "What do they say to your husband?" I asked.

"He has also changed. He helps. Last week we struggled once. But this week is good. We say to each other that if we didn't have this religion, we might divorce."

She had been in this religion and brought her husband into it with her. "Now he prays more than I do," she laughed. "We volunteer a lot, like cleaning Morioka train station or the river. It makes us busier but it makes my heart quiet. My work goes better. It is strange, but maybe it is because I am going by the power of Kami-sama [god in Shintoism] and not just by my own power."

In this new religion Kawahara-san found a systematic philosophy and an expert who urged her to be humble and take responsibility for her position in life. As a new religion, it is inferior in the dominant, middle-class discourse. Giddens (1991) would call this a cocoon in late-modern life in which to hide from the strong changes toward individualism. I prefer to think of it as a way of working out tensions and using religion to achieve a more stable form of ambivalence between various arenas of life.

Yamada-san found a different moral answer, but she too incorporated parts of an older system into her life. Her idea was to return to the countryside where she had grown up, with its rural practices and values. I talked with Yamada-san inside her chilly schoolroom as the fall dusk settled in and she chuckled as she sipped her warm tea.

"I used to hate living in the country and not having a TV and not going anywhere. I felt poor and couldn't wait to get out. But now that life looks rich to me. My parents are happy, but they live without things. My mother still makes pickles, miso, and tofu. I want my daughter to learn these old ways before they are lost and to understand these values. I don't want that culture to die." Yamada-san dreamed of retiring young and moving to live with her parents and starting a school "to read books, grow plants and not just sit quiet like in school." She thought that it would help her parents and improve her "psychological balance."

This exchange reveals the complex meanings of "rural" for this generation in Japan. It represents poverty and boredom, but within the moral debate on child raising and the continued evolution of "self," it represents values and practices lost in the transition to late modernity. Yamada-san idealized the rurality of her parents' farm as providing the moral balance to consumption, competition, and hyperindividuality. Here the lower-class life of the rural farm is reinterpreted as an antidote to overconsumption and a symbol of moral superiority; unlike Kawahara-san's new religion, it has appeal to the urban middle classes as an agrarian discourse (Kelly 1990). This alternative within this generation's ambiguous long-term resistance reoccurs later in the chapter.

Thus, both Kawahara-san and Yamada-san turn to older belief systems to use as mothers and workers in a late-modern world. They combine them creatively with new ideas to reconceptualize their own selves, and thus reach "psychological balance" for themselves and "moral balance" for their children. It is a process we see around the world in which people re-create and temper global-Western ideas into locally workable and appropriate forms (Appadurai 1996). As with all of the similar attempts in this book (such as Murayama or Yamazaki in Chapter 3), this effort attains to something better than the Western autonomous ideal, aiming toward interdependence, links with the past, and responsibility as part of independence. Gendered tension does not disappear in these discourses, as priestly directives to "not struggle" and "show appreciation to your husband" indicate; they are not unlike the doctor's command to Ishii-san (Chapter 5) to give herself to her daughter, though they exist in a broader religious philosophy. But even though the risk of returning to historical and seemingly natural gendered relationships remains, the opportunity does exist to live in the space in-between self and the universe of relationships, choosing the best of local ideas and ways.

Ironically, it is children, the very thing that these "new humans" were afraid would force them to sacrifice their selves, who created the new ambivalences that led them into alternative cultural fields. These women are still creating self-narratives, but improvising as they link their projects of self, which now include children, with older ways of being internalized from their upbringing and still extant in the regions. In their workshop of practical resistance, they are hammering out a strong form of practical ambivalence to live by.

In sum, I have used these case studies as indications that urban and regional/rural processes of working out the dilemma of simultaneous working and motherhood are more similar than different in their general characteristics. All struggle with the paradox of developing self as women and children as individuals while needing to raise children properly in a moral sense. All refute the postwar, emotional relations of dependency with their children and aim toward honest communication within their marriages. However, the processes here indicate that the urban experience is more affected by the pressure for class-based accomplishment and uncertainty about the adequacy of outside people's care even as educated experts are consulted; the rural experience exhibits trust in older systems of thought and practice, albeit reinterpreted, in a kind of residual resistance (Williams 1977). These systems can be demanding and are representative of "tradition" or inferior class status, but they also are available to use in innovative ways by professionals like Yamada and Kawahara who integrate them into a broadening of self. In comparison, Matsui's urban, middle-class project of mothering appears lonely and competitive, raising the question whether, ironically, it isn't the rural/regional experience that may offer creative options to the current disillusionment with a modern system of institutions and values built around rapid economic growth.

Working and mothering among the rice fields

Why do four of the seven full-time working mothers live in a rural village?[2] Regional fertility rates are higher than those in Tokyo, and rural village rates even higher. Gender roles are more conservative than in Tokyo. Why is it easier for mothers to continue working in the village? On the surface the answer is not different for Tokyo or Morioka: day care and parental help. However, the history lived by grandmothers and mothers, and inherited in the lives of daughters makes all the difference.

An older male teacher, with whom I first taught English when I came to Morioka in the seventies, drove me through pines and stubble of cut rice fields to his home village; he had introduced me to single women here in 1993 and continued to take me to see them. My plan was to visit the three women (other than Kawahara-san), who were full-time working mothers in this village area. All of these women had grown up in the village, one going to university and two going to work in the village right after high school graduation.

At the village hospital I met Shimura-san, a government bookkeeper recently transferred here from the village office, for an interview. In 1993, she had been a high school graduate trained on the job, claiming that she would quit when she married because, having been raised by her grandmother while her mother worked and did laundry at night, she wanted a different life. But here she was in 2004 following her mother's model, planning to continue her full-time work but with a four-year-old boy in day care. (The only difference in the model was that she and her husband did not live with her in-laws and the child was in day care.) However, because she often worked until seven, and even later at the end of the fiscal year, her husband, also a government worker, picked the child up at five forty and took him to visit with his parents, who lived next door to their house. That night they would all meet there for dinner, not an unusual occurrence. Except for the in-laws, whom she might have to care for someday, Shimura-san would be the envy of her generation.

After the interview at the hospital, Takahashi-san picked me up in her van, her two-year-old in the back seat. Dressed in jeans and denim jacket, with irregularly cut, reddish dyed hair with gray and black roots, she drove me to a coffee shop that had few customers in the off-season between winter skiers and summer golfers. We ordered cake and ice cream, and she fed the ice cream to her son.

"He loves ice cream!" she said in her gravelly voice. "I'm happy to have some time with him because I work most days at the retirement home." A university graduate, she had worked in Morioka for a year before she came back to the village and started at the retirement home.

"I remember when we first met there. Do you still like your work?"

With an embarrassed laugh, she admitted, "Yes, I like old people. It's a good job for this village. I work in the daytime now but have to do more office work. I am satisfied. My mother had to do everything and work outside while my grandmother raised me, so this is easy compared with that."

The air was thick with things unsaid. Takahashi-san had been full of marriage plans when we first met, but by 1998 she was divorced. Her ex-husband's parents got custody of her son with almost no visitation for her though they all lived in this area.[3] She had lost much of her characteristic humor, but her rough laughter burst forth when she described her new husband.

"We met playing volleyball. We drank and laughed together. He's thirty-three and I'm thirty-six. I wasn't sure about marrying again, but, anyway, a child got made (*dekichatta*), so we married."[4]

"Congratulations. That's wonderful."

"I am happy. I get along well with my husband. We still spend a lot on beer because we both drink at night!" she laughed.

"Who takes care of the child while you work?"

"He spends the day on the dairy farm with my husband and my in-laws. They rebuilt their old house, so we have a duplex right next to his parents. The foyers and kitchens are entirely separate but the boy runs in and out."

"That sounds perfect," I said.

"I can't do things just as I want (*katte ni*) anymore. I have to think of husband and children first, even on my vacations. His father is still in charge and he won't hire anyone to feed the animals, so we never get a night away. But when my husband becomes the manager, we'll change some things." Her raised eyebrows suggested that it was not only women who suffered from the effects of patriarchy in this farming village.

As her son got fidgety, I asked, "Do you ever meet your older son?"

"We meet with him four times a year. You have fun with your older brother, don't you?" She tousled her son's hair. "It's easier now that my ex-husband is with someone else."

Takahashi-san left me off at the apartment of my next interviewee, with whom she worked at the retirement home. Kawaguchi-san was forty-four and had two boys of six and eight. With only a high school education, she had risen from aide to care manager for home health care (Rosenberger 2001, 216–217).

While the boys played a rowdy mini-badminton game in the next room, her husband sat beside her listening to the interview. At one point her younger boy came in, climbed on her lap, and kept trying to grab her breasts; she just shooed him down gently. Her husband had wanted to meet me, perhaps suspicious of "feminists," which he asked me about. She supported him without a hint of his late nights that she had mentioned in 1998. "Japanese don't usually praise their husbands, but he is one hundred and eighty percent as husband and father. . . . When our children play they call out half for mother and half for father."

They laughed as the boys' shouts from the other room interrupted our talk. "Kids can be free here. My husband doesn't want them to do lessons after school. We want to just go slow and relax (*nombiri*) when we are all home."

How did Kawaguchi-san manage to raise her boys and continue working? I knew she had taken a year of maternity leave for both and had been on the line about whether to return to work in 1998. "I am entranced by the life of a 'full-time housewife,' " she had said, using the term popular in the sixties. "But I'd never be able to get a good job like this again around here." Despite her praise of her husband, it was her mother who had enabled her to remain a working mother. "The boys have been raised more than half by my mother. She lives nearby. Usually the children eat at my mother's house and then I make something for the two of us here."

Her husband had retreated to play room volleyball with the boys. She ended the conversation by asserting her late-modern belief in her own right to choose and her insight into the changing history of the family in the village. "My mother had to kill herself, always putting up with things. Now you can go toward your own goal. You may fail, but you can choose."

Why the village?

The processes reflected in these interviews point to answers as to why comparatively more mothers in this group work full-time in the village. The first is economic. Rural villages are poor, left behind in Japan's modern economic development, lacking employment, with agriculture earning meager profits and agricultural subsidies decreasing, and increasingly starved of tax money by central coffers (*Economist* 2011); so the stark need for money motivated these women to work. Their husbands had lower-paying jobs with local government, farming, or small companies; and women, also facing job limitations, had to covet their jobs once obtained. There were economic upsides, however. With fewer young adults in the village, even women with high school educations could move up at work. Because rural villages have a preponderance of elderly (Traphagan 2000), local governments are extremely generous in granting special allowances for helping families with birth and child raising—the more children, the more money given.

The second answer is cultural and historical. The "feudal" families that contemporary women so assiduously avoided because of strict mother-in-laws and hard work have learned to compromise. The alternative is losing their children to the city (which many have done) or never finding brides for the sons (which some did not). Takahashi-san's experience of losing her son through divorce shows that the learning process is painful for everyone and the younger generation does not always win. Patriarchal households and relationships have weakened, but because of the ongoing concern for ancestral land and graves their power continues. Both young and old must learn new scripts for living in productive tension with each other—the elders gaining grandchildren, and the younger sharing in the feeling of individualized choice that their generation in Japan has demanded.[5]

What is fascinating here is that certain aspects of these farming, land-bound, multigenerational families ultimately have adapted more easily to the changes in cultural codes demanded by Japanese women than postwar middle-class urban families. Historically, it was the younger women who worked and the older women who cared for the grandchildren. Now, however, this same arrangement fits the desire of younger women to work and the expectations of grandmothers to raise grandchildren. Most grandmothers have not acquired the habits of hobbies, friends, and travel like middle-class urban women, but the younger women even get to golf and go skiing with their husbands while the grandparents watch their children.

Making space in cross-generational relationships to preserve the semblance of nuclear families as long as possible is part of the new script. Tradeoffs wait in the wings: it is a sure bet that these women will care for and probably live with elders in the future, because all of them married eldest sons.

This rural script that supports full-time working mothers demands a caveat. Living in the village requires women to carry "self" and its pursuits lightly. Looking back at their interviews, they only referred to "self" with the double consciousness of their elders' view—as selfishness. In relation to getting her own apartment or doing karaoke in the city, for instance, the village woman would simultaneously laugh at herself: "I am selfish!" Takahashi and Kawaguchi both said that men and women should be equal, but they had to put up with male supervisors who thought differently.

Interviewees from Tokyo and Morioka also sometimes couched their self-narratives in words that implied their selfishness (*wagamama*, *katte ni*, *kimama*), but they also shed this and talked freely of self as a worthy goal. Ito-san, the single translator in Chapter 2, for example, never apologized for her focus on self; and Minami-san, the mother at the beginning of Chapter 5, felt a responsibility to plan for self. If a supervisor was too hierarchical, city women could change jobs.

To stay in the village was to accept emergence as an adult in the midst of practices and values embedded in hierarchical groups. Surely the dispositions they had been raised with made this adjustment easier. Takahashi-san mourned her mother's death in 2004, admiring her ability to endure (*gaman*) and live with all her might. Although tensions erupted and both generations fought for its own ways, these village women lived with the practiced double consciousness of ambivalence, pushed for certain changes, and otherwise waited for time to take its course. They will become the elder generation, with the power that entails, and it will be interesting to see what they expect from their children.

The third answer to why more mothers in the village work is related to class. Both insiders and outsiders evaluate rural village life as slower and more relaxed. This is not so much the privilege of tradition as a preference born of the necessity (Bourdieu 1984) of living on the periphery of a rich country. My interviewees labeled it with the word *nombiri*, implying laid-back and noncompetitive. It is a word that I heard in the 1980s in Morioka, used in relation to children who do not receive tutoring for high school and university exams, generally expressed with a light giggle to distinguish it from the class competition of mainstream Japan. In 2004, rather, these village women claimed *nombiri* as a kind of cultural capital of rural Japan that in some ways fits the tendency toward more creative play and less mindless devotion to work in the social movement of their generation. Although it places them and their children in a group of people who would not be winners in the larger landscape of Japan, it raises them in a humanistic sense. Urban people come here seeking relaxed *nombiri*, and rural people feel that they now have an advantage in the debate on morality and the ideal lifestyle that is quietly occurring in Japan. Thus, the long-term resistance of these village women, always accepted as more ambivalent than the urban version, fares well within their rural context of lower class expectations.

Part-time working mothers

Although married women in Japan often prefer part-time work,[6] this group yields only six. In general this trend is highest for women with children in school, and numbers may rise in future interviews. Much like the full-timers, the motivations and experiences of these part-timers raise issues of class and cultural redefinitions; they revisit the question of orientations to self and family, particularly husbands. Urban-regional issues do not surface as so important in these case studies; four of the six live in the regions (none in the village), but women's relationships with family vary in similar ways in both Tokyo and the northeast.

Differences in the type of part-time work do emerge as salient in the way that they increase or decrease the contradictions of long-term resistance. One woman is a contract worker with three children in school. The five with younger children are divided between artists and family workers, two categories of work that are acceptable for women. The difference between them, however, is stark: the artists create their own gravity against the "regular world" to keep their artistic talents alive, while the family workers struggle with the irresistible gravity of the family business that not only pulls them in but will determine their economic survival. Both work part-time, but the conversation with self varies tremendously, as do their relationships with husbands, his parents, and her parents.

I concentrate on the heterogeneity of part-time working mothers offered by the three artists and two family workers. The sixth woman, who delivers parcels in the rural northeast, signals the common denominator of tension between work and children that all these women's experiences take off from. She worries when snowy roads make her late cooking dinner for her three elementary school–age children, yet she finds work necessary because her husband is a farmer and factory laborer, and simultaneously satisfying because it makes her feel normal among her friends and gets her out into the world.

In this section, I explore how long-term resistance via self, generationally defined partly through work, plays out differentially in family workers and artists, and interacts differentially with parents and, to my surprise, especially with husbands. This contrast leads to interesting insights, marking extremes that exist within the overall term part-time working mothers and rendering the category in need of nuanced analysis (Kondo 1990). Two case studies will lay the groundwork for these insights.

Family workers

The two family workers both grew up in the northeast, but one remains there and the other married and lives near Tokyo. Both married into dental families whose businesses are struggling with competition—one is a brother-sister orthodontist business competing with an overflow of dentists in regional cities, and the other a father-son dental equipment business competing with larger, technologically advanced companies in Tokyo. In 2004 both had small children and lived separately from but quite near their businesses and their in-laws.

These family workers reveal the tensions of giving up work as an activity pursued for self, as imagined by this generation of women, and accepting work as a daily activity embedded in the larger family welfare. The challenge is to do it in a new way. New laws that require that all family workers be paid help, but legislation cannot change family dynamics or the nature of the work. Uchimura-san, the Tokyo woman, went to work Monday through Friday from her nearby apartment and received wages; she sent her son to day care and ate with her parents-in-law for lunches and on Saturday night. Having come to Tokyo originally as a dental technician, she understood the contrast with her generation's ideal: "Now I am doing work that I didn't choose. Because it's our own company, we immediately think of the profit."

In this case, tension for Uchimura-san did not emerge with parents-in-law directly but with the nature of the nuclear family constructed around the family business. They worried about profits, so having a second child seemed risky. Her chief complaint so far was that there was never time to relax leisurely with her husband because her father-in-law demanded too much in the way of effort (*gambaru*)—late hours and Saturday all day for her husband. She dreamed of a vacation together and family life after her husband took over the business, because at this point her generational ideal of family life with rich conjugal and father–children relationships was at the mercy of his father and the business.

The northeastern family worker exhibits more clearly the characteristic that I expected for family workers: tension between her "self" and her in-laws. However, the underlying tension with husband, devoted to her but also to his family and business's profitability, emerged here as well.

Nakamura-san, thirty-nine years old in 2004, lived in a small northeastern city in a tiny apartment where work papers and toys for her two daughters, three and nine months, lay helter-skelter all around. We talked amidst a flurry of activities: breast-feeding, her older daughter's scribbling in my notebook, phone calls about the account books for her husband's dentistry business, and changing diapers.

Nakamura-san did not feel a loss of a self actualized through work in the sense that she was already underemployed as a single woman, a four-year university graduate working as a museum guide. In 1993, she had already reduced her desires for success in the world, saying, "I don't desire much from life." However, she had an enjoyable singlehood, travelling and shopping with her widowed mother and sister. By 1998, she was ready to marry even "someone she didn't dislike" and have children, so marrying into a family business did not seem like a sacrifice.

However, her ambiguous sense of long-term resistance in terms of self sprang up in relation to mother-in-law, sister-in-law, and the business staff. Her mother-in-law lived with them at first, because it was economical, and she worked in the evenings so the new couple could be alone. Her sister-in-law was a dentist in the business and insulted Nakamura-san when she had conflicts with the mother-in-law. The staff resented her because she was brought into the business to work as an emergency dental assistant without training. Nakamura-san expressed herself with a directness I hadn't heard in her before. "No one here understood my own self (*jibun jiko*). . . . I had no place to be (*iruba*)." She brought her will to bear on her husband and they moved to this small apartment. Relationships improved and even softened after children came and she was working from home, but she worried about the future, when they would live above the new dental office now being built.

The family business always mediated her relationship with her husband. Having married at thirty-four, Nakamura-san had trouble getting pregnant, and her husband suggested that they forgo children; as the business was faltering and children were expensive, perhaps they should "bow to fate." Although she was practicing tacit accommodation in so many ways in her new family, she activated her own desires once again, insisting on fertility treatment and taking time off from the family business to travel frequently to Morioka an hour away.

In sum, both these family workers experienced encroachment into their territories of self and their nuclear family building as a place of rest apart from the work world. The relationship with in-laws was a predictable area of tension and negotiation, but the sticking point was the expected relationship with husband as chief ally and person who understood the wife's self. The family business infringed upon this relationship and forced the wife to temper her own wishes in relation to her husband and to the family business that was an integral part of him—and increasingly of her. Indeed, even the child rearing had to bend to the needs of the business. The business advanced into the territory of the wives' selves and their generational expectations, for the part-time work that had been intended to soothe the frustrating double binds experienced by these Japanese married women actually exacerbated the tensions in their efforts to build their self-narratives.

The artists

The artists exhibit an opposite phenomenon: their worlds of self, nurtured in their talents and creative work, tend to appropriate the worlds of their parents, their children, and even to a great extent their husbands. Especially husbands' support of their work has diminished the tensions of passing through the dilemmas of marriage and children and has enabled them to maintain their own talents and place in the world.

The most extreme example of this is Nakata-san, a dancer in the northeast who had danced her way "young and free" through university and theaters in Tokyo before returning to teach in Morioka. Her husband, a banker, fell in love with her when he saw her performing, and although he was an elder son with rural parents, he promised Nakata-san that he would let her continue dancing. "With many men it is just talk. But he didn't lie." He built her a home lined with wood—a large teaching studio with a locker room below and a sweeping kitchen counter above, and a large bedroom for them and a small bedroom for his parents to stay in when they visited. He did all the accounting work for her business on the computer and she did not have to wait on his parents; in fact, when his parents visited, her students were surprised that she did not run to clean up and greet them, but let them get their own tea. The house was ten minutes from her own parents, who picked up her daughter, fed her, and brought her home dressed in pajamas for bed. At five, she was starting to learn dance. Nakata-san chattered on about her students and the jealousies among dance teachers in the city, but added: "I am greedy (*yokubari*). At my last concert I told the audience, 'I talk so much, but I am not the heroine here today. My mother and father are the heroes.' " Her art had colonized her relationship with her family members, but her parents were happy and her husband remained devoted. If she felt tension, it was around her body, which at thirty-five was challenging her central meaning for self: "I am tired. I don't perform much anymore. I've gained weight!"

The other two artists have not molded their households to the same extent and experience more tensions with child raising, parents, and husbands. But the shifts that their artistic lives have engendered in their husbands are particularly interesting and indicate the importance of the husbands' attitudes to women's negotiation of long-term resistance.

The second artist, a piano teacher since junior college, was raised and still lives in Tokyo. Despite her marriage and daughter, two days a week she returns to her natal home an hour's distance away to teach piano while her parents care for her now four-year-old daughter. Her parents have their own hobbies and travel, and sometimes complain of the limitations, but they enjoy their granddaughter. Her husband, a salaryman, has always tolerated the arrangement and admired her hobby-cum-work. Perhaps in a similar bid to enjoy his life more, he asked her permission to risk changing jobs to a less secure but less conservative company. She was glad to assent, and he has shifted to companies where he likes the work and can develop his hobby of in-line skating on the side, sometimes with his wife and daughter. In short, this woman's life of self, expressed as a pianist, has encouraged her husband to find work and hobbies that nurture his self and help him to understand hers.

The case study of the third artist shows the change in a husband most clearly. Murai-san, raised and living in Morioka, married a government worker whose attitudes and career transfers made it difficult for her to keep practicing her art as a pianist. Her husband was the "hard" type (*katai*, strait-laced and old-fashioned) focused on his own work and his evening baseball games, and small regional apartments did not even have pianos in them for her to play. His parents supported his stable career. Her parents were busy artists themselves and gave her mainly moral support and a place to teach a few piano lessons. Even her six-year-old daughter did not like the piano much, perhaps feeling it to be competition for her mother's attention (Rosenberger 2001, 225–226).

The tensions between child and work were strong, but Murai-san felt compelled to continue her life of piano even if it was "a thin river" when compared to "blooming flowers" of the world of Nakata-san (whom she knew distantly). With her sister, Murai-san occasionally performed pieces that she herself had composed, accompanied musical groups, and taught a few students—but only within the interstices of child raising. Recently she recorded with her sister, but it was in a race with motherhood: "We got the studio to record it at nine thirty a.m. and I had to pick up the child that day at eleven thirty. We had only two hours, and we did it full steam." When she played in evening concerts, she fed her daughter dinner and raced to the concert hall. She felt "whirled about" by her daughter's activities, but was determined not to "think too much about children. You just have to do it." Tensions in her long-term resistance had heightened in spite of having married the man she loved since high school and wanting children.

The change in her husband came as a result of his experiencing international life in New York City on a two-year transfer. Murai-san had spent a year in the United States, where her love of piano had been confirmed, and she urged her husband, who made fun of her "doing just what she wanted" like an American, to work abroad. She had described her husband as a typical northeasterner—enduring, allowing himself little luxury, and expecting bad luck. After their return, she said, "He now wants to be a father raising his child and a husband giving an enjoyable time to his wife. I can leave my daughter with him when I have a concert to play in. He even dreams of changing his career to be self-employed."

This change in Murai-san's husband attests to the effect of an international experience outside of conservative, northeast Japan, and of the expanding impact of the generational discourse that pushes against confining institutionalized roles of men as well as women. But it also occurred because of the influence of Murai-san's ambiguous but steady long-term resistance as an artist with an alternative view of life.

In sum, the artists' part-time work nurtures the link between self and work popular in their generation and mediates the contradictions with marriage and motherhood that they have also chosen. This situation insists on itself to the extent that it can, spreading to and enveloping husbands and households. Respectful of their daughters' talents, the woman's own parents are supportive, and in-laws have no choice but to tolerate the situation. Although the artists attempt to expand their selves into their households, the family workers struggle just to stake out a small territory for themselves and their nuclear families in the household, albeit a larger territory than that inhabited by women of past generations. They have less influence on their husbands than most wives of this era, because their husband's household has staked its future on his work.

These examples show in an exceptionally clear way the contrastive ways that self and relationships can evolve as women tackle the dilemma of choice to marry and have children in the late-modern era. Furthermore, this contrast does not relate to an urban-regional split and its class implications, although socioeconomic differences are relevant in 2004 as family businesses struggle economically more than the salaried households of the artists. These case studies indicate both the mutual influences between husband and wife and the overarching influence of the economic environment as essential ingredients to consider in the long-term resistance of women.

Personal long-term resistance embedded in the organic movement

The case of Tsuchiya-san's life, committed to the organic farming movement with her husband, stretches the boundaries of her generation's challenge to the culture code more broadly than others in this book. As an organic farmer, she is part of a collective movement practicing a lifestyle that refuses to cooperate with the capitalistic economic frame of global corporate production and consumption. The social movement practices direct producer–consumer relationships, self-sufficiency for the farmer, and a local organic cycle on the land (Rosenberger in press).[7]

Tsuchiya-san and her farmer-husband also have resisted the cultural-legal code with respect to marriage requiring that a married couple share the same last name to enter one household registry (*koseki*)—the manner by which households are established legally in Japan. Joining others in a movement meant to push for changes, they did not marry under state law. Their three children belonged to her registry until recently, when they switched the children to his registry because his parents had no other grandchildren, whereas hers did.

Although neither of these collective movements has brought significant change to the status quo in Japan, they position Tsuchiya-san as someone who clearly understands gendered and economic contradictions in Japan and is not afraid to take chances in order to change things. Indeed, raised by a father who is a Christian minster, she grew up accustomed to taking marginal positions of belief in Japanese society.

Tsuchiya-san is without a doubt part of the long-term resistance of her generation to shift the status quo for women in family and society. The question is: Because of her conscious involvement in other resistance movements, has Tsuchiya-san overcome the ambiguity, ambivalence, and tension that others in her generation experience?

The all-encompassing work of organic farming—and three children

In 2004, Tsuchiya-san stands behind the counter pouring udon noodles made with wheat grown on their own farm from the boiling water into a sieve. Her youngest, a one-year-old son, is pushing soft carrots into his mouth beside me. The rain falls on the rice fields around their house—a rainy day is best for talking, she had told me, and I jumped on the train for the hour ride from Morioka.

"It's been ten years now since we came to this rural village and built this house. They are more open to outsiders here than in other places." Chickens roost on one side and two pigs wait with open mouths to recycle food waste on the other.

"We have no trouble giving parties because we always have lots of food. But it's busy. When we are planting and cutting, the children see it is terrible and want to help. Now, when they say the food is delicious, we tell them, you can't eat this in the city!" She smiles broadly.

"So can you basically live without money?"

"No, we need money like for day care and school fees, and now the oldest daughter wants to do some lessons. We deliver boxes of food to people in town in our consumer group."

Tsuchiya-san's husband joined us for lunch. They were both muscled from hard work and brown from the sun.

She added: "I didn't want to send our first daughter to day care because of the foods with pesticides. We would take her [with us] out to the fields. But in the summer we have to use day care now."

"How do people accept you around here?" I wondered. Tsuchiya-san bounced the baby on her lap while she ate.

"Well, they are glad to have young farmers around. I make *natto* (fermented soybeans) with a group of older farm wives at the community center. He does the accounting for the farmers' union. But there is prejudice here. They always want the man to be the representative of the household and the wife to be in the kitchen. Here we do it together." They glanced at each other.

"One thing they don't like is that we were never formally married. People here are conservative. The law was almost changed, but lost in the legislature recently," said her husband.

"It was a popular movement ten years ago, but now [for us it is creating] a problem with life insurance." Her tone was flat.

Her husband went out to work and Tsuchiya-san put the child to her breast.

"We used to do everything half and half, and we still make decisions together. I say what I think and we argue. We don't talk for a while and then figure it out. But it's getting harder to share everything. I feel my energy lessening with this third child, so I can't work in the rice field."

"Can the children help some now?"

"Yes, the oldest is eight and she helps care for the baby in the summer. We want them to be part of the farm, not just separate like in the city." The child had fallen asleep.

"What do you think as you look back over your life?" I asked.

"I think if I had done this or that, I would have a different life. But I made that decision according to that time (*sono toki*) and I understand why I chose that way. There is no help for it. I think back and then resolve to look toward the future."

"What are your dreams for the future?"

She hesitated. "I wasn't expecting that question! What have others said?"

"Some people talk about jobs and travel, and some don't want to answer it yet!"

"Well, I am searching for that," she said slowly. "We have reached our dream of ten years ago. We sometimes want to be more self-sufficient, but we would just get busier. We want to play with the children some. What will we do when the children want to do extracurricular activities? It'll take time and money. The oldest does piano and wants to do swimming. She's in a community play and they pulled me into taking a part—just this once. I would like to do more plays, but I have to choose. I can't do everything." she chuckled as if counseling herself.

"I try to think with a bigger vision, but I have trouble doing it because I am in the middle of everything. But I am very happy to be eating our own food that we have raised."

What kind of long-term resistance?

Has Tsuchiya-san overcome the ambiguity, ambivalence, and tension that others in her generation are experiencing? The answer has to be no. She is a full participant in her generation's experiences despite her work toward larger change, carrying feelings of ambivalence similar to those of other women. More than most she has passed through various dilemmas of choice as university-grad-turned-farmer, but even as she expresses continuing enthusiasm for her choices of safe food and the rural life, she experiences tension and a hint of ambivalent postdecisional regret. Tsuchiya-san is consciously writing a new script along with her husband and their allies in the organic social movement, but she still runs up against contradictions as a wife, a mother, a rural community member, and a citizen of a nation organized around consumerism and competition for personal success.

First, the organic movement devotes no explicit attention to making gender relations more equal. Although her husband, same-age female allies, and even some of the older couples attempt to practice equal gender relations, their practices remain implicit within the organic farming movement, which at times reflects typical hierarchical gender relations (Rosenberger 2011).

Second, both Tsuchiya-san and her husband have been raised in middle-class Japan and have internalized some middle-class ideals about the gendered division of labor. As the wife, she bears, breast-feeds, and feeds the children, and also takes major responsibility for the inside of the house. To also be an equal participant in farming with three children is impossible, and so she has had to step back from equal work while trying to remain equal with her husband in decision making. Even though this is organic farming, it is also like a family business, with all its financial and managerial difficulties that intersect with family life and conjugal relations; it takes effort not to give in to the default mode of male leadership.

Third, Tsuchiya-san's middle-class ideals of university education and extracurricular activities also contribute tension to her life. In addition to the values she conveys to her children through living on the land, eating their own organic food, and moving about freely without fear of urban crime, she wants them to have the opportunities she had to develop themselves through school and town activities and to receive university educations that are a leg up, if not a middle-class necessity, in today's Japan of winners and losers, even for organic farmers like themselves. She and her husband do not demand that the children follow them into organic farming and do not want to penalize them for following other paths. They need money to make all of this possible, which means working harder on the farm and collides with the time they need to take children back and forth to their activities. Tsuchiya-san herself realizes as she ages that her busy life as a farmer and her limited financial resources also impinge on her own desires to develop herself outside of farm and family, for example by acting in local theater productions and meeting with other female organic farmers around the country with whom she has special bonds. Like most people making their individualistic way in late-modern Japan, she reaches out for allies to make her way. Hints of a double bind arise in her interview as she wonders what the future opportunities for her children and herself will be.

Fourth, Tsuchiya-san has chosen to live in a very rural area in Tohoku, where gender relations are quite traditional. Even if she would like to represent her household in various village organizations, her husband is the appropriate representative and she is seen only as a substitute. Furthermore, village women's organizations consist of women in their sixties and seventies; the younger women have either left or opt for the dominant lifestyle of their generation, commuting to jobs in nearby towns. Tsuchiya-san teamed with the older women to make traditional food (such as *natto*) for a while, but has stopped. Almost all of the neighboring farms are conventional, nonorganic, and run by elderly people with part-time help from children. Many risks lie in this attempt to marry residual traditions with new ideas of ecology, gender equality, and life outside the market.

Thus, Tsuchiya-san experiences ambivalence and tension just like others in her generation and is a bona fide member of this ambiguous long-term resistance that is trying to write new scripts. This said, her life does overcome some contradictions that are key in late-modern Japan. As a cosmopolitan, educated person, her life reaches across the urban-rural divide, bringing a new meaning to rural life and offering a viable alternative to younger people who are disillusioned with consumption-oriented, middle-class urban life. She traverses class because she carries the idealistic hopes of the middle class for a meaningful life into self-chosen poverty. And, more than most, her work, play, and family form a coherent space in which to some extent she can grow as the self she wants to be. Yet, on the ground and in person, Tsuchiya-san still retains the ambivalence of her generation.

Conclusion

In sum, the processes in the lives of these working mothers show that women in this category have varied experiences. Urban full-time working mothers have a harder time than full-time working mothers in the village, where grandparents often care full-time for young children. Wives working part-time in family businesses have more difficulty seeing work as contributing to their long-term resistance as selves than those working as artists or in nonfamily pursuits. In all cases, these women try to shift the ground of their marriages in order to be able to value their own work as part of their long-term resistance and selfhood, but the women who do work that is more professional (teachers) or more self-actualizing (artists) are more successful than family workers and the Tokyo woman whose husband works in a prestigious bank in getting their husbands to help them balance work and family. However, mothers working for money also strive to express themselves and have personal time with their husbands in their marriages; in the case of family businesses or farms, this sharing bleeds over into scheming with husbands to change the nature of the business itself after he takes charge from his father or, for the organic farmer, holding on to the wife's decision-making role in the farm.

Overall, working mothers showed less concern about developing an emotional relationship of security and dependence for their children than stay-at-home mothers. All assumed that children would be somewhat separate from themselves. However, they were all active in the debate about how to raise children who would be individuals and also cooperative, moral beings. While the middle-class urban mother turned to herself in the role of mother-at-home as the answer, working mothers in the regions thoughtfully turned to reinterpreted versions of rurality and chosen aspects of the agrarian ideal that has shaped the psychosocial ideology of postwar Japan as the answer for them and their children.

CHAPTER SEVEN

The Nuances of Long-Term Resistance

IN THIS BOOK, I have traced the paths of Japanese women who in the beginning of the 1990s were single, over the accepted marriage age, and participating in their generation's form of resistance against the cultural code of postwar modernity. Throughout the 1990s and into the 2000s, these women have struggled both with external contradictions between historical and global influences in Japan and with internal contradictions between their desires to actualize an independent self in the spirit of late modernity and their wish for inclusion in the changing relations and positions of postwar family and work. This book has striven to help us understand the dilemmas of adulthood in the midst of economic decline and a shift to neoliberal ideas in Japan in the 1990s and 2000s.

Although these women have shifted and stretched the cultural rules they grew up with, and although the national statistics on marriage and childbirth and working women reflect these changes, their words and actions do not reflect a determined resistance to change the status quo, nor a feeling of agency that they are acting in a self-determined manner according to their own desires. Rather, ambiguous expressions, thoughts, and deeds fill their narratives, signaling what I call long-term resistance—a concept that catches the in-between space and time of gradual change described by the Comaroffs as ambivalent and full of tensions, developing along with accommodation, struggle, experimentation, and suffering within the contradictions of history (Comaroff and Comaroff 1991).

As opposed to a strong sense of intentional and immediate resistance, long-term resistance consists of vague movements such as tacit refusal and ambiguous perceptions of the contradictions within which people live.

Long-term resistance does not explode in protest or, usually, consciously aim to challenge the status quo, but simmers in personal dissatisfaction, stretching the limits of compatibility with the rules of the society through personal choices or non-choices (Melucci 1989, 1996).

My thinking about the nature of this long-term resistance owes a debt to anthropologists who have wrestled with the concepts of agency and resistance in ethnographic situations involving women around the world and have modified them to include ideas of conflict, limitation, contradiction, ambiguity, ambivalence, and tension. Shifting the lens slightly, I have focused on the concepts of ambivalence, tension, and ambiguity in contexts of contradiction as essential to understanding the nuances of long-term resistance. These concepts, imagined on continuums between structural norms and independent agency or stability and change, have given me the space to explore women's lives with flexibility and remain sensitive to differences among people, movement over time, and interactions between inner and outer forces working in people's lives.[1]

Indeed, ambiguous resistance that people dip in and out of over the course of their lives appears to be just the kind of social movement that women and young people enact in late modernity, where they do not feel comfortable in the cultural homes they grew up in and have new expectations and demands for self-responsibility and self-reflexivity, yet do not completely reject their past and its relationships. They wish to mold their cultural world into a new shape by simply living their personal lives differently from the postwar norms, and in many instances they succeed, yet their lives are forever marked by the points of resistance that they have experienced (Gupta and Ferguson 1997). Reshaping cultural codes even just at the personal level is a difficult feat to perform at key junctures where, blind to the future, people experience anguish in dilemmas of choice, or in certain periods of life when they harbor a sense of double binds—that their habits and dispositions do not fit the game as it is being played (Melucci 1989; Bourdieu 1990). Although the loneliness of the life of self emerges, a new flexibility in the cultural code also becomes visible.

In Japan, ambiguous resistance for women of this generation revolves around the concept of self as an ideal: to have choice in their life courses and to be relatively free from the conservative demands of family, schools, and workplaces where self-discipline, self-sacrifice, and harmony with the group spell maturity. But ambiguous resistance also revolves around the question of how to be happy and emerge as a new kind of adult in Japan. Embedded in various social and economic circumstances and living in urban, regional, and rural places, these women journey through a Japan of old ways that they both value and disdain, and new risks that open them to both creative possibilities and new problems. Neither the picture of women nimbly leaping over contradictory identities (Ueno 2005) nor the depiction of them as sinking into multilayered indecision (Miura 2005) is adequate to describe the undulating experiences of independence and dependence, self-actualization and self-cultivation, action for self, and endurance that these women experience over the long run. Yet bit by bit, they continue to attempt to shift the terms of their own lives, and unwittingly but inevitably change the conditions of other lives. Simultaneously (and in a mutual movement), political and economic shifts have occurred; what these women earlier experienced as consumer choice and self-development they now also feel as required self-responsibility against risk—an institutionalized individualism of neoliberalism that offers both self-actualization and, in Japan, moral obligation to community and family (Borovoy 2010; Beck and Beck-Gernsheim 2002).

In this chapter I focus on the question of how this study contributes to our understanding of the nuances of long-term resistance, particularly of long-term resistance by women in the shift from modernity to late modernity. As I indicate general points about long-term resistance, I also summarize how this has occurred in Japan for this group of women, both to illustrate life for women in Japan of the 1990s and 2000s, and to show a local example that may reverberate with the experience of ambiguous long-term resistance for women living through similar shifts in other parts of the world.

Time

In the case of long-term resistance, time is a constant factor, and with that, change, occurring irregularly in the political-economic environment, in one's own generation as they age, and even in the elder generation. As globalized imagination permeated these women and their generation, Japan slid from high economic growth and faith in its postwar sociocultural system into economic decline and doubts about itself. Worries about supporting the elder generation, about not being left behind in a more competitive society, or even about what is safe to eat placed the burden more completely on individuals and families to make the right choices for survival. The result has been that women in this generation who have achieved some success by making choices or non-choices for themselves have come to the realization that, because society itself has changed, they have no choice but to make choices—risky choices—in this new world. Not only they themselves have changed irretrievably from their points of resistance, but their world has also changed, making it necessary that they put their individualized strategies to use.

The time factor in long-term resistance brings change that is irregular in how it impacts various participants' lives, and thus the experience of societal contradictions and psychological ambivalence varies greatly among these women. For example, time has modified the actions and views of these women's parents' generations for some women but not for others, so some have parents as allies while others must battle and/or endure. New styles of work aid some women in their long-term bids for a different way of life but old styles of work hamper others. Often institutions such as schools and companies are in the midst of change or under pressure to change, but the change itself is uncertain, people are doubtful about it, and this ambivalence only adds to the tension of the long-term resistance that these women experience as teachers or mothers.

Time is also a factor in long-term resistance in relation to people's own aging. As single women age beyond accepted childbearing age, attitudes toward their unmarried state soften. Extraordinary choices that seemed fine when one was young and strong, take on a different caste when bodies begin to feel tired and minds are overstressed from the task of survival. Recognizing one's own eventual need for support when sick and old leads to new openness to interdependence with husbands, lovers, or parents. Focus also widens from one's own existence to children and/or parents, and questions of morality or situations of simple human need emerge. In addition, women begin to see themselves in relation to the next generation, observing women ten to fifteen years younger making choices that they themselves would not have made, as, for example, marrying lightly for money. In contrast, women begin to see the characteristic hues of their own generation. This results in moral judgments of the next generation in many cases, but in other cases a feeling that maybe the choices they have made in their long-term resistance are simply typical of their generation after all, related to a certain historical period of political-economic changes, and not so special to them as individuals.

Finally, time is useful to women in the fits and starts of their long-term resistance. Time allows change and acceptance of difference to occur just through the everyday living of life. They consciously use older ideas of life stages to guide themselves through motherhood, maintaining participation in the social movement, however ambiguously. The time factor allows for periods of relative stasis, such as occurs in an intense job when women are overwhelmed, as well as periods of self-reflection, imagination, and experimentation.

Space

Along with the effects of time on long-term resistance, space also makes a difference, offering actual geographies of difference and symbolic imaginaries of geographical differences. Despite the fact that the women of this generation share so much in their generational experience of growing up and coming of age into enjoyment and choices, they vary in how conflicted or ambivalent their long-term resistance is according to the geography of their lives and their use of geography, especially the rural/urban divide, to mark desires and actions.

Some of this difference is predictable. Working or studying abroad clarified women's ideas about the kinds of individuals they wanted to be at work and the kinds of independent partners they wanted. Large urban areas like Tokyo have made long-term resistance easier because of distance from regional families, faster acceptance of change and variety, markets and entertainment to experiment with, easier access to work for women, and work opportunities that offer more independent styles of work. In this study, it was far easier to be a successful single woman in the urban environment of Tokyo than in the regional city or rural village. Long love relationships that could be lived honestly and openly in Tokyo had to be hidden from all but close friends in the northeast; marriages of long-term singles and fertility treatment were both found in the northeast, where women felt more pressure to marry and have children.

Yet space does not always work in long-term resistance in a predictable fashion. Some aspects of the northeast aided women in their ambiguous struggles. Religion as an alternative channel for exploration was a phenomenon of the northeast. For women raising children, those in the rural village were the most likely to receive ongoing help from their own parents or their in-laws, enabling them to work full-time without feelings of guilt. Elders were used to such arrangements, but in addition, because change has hit rural villages hard as young people leave and population plummets, elders realized that they had to make adjustments or lose their children. In contrast to those in the city, most women in the village and regional city trusted others to raise their children, and the cocooning mothers who hailed from the northeast wanted to return there to raise their children in a safe and friendly environment.

Women involved in long-term resistance in late modernity also look to the peripheral areas of their developed countries for values they feel modern life has lost, drawing on a nostalgic discourse of agrarian and rural village ideals as the center for morality in Japan yet adapting its meanings to an age of individualized risk. Rural areas or their values attracted some Japanese women in this study because they considered rural life closer to nature, more laid-back, friendlier, safer, simpler, and less materialistic. Rural space and its values tempt many for short trips, but only a minority interprets rural or regional life as being able to help them be persons who live with meaning beyond the postwar modern scripts by which they feel trapped. Some mothers reasoned that it was the race to compete in the cities that was the problem in rearing children who were both moral and individual. In contrast, they favored the quality of *nombiri* (relaxed, laid-back), identified with lower-class and rural people but recharacterized in terms of caring relationships, a closeness with nature, and old technologies rather than material consumption.

Disadvantages in the rural choice emerged, however. Women who made the move, like the organic farmer, found themselves lonely in their ideals, as other young people around them yearned for the dominant generational ideals of consumption, enjoyment, and choice. Although the organic farmer's ideas about societal contradictions and ways to change the status quo in broad ways were clearer than those of other women because she participated in other social movements, ultimately she found it difficult to practice her ideas about gender equality in her rural area. The women who grew up and still live in the village are aware that the accepted views of men as authoritative leaders and of women as caretakers in multigenerational households are social realities for them, but they still hope that these will prove more flexible than they have been in the past, because in fact the rules of the game have loosened and these responsibilities may be more widely shared.

Class

In terms of educational level and income, class makes a difference in the experience of long-term resistance and the ability to make choices over time, but certain cultural proclivities mitigate these differences. Class intertwines with urban-rural/regional differences, offering fewer opportunities for education and income in the regions yet less pressure, especially in rural areas, to achieve solid middle-class success.

No matter where they lived, less education clearly made a difference for single women as far as their ability to support themselves adequately, let alone travel and enjoy themselves or work and advance in a meaningful career, as their new generational values suggested. Singles used their educations to hoist themselves up in the world. Most successful singles had four-year university degrees, with the notable exception of the regional high school graduate in Chapter 2, who was nonetheless able to rise in the hierarchy at work.

Most singles educated through high school in the northeast earned low incomes and were relieved to marry, even though they married later and to men who had household responsibilities such as elder sons, and even though they had little chance of having children of their own. In short, less-educated women with lower incomes were left taking up some of the overflow of older men who had avoided marriage or had found it difficult to marry because of household circumstances.

Women with higher educations not only had better jobs, they were also able to marry men with high income-earning potential and, in the cases of regional women, move to a more urban area. This entailed mixed results for the tension of their long-term resistance, however, because these educated men and women were intent on having highly educated children, an enterprise that demanded attentive, at-home mothers. Thus, Japan's unique situation among developed countries—that highly educated mothers actually work less than their counterparts in other nations—is a cultural situation that challenges any assumption that women of higher education and income can manipulate their attempts to change the cultural code completely as they wish. Women with young children in this study were not able to realize the generational ideal of mothering and working simultaneously, in some cases because of their own ambivalence, but also because wife and husband could not both continue to hold down good full-time jobs and nurture firmly middle-class children. Except for the few women who were artists, or those who used marriage as a way to escape country life and enjoy the city for themselves via their children, ambitions to remain middle-class or better made these well-educated women bow out of the obvious process of long-term resistance except in the areas of perceptive awareness and planning long-term for self.

Old and new ways

The old and the new work together in long-term resistance. Old ways—so-called tradition or the older cultural codes with which these women were raised—are salient over the course of long-term resistance: first, because long-term resistance occurs in the ambivalent space between old and new; and second, because long-term resisters have the capability of reinterpreting or reshaping the old for new uses. Parents with whom women have maintained fragile relations over time make continuing work possible for mothers because day cares and schools rarely give quite enough care to children. Single women assume typical male roles, working long hours at work and buying expensive apartments, but in so doing prove themselves as successful singles and mature adults.

The opposite is also true as a characteristic of this vague impetus for change over a lifetime: the old ways can seize upon the new ones and cause difficulties for women experimenting with new ways of being. The old ways may extend their own older cultural codes through taking advantage of what has been created anew in the younger generation. An example in Japan is the way in which elder parents, and even siblings, have taken advantage of single women to be the main caretakers for parents. Single women have also been used harshly by employers, who expect unlimited work hours from them because they have no evident family to care for.

Long-term resistance takes place in the social, cultural, and psychological spaces between historical local values and newer global values, and thus will always have to come to terms with certain deeply embedded feelings and practices at the core of local life. Although there are different nuances to these concepts around the world, in the conflicted shift between modernity and late modernity, ideas such as responsibility to the group, social roles as paths to power, care for others, and prescribed differences between men and women vie with ideas popularized in the global media concerning freedom, independence, individuality with unanchored identities, consumption, and women's equality with men.

Independence and dependence (amae)

In Japan, women in the process of long-term resistance to shift the cultural code have to cope in some manner with ideas about how women are supposed to act—as their mothers have acted in close, long-term relationships and as they have been taught to act. In this study Japanese women faced the challenge of dealing with the well-entrenched practice of *amae*, the communication of affection and love through the indulgence of the other as a dependent being in physical and emotional terms. Women's lives have illustrated a variety of strategies that they have employed. Successful single women claimed they had achieved a new kind of independence as individuals who are not emotionally or financially dependent on others, and on that basis are seeking mutual respect between them and their boyfriends, future husbands, and mothers. Meanwhile, struggling and crashing singles gave themselves over to a new kind of dependence on religious figures and their philosophies, or on artistic worlds that they hope will lead to an entirely different kind of independence in the nonrational realm.

Married women without children have their own interesting experience with this local value of dependence in the marriage relationship that is now, ideally, a union between two individuals who respect each others' developing life narratives and have created a place of psychological rest for both wife and husband (Giddens 1991). Some married women without children wove elongated romances with their husbands in a satisfying mutual dependency that was not overwhelming and that allowed their relationship to meld with their generational values of conjugal love and enjoyment. Other married women without children found themselves victims of old ways, as their childless husbands claimed roles of dependence on their wives as the comfortable husband–wife relationship. The wives maintained awareness of the problem, but as yet had not figured out how to escape it and resisted only through pursuing individual activities when possible and through sickness. In one surprising example, a couple with no children and intense careers both attacked each other as being too dependent or spoiled in their lifestyles, oriented to themselves rather than others, in essence raising the question of whether people who have been able to fully follow the shifts in the cultural code called for by their generation are capable of being adequate parents! All of these examples indicate that a certain degree of ambivalence and ambiguity in women's long-term resistance is not just a characteristic of long-term resistance, but a requirement demanded by generational counterparts in marriage and parenting.

In a similar way, the ambivalence of long-term resistance in regard to independence and dependence emerged clearly when it came to ideas and practices about raising the next generation. The narratives of mothers revealed a debate around what kind of children they should be raising and how that should happen. Working mothers in urban, regional, and rural spaces tended to argue that their children should become individuals like them, with their own worlds; too much dependence would keep children from standing on their own two feet. Mothers who quit work and stayed home with their children tended to want to raise children who were more dependent on them because that would make the children more caring, stable people, and because children were the mothers' projects for the time being. A small group of mothers were highly protective of their children in the face of the dangers of the late-modern world and watched their every step, employing the emotional dependency of the past to guard their children in the contemporary world.

Urban women practiced goal-driven dependence with their children in relation to education and future success in this late-modern society of winners and losers. The mothers who quit work and stayed home felt their children would succeed better because of the advantages they could give them in schooling and extracurricular activities. However, in the rural village, where most women worked full-time, mothers cherished a relaxed upbringing that did not get hung up on urban ideals of success and gave their children more independence, at least when young. Thus, the contemporary conditions of risks for urban children in terms of both success and safety called women to reenter relationships of dependence with children and challenged them in their task of raising adequately independent children, while, ironically, rural children and mothers seemed to enjoy greater independence.

Emotional expression and endurance (gaman)

Endurance (*gaman*) is another core local value, salient in the past for women sacrificing self for others in Japanese families and an inevitable center of struggle for women involved in the long-term process of ambiguous resistance. The necessity to call on old traits of endurance surfaced particularly in relation to the care of sick and aging parents wherein daughters, single and married, had to devote major parts of their lives to this endeavor. The case of the married woman whose young daughter also had to learn endurance because her mother was too busy caring for her grandfather to give her affection was particularly poignant. The mother basically stopped feeling anything, she reported, her case indicating that the opposite of endurance is feeling and acting on one's emotions.

Indeed, being an individual who acts according to what one feels (one's emotion) and also according to what one's self desires (*katte ni*) are important aspects of the way in which these women wanted the cultural code of their mothers to change. Women challenged by the need to endure combined these new values with the old value of endurance in an interesting synthesis. Most important was that in all cases they were caring for their own parents, a new tendency in kinship in Japan that itself rests on the popular idea that daughters make better caretakers because they truly do care in an emotional way for their parents (unlike daughters-in-law). Thus, endurance was already married with emotion.

In one case, a woman who claimed she found her enjoyment by traveling with her father (who helped her care for her sick mother) combined her endurance with the idea of choice. Claiming that she could have made other choices and that she had willingly chosen this route in life to remain single and care for her parents, she felt that she remained within the discourse of long-term resistance for her generation. Thus, people maintained the sense of their long-term resistance in frameworks of traditional obligations such as parental care by interpreting their actions as the playing out of individual emotional will and of individual choice.

In sum, these women show that part of the ambivalence built into the process of long-term resistance involves the process of figuring out how to integrate local values with global values in a way that allows them adequate satisfaction. It is a process of interpreting and reinterpreting the old and the new; of tacitly living out the compromises that feel acceptable within their "specific modes of being, responsibility and effectivity" (Mahmood 2001, 212); of keeping perceptions of contradictions at just the right point of hazy realization; and of maintaining hope over time in what appears as the nondirectional ambivalence of the "not yet" (Miyazaki 2010).

Debates and friends

As people in this vague social movement make life choices that make their world feel like home, intragenerational debates emerge about just how this integration of local and global, old and new values should occur. We might call the questions that confront these ambiguous resisters as they realize the limits of life and the stakes of the games they play questions of morality. How much dependence, given or taken, can independence take? How much endurance can emotional individuality afford? How much choice can live in a forest of obligations? These narratives show that the range of tolerance in this generation varies greatly—a testament to these women's broad movement over time in their particular historical space of double binds and contradictions.

In the midst of these debates, women of this generation turn to experts such as teachers, doctors, religious leaders, and authors for help in making individual decisions, a process that is typical of the decentralization of individual governance in the neoliberal era (Dean 1999). Saturated with information, most participants in this social movement listen to experts rather than parents, often letting the experts' claim to knowledge and their skill in dressing old ideas in new jargon (Foucault 1980) nudge them toward decisions to abide by older norms, at least for the time being. Both trust and distrust emerge in these relationships, however, as people also turn to the reflexive awareness of themselves, their friends, and siblings.

Reporting their voices and consultations with them in narratives, women name friends and siblings as all-important allies who give support but also critique as they watch each other from the Panopticon towers at the center of this scriptless life they are trying to hammer out together. The value of friends' points of view relates to the facts that they have passed through similar disciplines, desires, and points of resistance in the past, and that they too are figuring out how to be responsible individuals in their own lives, in families, and at work. In this study, friends emerge as lending both stability and ongoing incitement toward change. The voices of their generation in both city and country sometimes urge friends to adhere to older norms to achieve certain moral ideals and obligations with the consciousness of time changing the situation. Yet, when the time is right, friends' voices can also be depended on to encourage alternative actions that support desires for more individual autonomy. In short, friends help friends to write new scripts that fit their ambivalent long-term resistance.

The presence or absence of friends and siblings that women can confide in and trust eases long-term resistance. Single women in the large city grapple with their anomalous status in terms of old norms better than single women in the north because of available friends with whom they may talk and enjoy life. Although this social movement is vague because it works through individuals attempting in small ways to shift the cultural codes in their personal lives, the collectivity of same-age allies contributes psychological strength and increases external acceptability. Likewise, in the north, more single women married regardless of risky husbands and in-laws in part because they had few allies left, and friends kept introducing them to prospective marriage partners.

In general, the process of long-term resistance increases in loneliness as one ages because the particularities of one's life conditions intensify and people must face the challenges of work and family on their own. However, social media connections with friends were important for isolated mothers, and some singles held on to the hope of living with friends in old age. As the children of these interviewees grow up and move on, I expect that relationships with friends will surface once again in a more active way, as women work out scripts for their continued dilemmas of adulthood after child raising and retirement.

Family

Family is a key institution for these women in their long-term attempts to shift the cultural codes toward independence and choice, but ambivalence is central in this arena where adaptation to family or household traditions pairs with the ongoing push to live by late-modern values. If these women can be seen as suggestive of global trends, their ambiguous long-term resistance has been fairly successful in forcing some change in the attitudes of their parents. The ambivalence of their mothers toward their own marriages and care of elders often came to these women's rescue as their mothers negotiated with fathers to gain tolerance for what they saw as their daughters' transgressions in the form of seeking enjoyment, boyfriends, continued work or education, and time spent abroad. Furthermore, the women's own wills to power were most vulnerable and ambivalent toward those who first loved and recognized them—their mothers, who gave them time, unselfish love, and close physical relationships when they were young (and fathers, who were close advisers for some). Put this complex of ambivalences together and it adds up, not only to ongoing conflict between mothers and daughters, but also to mothers' wishes to give help to daughters, daughters' ability to accept help from mothers, and daughters' willingness to help mothers when they grow old. They mended their fractured relationships, finding creative means for a different relationship to emerge. In fact, rather than the overdependence or parasitism of which Japanese women are accused, I found many single and married women who were in relationships of mature give-and-take with their mothers over the long term.

Women's long-term resistance also affected their relations with parents-in-law; the divorced woman in the village lost her son to one family but managed to get separate living quarters for her nuclear family with her present in-laws. Nonetheless, these women far preferred the emotional relationship with, and even elderly care for, mothers rather than mothers-in-law. In the most dangerous position with in-laws were the women married without children who faced household gridlocks around how to get heirs. At this point in this longitudinal study, almost all the women were able to avoid living with their mothers-in-law, but future pressure or obligations to do so loomed in both rural and urban areas.

With ideals of respect for self and expectations for love or special connections in relationships central to this ambiguous resistance of late modernity, the husband is a pivot for the ability to stay on track with the task of manipulating cultural codes in one's life. The success of this process for this generation has to be qualified. On a personal level of interrelationship between husband and wife the majority of women in this study were not ecstatic but satisfied, conveying that their husbands understood them and supported their ability to maintain some space for self. Unlike many of their mothers, they enjoyed their husbands' presence at home and had time to do things together on the weekends. In many cases, they reflected that their husbands did not like going on late-night drinking bouts or weekend retreats any more than the wives wanted them to, but company practices required less of this than in the past. On a structural level of actual practices in time and space, however, women had no choice but to accept work demands made on their husbands who arrived home at nine or ten p.m. at the earliest, and they seemed to tolerate these, much as their mothers had, as inevitable conditions of employment in Japanese institutions.

With men, women sometimes shared feelings and actions of long-term resistance, but such alliances with husbands or lovers could not be assured just because they were in the same generation. Women in this study put up with husbands whose consciousnesses had changed little, just as the women had feared when they were younger, and the fact that most men are the main breadwinners in this study reinforces this. Married men who were not fathers seemed to use the situation to revert to dependence on their wives. The regional male lover who tacitly refused marriage is one who himself hung on to his ambiguous resistance but never clearly communicated its nature to his girlfriend. However, the long-term resistance of women did contribute to changes in men in some cases. Some husbands loosened up and gave more time to their families over time, changed jobs, or engaged in hobbies for themselves much as their wives did. Too much time devoted to hobbies on top of work, however, could backfire on the wife.

The opposition to the cultural code lived out by most women in this generation did not include a wish never to have children, but rather objected to women's self-sacrifice to family and the idea that their maturity would be measured by expunging desires for independent self. Yet ambivalence toward child raising is inevitable, because in this form of long-term resistance between modernity and late modernity, women find themselves being judged as mothers by teachers, doctors, and the nation even as they simultaneously try to enjoy themselves with their children and find new, interesting selves while raising them.

I find Japanese women experiencing child raising as both a demanding responsibility and a satisfying joy, challenging and expanding the ideas of self. Children deliver these women from a narrow vision of growing only through consumption, enjoyment, and work centered on self. Women who have been successful singles in the past and quit work tend to define their child-rearing period as a limited time in their lives—a time of less stress, or a time of information-gathering for self and children. Other nonworking mothers are consumed by child raising, giving themselves to it completely to minimize risks for their children and save Japan. They suggest that cocooning may well carry with it insights into the risks of the late-modern era.

Work, companies, and government

The workplace is also a key institution in the lives of these ambivalent resisters, some of whom invested it with great potential for self-actualization. For most, however, work for women is not the panacea that some had hoped for, not only because of the unrelenting contradictions between work and mothering, but also because work itself has changed in the unstable and globalized economy of the late-modern era. Fewer jobs, fewer satisfying jobs, and more part-time service jobs with fewer benefits and more individual responsibility typify this period. Most successful singles either work in freelance or independent employment or for a modern type of company that allows flexibility; for them, the late-modern style of work has leveraged their independence. For others, work is simply the way to hold the line financially or psychologically against total accommodation. Work as a strong meaningful core to life or as the lucrative basis for enjoyment on the side has failed single women in the northern regional city as well as a few women in Tokyo working in educational institutions. In these cases, enjoyment of work and of being single is hampered by demands for loyalty, emotional dependency, and long hours of work from bosses who expect women to prove themselves, do the dirty work, or overwork. Overwhelmed, the women can do little more than remain aware of the double bind in which they find themselves.

Part of the experience of ambiguous long-term resistance is the acceptance of a certain degree of structural intransigence and the power of institutions in late-modern society. These Japanese women accept the idea that the larger structure is dominant and there will be little meaningful change, especially in companies and schools. Women must work hard in their own jobs, yet companies do not give them special help with children in order to advance, and glass ceilings remain for singles, even though some in this study have done reasonably well. Husbands must give their jobs priority rather than helping around the house. Children's success in schools still depends on mothers' roles as organizer and coach because schools remain ranked and competitive, with high school and university exams being major turning points in their children's lives, and outside education necessary to succeed. To maintain their middle-class status, women's long-term resistance must be ambivalent, because it is permeated by frameworks of institutionalized power that privilege men in the public world.

Women view the government with vague hopes for changes in policies that might help them, but generally they reflect that policy changes have not helped them in their long-term resistance and thus it is useless to put faith in the government. Ironically, the relationship with the government reinforces these women's idea that they must be independent and figure out their own best choices. Government cannot be trusted to help the people with their real problems. Thus, they implicitly recognize the neoliberal governance that they must deal with in this era—a governance that deals out policies that depend on citizens, particularly women in Japan, to be entrepreneurial in their work and to act as the basis for child and elder care at home.

Self

This long-term resistance movement has centered on shifting society just enough to accommodate individuality, independence, enjoyment, and expanded opportunities for women. In Japan, self, with its development and actualization outside of daughterhood, marriage, and motherhood, is the core concept. How has the concept of self fared in the longitudinal narratives of women in this study?

The dilemmas of adulthood in Japan have molded this concept of self into various shapes in women's lives. For singles, the aims are to normalize the anomalous identity of singles so they are no longer liminal people who have not yet emerged as adults and to live their singlehood in ways that enable them to maintain the integrity of their generational aims. Successful Tokyo singles experience a version of self that shines with independence, a new form of middle-class identity (Muraki 2007) and the ability to move freely among multilayered identities, while up north singlehood is similar but is experienced as a manual for self that singles are still writing. Consumption was more important as a symbolic bootstrap in early years of working toward a free-floating selfhood, but appears in larger forms like apartments and recedes as an everyday concern as singles age.

In the process of the long-term resistance of this generation, the emphasis on self has mellowed—as one might expect in ambiguous, long-term resistance such as this, and especially in Japan where self is laden with meanings, including realizing self as flexible and part of the whole as the apex of maturity (Rosenberger 1992). One successful single even plays with ideas of integrating her ambitious small self with the larger self of the universe. There is no other way for the struggling, crashing singles whose identities have literally fragmented, double binds imploding inside them. Religion offers them a fresh interpretation of self-awakening, as they are reborn into a new sense of what non-self means. Art affords the opportunity for irrepressible expressions of self, and theater in particular offers the ability to try out random, marginal identities on- and offstage.

Despite their renunciation of singlehood, married women without children find themselves still trying to normalize an anomalous identity. Having passed through the biggest dilemma of choice, however, their way is not as difficult as that of singles because the values of their generation have penetrated society to the extent that couples living for their own enjoyment are accepted; some enjoy themselves with a fierce determination, but if they care for elders, they gain even more acceptance. The problem is that they themselves sometimes feel stuck in a no-man's land between friends who are married with children and friends who are single, or between freedom from children and the dependence of demanding husbands. They do not have the ideal of independent self for their generation, the ideal of a self that might grow with their children, or the ideal of a future that might leave more room for self-development once their children have grown.

Nonworking married women with children have the task of defamiliarizing this postwar role of full-time housewife as they fit it to their own generation's values. Outside of an anomalous identity, the ambivalent mind becomes hard to hold onto and action toward self causes disharmony. At the center of their households, these mothers use the skills that they learned as singles in their conscious performance of an identity that includes manipulation of husbands and children and care of the household in a risky, neoliberal world. Some women would say that they have taken a hiatus from self, but their narratives show that they remain aware of it, most of them planning how to take up the pursuit of self in the future. They are cautious about portraying themselves as presently capable of building self—certainly not a self independent of family, as they once imagined it, but rather one of traveling with children or building and decorating new houses. Yet they do imagine growing self through low-income jobs and volunteer activities that involve them in society beyond family, some feeling that this may allow them to do something more meaningful than they did when they were young and working in companies. In this sense, their children have served as a symbolic means to make this shift out of the male-defined world of work. Moreover, their desires fit with the increase in volunteer activities that Japanese communities offer, even demand (Ogawa 2009).

Married women with children who continue working voice the concept of self more than their nonworking counterparts. The full-timers still have a world of their own where they see their selves existing if not actively growing, but their long-term resistance fights to fashion the independence of their children as well as themselves. Perhaps the dance teacher–mother whose husband and parents support her, and the organic farmer with her strong sense of the societal importance of the work she does with her husband, have the strongest concepts of self among the mothers interviewed. Although both feel the tug between work and child raising, they have never lost sight of themselves as individuals with choices and purpose in the world. On the other end of the spectrum are the part-time family workers whose jobs are embedded in their husband's family's work and thus, for the present, have lost connection with their paths of self via work.

In short, self remains a viable concept in the discourse of this generation, although it decreases in importance over the years. It takes on different meanings and practices for different members of this generation as their lives assume firmer shapes through the choices they have made or not made. Gazing on these very differences keeps the question of self alive in this generation. Self has neither flown to the flexible heights that Ueno (2005) imagined nor died in the depths of conservative Japan; yet the concept continues to be salient for women as a measure of their journeys along the path of ambivalent long-term resistance.

This longitudinal study has illustrated the myriad angles of long-term resistance for women trying to shift the cultural code in the turn from modernity to late modernity. The ambivalence and tension that lie at its core frame the dilemmas of adulthood for women who feel they are writing their own manuals for life within the contradictions of the life they were raised in and the life they have discovered through both their experimental choices and the turns of history shaping their lives. In the economically unstable and culturally changing life of the 1990s and 2000s in Japan, this generation of women finds that their long-term resistance takes them places they never dreamed of, both because they are so different from how they imagined their lives would be when they were young, and because they are more similar to their mothers' lives than they imagined as young adults. There is no turning back, however, because what they have become answers to the ongoing struggles within them as well as to the larger contestations and shifts in late-modern Japan. They feel they have choices, and yet simultaneously they have no choice but to negotiate their way with practiced ambivalence through the dilemmas of their adulthood.

Through the making of their personal life narratives, not intended to challenge the status quo in any revolutionary way, have these women brought change? Undoubtedly, the answer is yes, that their small ambiguous choices and silent refusals, practiced within a generational discourse that has spread from mouth to mouth, have been an impetus toward larger change, not least because the political and social body was depending on their bodies to make babies. This story of long-term resistance has also revealed long-term shifts in power, with change itself best imagined as a spiral of intertwining cables, some tugging toward reproduction of the old and others straining toward innovation, but always with mutual effect on each other in conflict and symbiosis. Over the course of these women's lives in Japan, consumer choice and global information increased; women responded with ambivalence toward postwar cultural codes; the government reacted with new policies; a sense of risk grew with economic decline and globalization along with a sense of rising inequality; many men joined women in their ambivalent long-term resistance; and governance turned increasingly to dependence on experts, self-responsibility, and a continued sense of morality in families and communities. Change has undoubtedly occurred; but, as in many places around the world, change is uncertain, imbued with "tensions and ambivalence that subjects face as they position themselves simultaneously within emerging neoliberal regimes and in relation to social contexts that may be governed by alternative ways of conjoining subjectivity, social relations, and politics" (Goodman 2009, 206).

By the time the earthquake, tsunami, and radiation of 2011 occurred in Japan, individuation, a sense of risk, and distrust of government were already well developed, and these events boosted them sky-high. The ambivalences of long-term resistance honed by these women have come to permeate Japan, producing negative tension, disbelief in nation, and profound uncertainty about the future—but on the positive side yielding reflective awareness, increased tolerance of difference, and a conscious search for new kinds of human linkages.

Epilogue

I WAS NOT ABLE to interview these women again until 2012, almost exactly a year after the earthquake, tsunami, and nuclear plant explosion of March 2011 in Japan. Although the results are not fully analyzed, I want to share some of the women's experiences and thoughts connected with these tragedies. This brief report serves as a fitting epilogue to this book, because for many women, the quake, tsunami, and radiation marked a high tide of risk in their lives as individuals, families, and citizens of a nation, revealing their reactions along the continuum of risk and stability in their lives.[1]

The shaking that women felt from the earthquake in Tokyo was quite pronounced, but other than the destruction of a few books and plates, little damage was done. The single department-store manager in downtown Tokyo walked for more than three hours to a friend's house, rested there, because "you don't want to be alone at such a time," and reached home late at night. An only child, she kept trying to telephone her parents in Tokyo, but it took a long time because they had refused to get mobile phones. Matsui-san, the woman working at Toyota, got a ride home with a friend, and luckily her young son's friend's mother had taken him home: "They were playing as if nothing had happened when I walked in at eleven p.m.!" Convenience stores, ubiquitous in Tokyo, as well as supermarkets, soon were running out of tofu, yogurt, bread, and rice, but a few women were well-prepared enough to have a stock of water and rice or lucky enough to have relatives down south who sent them food. Tokyoites had to put up with lack of electricity at first and rolling electricity stoppages throughout the next months. One single woman found the dark subway stations spooky, and her strength was challenged by having to carry water up to her seventh-floor apartment because the water pump did not work. In the following summer's rolling electricity outages, if she worked during the two hours of electricity she received, she still had to haul up her water.

In the Tohoku city of Morioka, the shaking was worse than in Tokyo, although no widespread damage occurred; afterwards people lacked water as well as electricity. Nakajima-san, the medical technician, was giving medical tests to patients who got stuck in MRI machines for a time. Kawai-san at the assisted living home stayed all night and into the next day, piling blankets on the old people who were there on short- and long-term stays, carrying water over from neighbors' wells, and feeding the elders only twice a day with food on hand and extra rice brought by workers' relatives. Both of these women learned that in a crisis the true personality of people shines through. Nakajima-san was disappointed in fellow workers who left patients to grab food from the convenience stores. Kawai-san's boss left her there to help the patients all night without a word of apology or appreciation and then attacked her the next day for dispatching home helpers to continue to check on elders whom their employees served in their homes and who often lived alone. The boss seemed to care more about finances than about helping the elders of the local area, and Kawai-san vowed to quit her job as soon as she could.

The small village also shook fiercely, but the retirement home where Takahashi-san worked stood firm. She had to stay to help with patients until ten p.m., and at first she could not get in touch with her family, but when she did her sister-in-law had picked up her children and taken them home. "That night we all got together at our place, fifteen people or so. Our hearts felt assured (*anshin*) to have all the family together. We were so relieved. We have bonds with each other now thanks to the quake."

In Tokyo and the northeast, depending on how long their electricity was out, people did not find out about the tsunami for one or two days. When people in Tohoku realized the enormity of the tsunami, their own woes faded in significance. Because of the closeness of the tsunami-hit coast in Iwate Prefecture where Morioka and the village are located, women lost friends and relatives; they saw refugees flowing into their areas and helped out as best they could. The musician in Morioka lost an aunt and uncle, who were doctors on the coast, in the tsunami, and Nakajima-san lost a doctor friend with whom she had graduated from high school. "He went back to search for his cat and died. Why?" she asked herself. She went to a coastal town to help clean up the mangled debris on the coast where houses had been, feeling less sad when she was there.

One of the "romantics" discussed in Chapter 4, who had married late and moved to live with her husband in a mountain town in Iwate Prefecture only two passes over from the coast, was working in the city hall that became the refugee center. With her husband's permission, she stayed on for several weeks, sleeping in a sleeping bag, making rice balls (tiny, to conserve their small stock of rice), and holding the flashlight at the toilets for old people who lived alone and could not survive without electricity and water. "There was a little girl who made a rice ball bigger and bigger, trying to make it for everyone, saying the names of her parents, grandparents, and siblings. Everyone listened to her and cried." Over the next days, as refugees from the coast came in, she heard tragic stories of people such as a man who reached out his hand to save his mother but failed to reach her as she got washed away. This woman, always very sensitive to human and animal suffering, felt depressed for many months afterwards.

Japanese heard about the explosion of the nuclear plant in Fukushima Prefecture, and because of slow government reportage, very gradually came to realize how serious it had been. Negishi-san, the single woman who had played Maria in *West Side Story* in her youth and had since returned to train nursery-school teachers in Fukushima City, said that they received no official announcement of the explosions and their severity until one month after they had taken place. She said, "Even the kids don't believe anything the government says anymore. Mothers of young children at our nursery school cry to think that they allowed their children to play outside when the radiation was so high, but they didn't know." Tears rolled down her cheeks. However, she was thrilled that all the students she was responsible for survived, and only one of their university students died in the tsunami. She and her sister (who lived nearby with her family) were scared without water, but country people shared from their wells, and the landlord of her apartment building brought Negishi-san water.

Glad to be near her family at such a time, Negishi-san and her sister, who has three children, adopted a resigned point of view. "We live here and we are staying here. We eat the food and drink the water. You can't worry about everything you eat and drink." At their home, their mother served me beef from Fukushima and fish from the Pacific coast, and although I admit that I hesitated, I ate it. Negishi-san's nieces and nephews had played inside all summer after the explosion, wearing radiation counters around their necks and roasting in schoolrooms with no windows open, but when given the chance to spend a week with their school friends away from the radiation, they said they would rather stay home with family. Many friends have left, some families split, with fathers staying on to work and mothers and children fleeing to the next prefecture that has lower counts of cesium.

Ever the optimist even when almost defeated by depression and fatigue, Negishi-san encouraged her niece and nephews with the only antidote she had: "Just laugh and eat miso soup and it will be okay!" Indeed, there was a general wisdom, often reported as having come from the Hiroshima experience, that miso and other fermented foods Japanese treasure as part of their culinary heritage are helpful to bodies fighting radiation. Women advised me, "Eat fermented food and get things through your body quickly."

A single woman working in Tokyo was relieved to hear that her parents, living on the coast just south of the nuclear plant, had survived the tsunami and that the wind from the nuclear explosion had not showered where they were as much as areas to the north and west. Her brother went up to bring her parents to Tokyo soon after the incident, but her parents were not happy staying there with their children. Their main worry was the graves of the ancestors, and when the equinox (*o-higan*) came in late March, an important time for people to visit and care for the graves, it was all the children could do to convince their parents just to visit an aunt's grave near to Tokyo to "tell her that everyone had survived" rather than to go home. After Golden Week in May, they did return home, and found their ancestors' graves on the coast toppled by the tsunami. They raised them and quickly ordered a new Buddhist altar for the house of the eldest son, which had been badly water-damaged. This woman was shocked to find out how important the ancestors and their graves were to the elder generations. "For us, the living are important, but for them it is the dead."

As of the writing of this epilogue, two nuclear plants are working in Japan, and the debate continues as to whether, to what extent, and how gradually nuclear energy generation will be phased out. The mood when I was there a year after the nuclear explosion was extremely ambiguous, and although many people had serious doubts about nuclear power, they were hesitant to express their points of view publicly. Baba-san, the single interpreter in Tokyo, had gone to an antinuclear demonstration in Hibiya Park (her first such demo) and strongly criticized the Japanese media for not reporting on anything much at all about antinuclear activities. Telling me that a journalist who had expressed an antinuclear sentiment had been sacked, she complained, "I thought Japan was a liberalized country! There is no freedom of the press here!"[2] She felt shock that, given what had happened, people were not supporting antinuclear politicians. Like others, she looked around and asked, "Don't we have enough electricity now without nuclear power?"

Oyama-san, a housewife and mother of two in Sendai who grew up in Morioka, was the most expressive in her antinuclear sentiments, influenced, she said, by a friend who was strongly into the movement. Sendai received radiation by wind from the nuclear explosion and part of the city was damaged by the tsunami. "We aren't sure exactly how bad things are here. We got radiation, but not as much as elsewhere and now in the air we have about .7 microsieverts. I would flee from Fukushima City with my children if the microsieverts were 5 even if my husband didn't want me to," she declared.[3] In meetings with groups of mothers from her children's classrooms, Oyama-san has cautiously raised the question of radiation and its effects on school lunches and even on playing outside; she is careful not to take a clear, antinuclear stance, but nevertheless mothers say nothing and shift the topic to something else. Although her husband is not antinuclear, feeling that nuclear energy is necessary for industrial growth, he agrees with her decision to order vegetables from a farm in a southern prefecture with no measurable problem of radiation. The explosion seems to have radicalized her: "People are just going back to their regular lives. They can't be bothered, but I can't get used to it!"

However, another housewife and mother of two in Tokyo who also grew up in Morioka took the opposite stance. As we sipped coffee, she broke out into a diatribe against the media that she thought was blatantly antinuclear and began to argue that radiation is not so bad for us, that it is in the air anyway, and that our bodies get used to it. It turned out that her husband worked for a nuclear power plant on the coast of Japan opposite from the Fukushima explosion, and he was enduring strong attacks from antinuclear protestors who came in boats, beating drums and throwing things. He is overstressed trying to defend the nuclear power company in that area to protestors and to the local townspeople around his plant. She explained that he had taken this job because of his mission to save Japan from dependence on oil through using nuclear power, and now he felt that people were ignoring his contributions. "There are always dangers," she said. "We have to think of the happiness of the whole."

She was the only woman among the interviewees who argued for nuclear power, but only seven openly expressed feelings or participated in activities against it. Most took the ambiguous middle road of not really being in support of nuclear power but persuaded by government representatives that Japan's economic stability would suffer in the long run without it.

Because I was in Japan a year after the quake and eating food that could have been contaminated by radiation, but also because I was doing research on organic farmers in Japan who were trying to sell their crops, I asked how these women felt about the danger of radiation in food. About two-thirds said that they did not worry much about it in the food that they buy and eat. Some stated firmly, "I don't worry about it all!" A Tokyo single woman said: "I eat what I want. Japanese women live a long time anyway." A Tokyo mother who lived in an area in Chiba that was a hot spot for radiation also declared: "I feel I can't worry much—we are an older couple and our child is in junior high. I buy delicious food and don't worry about where it comes from, and we drink the regular water."

Thus, the majority were only slightly hesitant: "I can't worry about it [the radiation] all the time. If I did, that too would become a source of stress." "You have to go on living. You have to buy the food or it will disappear." Yet women were careful, many studying store labels at supermarkets and buying vegetables, meat, and fish from prefectures far from Fukushima, the center of the explosion, if they were available. Shopping in Tokyo, however, I noticed that many vegetables, pork, and chicken came from prefectures north of Tokyo that had received radiation. By this time, women had realized that, according to the wind and the rain at the time of the nuclear explosions, various areas had received different doses of cesium, the main source of radiation in this explosion, so the name of a prefecture did not tell the whole story. In Iwate Prefecture where half the interviewees live, the very southern part was showered with radiation but the north was not, except for an area just below Mount Iwate. In fact, the women living in Iwate Prefecture in the northeast, although closer to the nuclear power plant in Fukushima than Tokyoites, did not worry about their food because they actually had not received as much radiation as Tokyo. The milk sold by the dairy farmer–husband of one of the village women measured below the legal limit for cesium. A few wondered about the fish off the coast where cesium may still be leaking from the damaged nuclear power plant, but most ate what seemed delicious and hoped that "I am being safe by living a regular life."

Although trust in the government was low, those who were worried turned to the institutions they shopped at to protect their safety. "I am just trusting the Seikyo to have safe food. They measure the radiation in the food." The Seikyo is a nationwide cooperative market with local member branches that is known for the attention it pays to selling safe, healthy food, although it varies a great deal among its branches and was involved in poisoned food incidents in the recent past (Rosenberger 2009). Others simply trusted the system, for spot-monitoring of food was being done and the government's legal limit on cesium in food was soon to tighten.[4] Furthermore, in Tokyo, some women were more concerned about how to protect themselves from the next big quake and tsunami, which are predicted for Tokyo over the next four to five years, than with the present-day danger of radiation.

Two Tokyo mothers were being very vigilant. One, Matsui-san, the Toyota worker, said, "I read about Chernobyl and worry that my thirteen-year-old will get leukemia by thirty, like those children who didn't flee during the Chernobyl radiation leak." Distrusting local supermarkets, she paid more for her food from Radish Boya, a company that contracted with farmers to grow safe food in Japan, than she would pay at local supermarkets. The second Tokyo housewife, a part-time family worker, has bought all of her drinking and cooking water from Hawaii ever since the explosion, even sending water with her daughter to day care. "An announcement has come saying the water here [in Chiba near Tokyo] is okay to drink, but I still buy water from Hawaii. Everything is confused." In addition, she feeds no fish at all to her children.

People sympathized with the plight of people in Fukushima Prefecture where the explosion occurred. Some food companies and nonprofits have taken up the cause of Fukushima farmers and urge people: "Help Fukushima! Buy food from Fukushima!" Three of the single women said, "I feel apologetic to the people of Fukushima, 'cause we also use electricity made there, so I buy Fukushima food." Two bought it when it was available, but the single from the village, Hasegawa-san, special-ordered it; she was so moved by the plight of people in Fukushima and had such good memories of her time spent there in college, that she hoped to move to a retirement home in Fukushima when she was older. Three other singles, however, refused to buy food from Fukushima, and one in Tokyo commented: "I give my apologies to Fukushima, but I am not going to buy their food. In this situation there is nothing to do but protect one's self."

To close, talking with these women revealed that the triple whammy of earthquake, tsunami, and nuclear explosion was a turning point for many, who felt that they had learned lifelong lessons. Predictably, the importance of family emerged, with one Tokyo mother saying, "I really want to take good care of my family now—especially my daughter and mother-in-law." A single teacher in Tokyo said: "Priorities came into clear relief. People learned to care for each person." Likewise, a Morioka teacher noted, "The students learned that life itself is important (*inochi ga daisetsu*) and that everyday life is valuable." The pronuclear mother above told me that since the earthquake she and her old friends got together more often than before, attesting to the bonds (*kizuna*) that became the positive watchword of the whole incident. Several mentioned, "We learned that luxuries are not so important if you have your basic needs met," and Yamada-san, the Morioka teacher who idealized rural life, recommended that if people would learn the traditional food knowledge of their parents and grandparents, they would survive.

Women also worried about the image of Japan itself. "I feel apologetic to the world for what has happened in Japan. The world must have bad impressions of Japan now," sighed Baba-san. Another single woman in Tokyo puzzled over what she could do to help Japan become energetic (*genki*) again. Yet women also had learned to distrust the Japanese government more than before, and Oyama-san from Sendai said: "As a graduating senior from a tsunami-hit town said, we can't resent this huge disaster sent from heaven. But I do feel resentment about this man-made nuclear explosion."

In sum, the lives of these women have become newly burdened by forms of risk that they had not been aware of before; the possibility of further earthquakes and tsunami, simulated on Japanese television, are on their minds. These tragedies have deeply affected the thoughts and activities of some and have put the personal dilemmas of all in perspective. But a year later most of these women are finding a fulcrum on the continuum between risk and stability where they remain aware of risk but feel they can still care for families and self adequately, while slowly returning to consideration of their own futures.

Appendix

In an attempt to represent the ideas that constitute the movement of long-term resistance used in this book, I have developed two sets of double axes of intersecting continua. One represents psychosocial movement at the individual level and revolves around the concepts of ambivalence and tension. The other represents cultural political movement at the societal level and revolves around the concepts of ambiguity and contradiction. The point here is to foreground the in-between space that accommodates various experiences among my research participants and the multiple experiences that research participants undergo over time. At each end of the continua are parameters that represent concerns that frame long-term resistance in this era of late modernity.

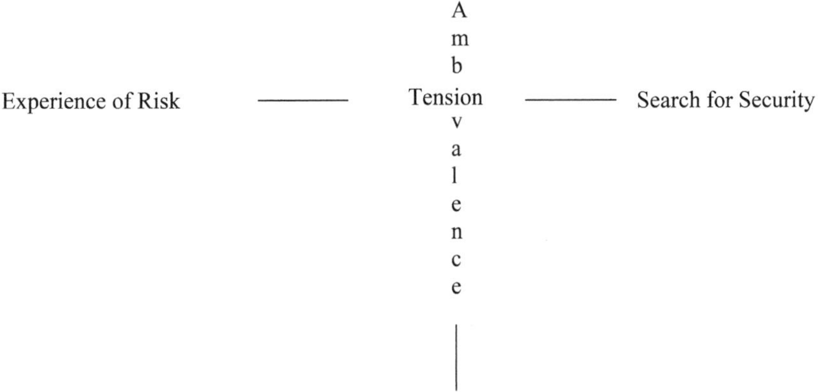

Late-modern Differences (heterogeneity)

|

A
m
b
i
g
u
Global Risks ——— Contradictions ——— Nationalistic Protection
t
i
e
s

|

Postwar Institutional Order (homogeneity)

Notes

CHAPTER 1: WHAT IS LONG-TERM RESISTANCE?

1. In contrast, the U.S. fertility rate in 2010 was 2.1 (Google Public Data 2011), a rate at which the population is reproducing itself. In the United States this depends in part on the high degree of immigration, which Japan does not have. The mean age of women at first marriage in the United States was below Japan at 26.1 in 2010 (Info Please 2011), and the mean age of women at first birth rose from 21.4 in 1970 to 25 in 2006, again well below Japan (Center for Disease Control and Prevention 2011).
2. Kaori Okano (2009) has done a longitudinal study of Japanese women high school graduates from 1989 to 2001, tracking their progress in their twenties through employment, family, and relationships, as they seek comfort. The inclusion of people with working-class background and Koreans in Japan adds special interest to her study. Yoder (2004) has done a long-term study of deviant youths in Japan.
3. They prefer to remain anonymous.
4. Lila Abu-Lughod (1990) wrote that often the resistance that Western researchers track shows more about the various effects of power than it does about resistance. She describes young Bedouin women who have moved into the cities in Egypt. They resist old norms about marriage based on parents' choices and on social stability rather than love, but as they shop for sexy lingerie to seduce their husbands, they enter a new set of media-led norms about women, sexiness, and marriage based on sexual bonds rather than family and community ties. Similar observations can be made about the use of media as part of resistance in Japan or the United States as well.
5. Saba Mahmood, an Egyptian anthropologist, criticizes agency as a Western feminist/liberal idea that is "a synonym for resistance to relations of domination" (2001, 206). She studies the Mosque Islam movement in Egypt and claims agency, but within the self-cultivation and discipline of Islamic norms. It is the religiously based patience and modesty of these women that allows them to deal with social suffering even as they cry about it with a friend. Her definition of agency aids in analyzing

actions in contexts that are non-Western: "capacity for action that historical relations of subordination enable and create" (2001, 203).

6. Sherry Ortner points out that agency and resistance are full of tension between a person's intentions and socialized norms (2006, 77). Ethnographers should listen for details in people's narratives in order to hear the ambivalence inevitable in agency because "people are reacting to more than one form of domination and individuals are themselves heterogeneous with internal contradictions and ambivalences" (Ortner 2006, 179). Here Ortner accepts the argument of Shahbono's multiple identities, but emphasizes that she is "at the low end of every form of power in the system" (Ortner 2006, 56).
7. Laura Dales writes that Japanese women have "limited agency . . . bounded by context" (Dales 2005, 150). Lyn Parker (2005), whose book *The agency of women in Asia* Dales writes in, uses the term "conflicted agency" for the women in Bali she studies, who want to use biomedical clinics for childbirth because they are safe but often end up with traditional healers because they treat the women more respectfully.
8. Talal Asad (2003, 79) attacks the idea of agency as a Western notion that Western scholars cannot give up because they are imbued with the historical idea of freedom. Yet he cites hypocrisy, because the same scholars want a subject who is historically constructed.
9. Nandini Gunewardena (2007) suggests that we avoid seeing women as either "wholly antagonistic or fully compliant to the gender norms of the day. . . . In my long-term ethnographic observations . . . ambivalence is a far more common response to encounters with power than is wholesale antagonism."
10. Ortner (2006) speaks of agency and resistance in relation to tension; Gunewardena (2007) and Ortner (2006) use the term "ambivalence"; Parker (2005) qualifies agency as conflicted, and Dales (2005) as limited.
11. Gupta and Ferguson (1997) take off from a footnote of Foucault's that claims that points of resistance are earth-shaking experiences. not because they change the era's truths, but over the long run because they "cut across individuals themselves . . . fracture unities and make new groupings" (Foucault 1980, 56–57, n.13). They write that experiencing these small points of resistance leaves traces of tension in individuals and relationships that change people in terms of how they are subject to others and how they are linked with their own identities through how they think about themselves (1997).
12. "Games" here means the social fields of power that people live and compete in. The rules of social games are complex and strong, but games may change over time, causing dilemmas for some people (Bourdieu 1990).
13. Raymond Williams (1981) uses the phrase "structures of feeling" to name this ambiguous arising, and the ideas and practices that take form he calls "emergent discourses." They are uncertain and may or may not become social movements.

They vie or combine with other powerful sets of ideas and practices: dominant discourses—powerful in everyday society now—and residual discourses—powerful from social and cultural history.

14. Butler proposes that small changes occur in the margins of society as people fail to enact or act differently from certain societal expectations of their identity, especially gender identities. In her story of a hermaphrodite, the courage and risk involved in such "slippage" is clear.
15. In 2004, 9.7% of university professors were women, 16.1% of assistant professors, and 22.9% of lecturers. Nearly 30% of students in PhD courses were women (Sodei 2005).
16. Bourdieu experienced two games of power in his life, one in his peasant village and another at the Sorbonne in Paris. He knew how to play the village game in his bones because he had been raised in it, but he had to learn, and always felt out of place, in the academic game. He described this as a double bind, which presents dilemmas in people's lives as they try to adjust (Charlesworth 2000).
17. Das (2007) writes of the poignant silences of wives kidnapped by the enemy and sometimes impregnated during the partition of India and Pakistan. These silences are another aspect of agency for Das.
18. Ryang (2006) accuses the Japanese postwar economic, political, and social system of making women endure loveless marriages for the sake of the nation.
19. I have chosen to use the term "late modernity" in this book after the style of Anthony Giddens (1990). I have settled on late modern as an indication that this is an era that has lost faith in the institutions of modernity as a path of progress. Globalization has increased information and risk, broadening people's imaginations. Dynamics of consumption and production have changed, but the institutions and values of modernity still have a strong claim on the era (Harvey 1990).
20. Meanwhile, single men were also increasing, though more gradually, with the increase starting from 1975, according to the *Kokusei Chosa* of 2005. Although men tend to marry later than women, single men in the thirty to thirty-four age group were 32.8% in 1990 and 47.1% in 2005. At age fifty, 5.6% of men were single in 1990, but by 2005, this had risen to 16% (*Shakai Jitsujo* 2011). By 2010, 46% of men were single and never married between the ages of thirty and thirty-four; 35% between thirty-five and thirty-nine; and 28% between forty and forty-four (Statistical Survey Department 2012).
21. Japan has the highest proportion of mothers who earn less than 20% of household income when compared with Taiwan, Germany, Italy, Sweden, the UK, and the United States. Taiwan and Italy are more like Japan in having a lower percentage of working mothers with small children. Among working mothers, the United States has a comparatively high proportion of full-time workers (two-thirds), whereas part-time workers are high among working mothers in the UK and Germany (Shirahase 2007, 46–47).

CHAPTER 2: AMBIVALENCE AND TENSION

1. Butler takes off from Foucault's idea that there is "an ambivalence at the site where the subject emerges," arguing that everyone is brought into ambivalence from the beginning—"a strong vacillation between subordination and a will to our own power" (1997, 7, 17). We are vulnerable to subordination in the complete relationship with mother or caregiver, but we do have the potential to "transform the social terms that have spawned us" (1997, 29).
2. Louis Althusser (1970) argued that the subject, especially the modern "individual," comes into being through structures and social practices tied to economics and politics. Thus, "ideological state apparatuses," such as the policeman pictured here as hailing the subject, constitute the subject and "interpellate" a person into being in ideological form. He is now criticized for overdrawing the power of ideology, but Butler uses this example as one aspect of the process of psychic ambivalence.
3. One in three women between the ages of twenty and sixty-four living alone were in poverty in 2010, defined as earning under 1.25 million yen per year for a single-person household. Married women experienced a poverty rate of 11% compared with the poverty rate of 31.6% for single women living alone (Aoki 2012).
4. Kitamura (2007) finds proof of just such a dilemma of choice. Japanese men and women attend parties that are arranged meetings for potential mates between groups: women graduates from a particular university and men who are lawyers or doctors, for example. She finds them unable to commit, forever searching for the ideal spontaneous encounter (*en*), and thus, perhaps conveniently, keeping themselves out of the formal familial roles they reject. She describes them as in an ongoing liminal state, always within the rite of passage to adulthood but never willing to cross the threshold that would commit them to identities in modern society.
5. This generation is slightly older than the generation of "cuties" studied by Kinsella (1995), who resisted by refusing to grow up and remained childless as a way of protesting the narrow roles of postwar Japanese society.
6. Although the regions lag behind large urban areas economically, after the tsunami of 2011 Tokyoites were surprised to find out that Tohoku (northeast) has an economy the size of Argentina's, with many labor-intensive suppliers of small parts. Its problems affected the national economy. Several such factories near small regional cities employ husbands of women in this book as blue-collar laborers. The economy of the larger Tokyo area, however, is the size of Russia's (*Economist* 2011).

CHAPTER 3: LIVING WITHIN THE DILEMMA OF CHOICE

1. In 2011, a government survey of singles aged 18–34 found that 61.4% of men and 49.5% of women had no girlfriends or boyfriends respectively. Forty percent said

there was no need to marry. Furthermore, a quarter of unmarried men and a quarter of women aged 35–39 said that they had never had sex (Buerk 2012).

CHAPTER 4: NO CHILDREN DESPITE RUNNING THE GAUNTLET OF CHOICE

1. Like others, they inherited the ideology of the mother that has grown strong in the last century in Japan. In the late 1800s, "wise mothers" began to be valued for the growth of the nation (Uno 1991), and the idea grew with the increase in middle-class urban mothers in the twenties, honor given to war mothers in World War II, and importance of professional housewife-mothers in the 1960s and 1970s. Mothers' value in time spent with and for children ratcheted up postwar, because mothers supposedly gave the physical and emotional stability, along with gradual discipline, that would produce children with the idealized Japanese psychological characteristics of cooperation, empathy, emotional dependency, and perseverance. The success of postwar institutions in Japan was supposed to depend on mothers' contributions and made them significant.
2. The popular way of quickly labeling a person who is divorced is to refer to them as having an X (*batsu*), a word that can also mean a penalty.
3. "Old miss" is used in Japanese as a derogatory term for an unmarried woman and is spoken with a Japanese pronunciation of the English words. Americans would use the phrase "old maid."
4. A survey done by the Asahi Newspaper Company of 600 wives in 2005 showed that 26% of married women had not had sex with their husbands in the last year (Cameron 2005). Other surveys of men and women have shown even longer time statistics.

CHAPTER 5: PLANNING AND COCOONING

1. If just considering women who have had children in this study, the overall rate of children per mother is 1.63, with a rate of 1.72 in the regions and a rate of 1.44 in Tokyo.
2. I have used the fertility rate for Iwate Prefecture, where Morioka and the village are located. However, by 2004, four married women (all with children, nonworking) lived in the regions, but outside Iwate. Two were in Sendai, a large northeastern city, and two in other regional cities. The fertility rate for Miyagi Prefecture where Sendai is located is 1.25, while the other two prefectures have rates of 1.44 and 1.51 (Naikakucho 2008, 13).
3. Rayn finds that child raising is understood as a "part of individualistic formation of self" and developing potential resources of self among young women in Norway (2005, 39).

4. Goldstein-Gidoni (2012, 103) found that the generation behind this one is insistent on enjoying life as housewife-mothers.
5. Ishii-san's father is registered as a disabled person. His disability is classified as fourth in a five-tier system. A plan manager makes a plan for him: a home helper takes him back and forth to an adult day service twice a week where he is bathed, and to a dialysis center three times a week. They pay 10% at 10,000 yen per month, and the rest comes from the government's tax program known as "care insurance," paid into by everyone over age forty. A commercial company delivers his special-diet meals to him for $700–$800 per month, which was expensive for the family.

CHAPTER 6: WORKING AND RAISING MORAL CHILDREN

1. Shinnyoen is a new Buddhist sect founded in 1936 by Shinjo Ito in Japan and is now headed by his daughter Shinso Ito. It follows Buddhist ideas of spiritual awakening to the nature of reality, but places special emphasis on altruism through individual contributions to the planet and philanthropic foundation. It is active in the United States, Taiwan, France, and Japan (Shinnyoen.org 2011). Like other new religions in Japan, it is focused on the founder or leader as a prophet/ess, a position that often is inherited within the family, and it is viewed perjoratively by mainstream Japanese.
2. I am including the teacher Kawahara-san in these four, but in this section I discuss the three retirement home workers who grew up in the village and have both parents and parents-in-law there.
3. This is the only woman in this study who had gotten divorced by 2004. The divorce rate has risen significantly since the 1960s. It reached a peak of 290,000 divorces in 2002, and in 2009 there were 253,000. The divorce rate in 2009 was 2.10 per thousand population (*Statistical Handbook of Japan* 2010).
4. The number of children born to couples married after pregnancy has risen in Japan. In 2004, 26.7% of births were in this group—2.5 times higher than in 1998 (*Mainichi Shimbun* 2006).
5. Rosenbluth (2007, 13) states that rural prefectures have a flatter M-curve, indicating that women take less time off from work as they raise children. The correlation between residence in relatively rural areas and female labor-force participation goes beyond the positive effect of grandparents caring for children.
6. In 2012, a survey of married women aged twenty to forty-nine with children under nineteen found that 45.3% wanted to work part-time and 25.8% wanted to work full-time (*Japan Times* 2012).
7. This organic movement is associated with the Japan Organic Agriculture Association. Its principles include *teikei* or community-supported agriculture (CSA) outside of the commercial system. The first CSA operated in Japan in the early seventies. It challenges organic farmers to live entirely off the products of their

land and eschews moneyed economy. Finally, the movement stands for a local cycle of plants fed by compost made from local plant and animal waste without any chemical fertilizers or pesticides. Tsuchiya-san and her husband run a CSA for people in the small nearby city where they go to distribute vegetables and some pork and traditionally processed foods in boxes every week; the members pay for these boxes weekly, but they can refuse for that week or just order half-boxes, thus cutting down on money for the farmers.

CHAPTER 7: THE NUANCES OF LONG-TERM RESISTANCE

1. Anthropologists who rethink agency and resistance include Abu-Lughod (1990), Asad (2003), Dales (2005), Gunewardena (2007), Mahmood (2001), Ortner (2006), and Parker (2005). Studies of psychosocial development and of sociocultural development have lent explanatory concepts for delving into these ideas of ambivalence and tension in people's lives and how people deal with them over time: vulnerability to subordination and a will to power in development (Butler 1997); symbolic bootstrapping with objects (Vygotsky 1966); mental orchestration of various social voices (Bakhtin 1981); and double binds (Bourdieu 1990).

EPILOGUE

1. In her study, Okano (2009) also shows how women in her long-term study got on with their lives after the Kobe earthquake of 1995.
2. At that time, only the *Tokyo Shimbun* (Tokyo Newspaper) was giving full coverage to the nuclear demonstrations and was openly antinuclear in its reporting, although the *Asahi Shimbun* had declared it was against nuclear power.
3. Microsievert is the amount of ionizing radiation required to produce the same biological effect as one rad or gray of high-penetration X-rays. This is measured in the air in various places throughout Japan to estimate how much radiation people are receiving.
4. On April 1, 2012, the Japanese government tightened restrictions on the amount of cesium allowed in food. For general foodstuffs, the limit is 100 bequerels of radiation per kilogram, down from 500; for milk 50 bq, and for water 10 bq (*Japan Today* 2012). A bequerel equals one unit of nuclear decay or other nuclear transformation per second and is used to measure the radiation present in things such as food.

References

Abu-Lughod, L. 1990. "The romance of resistance: Tracing transformations of power through Bedouin women." *American Ethnologist* 17, no.1: 41–55.

———. 2006. "Writing against culture." In *Anthropology in theory,* ed. H. L. Moore and T. Sanders, pp. 469–479. Malden, MA: Blackwell.

Alexy, A. 2011. "Intimate dependence and its risks in neoliberal Japan." *Anthropological Quarterly* 84, no. 4: 895–918.

Althusser, L. 1971. "Ideology and ideological state apparatuses." In *Lenin and philosophy and other essays,* pp. 121–176. New York: Monthly Review Press.

Aoki, M. 2012. "Poverty a growing problem for women." *Japan Times,* April 19.http://www.Japantimesco.jp/news/2012/04/19/national/poverty-a-growing-problem-for-women/#.UR_ED45wyqy (accessed 2/24/13).

Aoki, O., and D. M. Aoki. 2005. "Invisible poverty in Japan: Case studies and realities of single mothers." *Journal of Poverty: Innovations on Social, Political and Economic Inequalities* 9, no. 1: 1–21.

Appadurai, A. 1990. "Disjuncture and difference in the global cultural economy." *Public Culture* 2, no. 2: 1–24.

———. 1996. *Modernity at large: Cultural dimensions of globalization.* Minneapolis: University of Minnesota Press.

Arnett, J. 2004. *Emerging adulthood: The winding road from the late teens through the twenties.* Oxford: Oxford University Press.

Asad, T. 2003. *Formations of the secular: Christianity, Islam, modernity.* Stanford, CA: Stanford University Press.

Bakhtin, M. 1981. *The dialogic imagination: Four essays.* Austin: University of Texas Press.

Bardsley, J., and H. Hirakawa. 2005. "Branded: Bad girls go shopping." In *Bad girls in Japan,* ed. L. Miller and J. Bardsley, pp. 115–125. New York: Palgrave Macmillan.

Bauman, Z. 1991. *Modernity and ambivalence.* Ithaca, NY: Cornell University Press.

Beck, U., and E. Beck-Gernsheim. 2002. *Individualization: Institutionalized individualism and its social and political consequences.* Thousand Oaks, CA: Sage.

Befu, H. 2001. *Hegemony of homogeneity.* Melbourne: Trans-Pacific Press.

Berque, A. 1992. "Identification of the self in relation to the environment." In *Japanese sense of self,* ed. N. Rosenberger, pp. 93–104. Cambridge: University of Cambridge Press.

Birmingham, L. 2012. "As its single ranks swell, Japan wonders 'Where's the love.'" *Japan Times,* Feb. 14. http://www.time.com/time/world/article/o.8599.2106704.00.html (accessed 2/24/13).

Borovoy, A. 2005. *The too-good wife: Alcohol, codependency and the politics of nurturance in postwar Japan.* Berkeley: University of California Press.

———. 2010. "Japan as mirror: Neoliberalism's promise and costs." In *Ethnographies of neoliberalism,* ed. C. Greenhouse, pp. 60–74. Philadelphia: University of Pennsylvania Press.

Bourdieu, P. 1984. *Distinction: A social critique of the judgment of taste.* Cambridge, MA: Harvard University Press.

———. 1990. *The logic of practice.* Cambridge: Polity Press.

Budgeon, S. 2008. "Couple culture and the production of singleness." *Sexualities* 11: 201–235.

Buerk, R. 2011. "Japanese singletons hit record high." *BBC News Asia.* www.bbc.co.uk/news/world-asia-.5915118 (accessed 2/24/13).

Butler, J. 1997. *The psychic life of power: Theories in subjection.* Stanford, CA: Stanford University Press.

———. 2004. *Undoing gender.* New York: Routledge.

Cameron, D. 2005. *A nation where marriage beds have gone cold.* Feb 5. http://www.Theage.com.au/news/World/a-nation-where-marriage-beds-have-gone-cold/2005/02/04/1107476799599.html (accessed 9/1/12).

Center for Disease Control and Prevention. 2011. http://www.cdc.gov/nchs/data/databriefs/db21.html (accessed 6/12/11).

Charlesworth, S. 2000. "Bourdieu, social suffering and working-class life." In *Reading Bourdieu,* ed. B. Fowler, pp. 49–64. Oxford: Blackwell Press.

Collins, P. H. 1998. "It's all in the family: Intersections of gender, race and nation." *Hypatia* 13, no. 3: 62–82.

Comaroff, J. L., and J. Comaroff. 1991. *Of revelation and revolution: Christianity, colonialism, and consciousness in South Africa.* Chicago: University of Chicago Press.

———. 1992. "The madman and the migrant." In *Ethnography and the historical imagination,* pp. 155–177. Boulder, CO: Westview Press.

Dales, L. 2005. "Agency and the parasite single issue." In *The agency of women in Asia,* ed. L. Parker, pp. 133–157. Singapore: Marshall Cavendish.

Das, V. 2007. *Life and words: Violence and the descent into the ordinary.* Berkeley: University of California Press.

Dean, M. 1999. "Risk, calculable and incalculable." In *Risk and sociocultural theory: New directions and perspectives,* ed. D. Lupton, pp. 131–159. Cambridge: University of Cambridge Press.

———. 2007. *Governing societies: Political perspectives on domestic and international rule.* New York: Open University Press.

deCerteau, M. 1984. *The practice of everyday life.* Berkeley: University of California Press.

Delueze, G. 1993. *The fold: Leibniz and the baroque.* Minneapolis: University of Minnesota Press.

Doi, T. 1971. *Anatomy of dependence.* Tokyo: Kodansha.

DuBois, W. E. B. 1994. *The souls of black folks.* New York: Gramercy Books.

Economist. 2011. "Japan's recovery: Who needs leaders?" *Economist* 399, no. 8737: 27–30.

Ezawa, A. 2002. "Motherhood, family, and inequality in contemporary Japan." PhD diss., University of Illinois at Urbana-Champaign.

Farrer, J., H. Tsuchiya, and B. Bagrowicz. 2010. "Emotional expression in *tsukiau* dating relationships in Japan." *Journal of Social and Personal Relationships* 25, no. 1: 169–188.

Foucault, M. 1979. *Discipline and punish: The birth of the prison.* New York: Vintage.

———. 1980. *The history of sexuality.* New York: Vintage Books.

Fujimura-Fanselow, K. 1995. College women today: Options and dilemmas. In *Japanese women: New feminist perspectives on the past, present and future,* ed. K. Fujimura-Fanselow and A. Kameda, pp. 125–154. New York: The Feminist Press.

Fukuzawa, B. 1994. "The path to adulthood according to Japanese middle schools." *Journal of Japanese Studies* 20, no. 1: 61–86.

Gandy, O. H. 1993. *The panoptic sort: A political economy of personal information.* Boulder, CO: Westview Press.

Genda, Y. 2005. *A nagging sense of job insecurity: The new reality facing Japanese youth.* Tokyo: International House of Japan.

Giddens, A. 1984. *The constitution of society.* Cambridge: Polity Press.

———. 1990. *Consequences of modernity.* Stanford, CA: Stanford University Press.

———. 1991. *Modernity and self-identity: Self and society in the late modern age.* Palo Alto, CA: Stanford University Press.

Goldstein-Gidoni, O. 2007. " 'Charisma housewives' and 'fashionable mothers': Symbols of ideological change in contemporary Japan?" Paper presented at Conference of Japan Anthropology. Tokyo, November 17–18.

———. 2012. *Housewives in Japan: An ethnography of real lives and consumerized domesticity.* New York: Palgrave Macmillan.

Goodman, J. 2009. "Performing laïcité: Gender, agency, and neoliberalism among Algerians in France." In *Ethnographies of neoliberalism,* ed. C. Greenhouse, pp. 195–306. Philadelphia: University of Pennsylvania Press.

Google Public Data 2011. http: //www.google.com/publicdata (accessed 6/12/11).

Grosz, E. 1994. *Volatile bodies: Toward a corporeal feminism.* Bloomington: Indiana University Press.

Gunewardena, N. 2007. "Disrupting subordination and negotiating belonging: Women workers in the transnational production sites of Sri Lanka." In *The gender of globalization: Women navigating cultural and economic marginalities,* ed. N. Gunewardena and A. Kingsolver, pp. 35–60. Santa Fe, NM: School for Advanced Research.

Gupta, A., and J. Ferguson. 1997. "Culture, power, place: Ethnography at the end of an era." In *Culture power place: Explorations in critical anthropology,* ed. A. Gupta and J. Ferguson, pp. 1–29. Durham, NC: Duke University Press.

Hall, S. 1996. "Introduction: Who needs identity?" In *Questions of cultural identity,* ed. S. Hall and P. duGay, pp. 1–10. Thousand Oaks, CA: Sage.

Hall, S., and T. Jefferson. 1976. *Resistance through rituals: Youth subcultures in postwar Britain.* Birmingham: University of Birmingham.

Harvey, D. 1990. *The Condition of postmodernity: An enquiry into the origins of cultural change.* Cambridge: Blackwell.

———. 2005. *A brief history of neoliberalism.* Oxford: Oxford University Press.

Hashimoto, K. 2003. *Class structure in contemporary Japan.* Melbourne: Trans-Pacific Press.

Hirota, A. 2004. "Kirishima Yooko and the age of non-marriage." *Women's Studies* 33: 399–421.

Ho, L. 2008. "Private love in public space: Love hotels and the transformation of intimacy in contemporary Japan." *Asian Studies Review* 32: 31–56.

Holland, D., W. Lachicotte Jr., D. Skinner, and C. Cain. 1998. *Identity and agency in cultural worlds.* Cambridge, MA: Harvard University Press.

Honda, Y. 2006. "Freeters: Young atypical workers in Japan." In *Perspectives on work, employment and society in Japan,* ed. P. Matanle and W. Lunsing, pp. 143–167. New York: Palgrave Macmillan.

Hook, G., and T. Hiroko. 2007. " 'Self-responsibility' and the nature of the postwar Japanese state: Risk through the looking glass." *The Journal of Japanese Studies* 33, no. 1: 93–123.

Info Please. 2011. http://www.infoplease.com/ipalAoo5061.html (accessed 6/12/11).

Ivry, T. 2007. "Competing models of becoming a person and pre-natal diagnostic technologies in contemporary Japanese society." Paper presented at Conference of Anthropology of Japan. Tokyo, November 17–18.

Iwao, S. 1993. *The Japanese woman: Traditional image and changing reality.* New York: The Free Press.

Japan Times. 2010. "Japan high in gender inequality." October 13.

———. 2012. "Editorial: Married women want to work." June 4. http://www.japantimes.co.jp/text/ed20120604a1.html (accessed 9/1/12).

Japan Today. 2012 "New safety standards for radioactive cesium in food products go into effect today." April 2. http://www.japantoday.com/category/national/view/new-safety-standards-for-radioactive-cesium-in-food-products-go-into-effect (accessed 8/31/12).

Japp, K. P., and I. Kusche. 2008. "Systems theory and risk." In *Social theories of risk and uncertainty: An introduction,* ed. J. O. Zinn, pp. 76–105. Hoboken, NJ: Wiley-Blackwell.

Jolivet, M. 1997. *Japan: The childless society?* New York: Routledge.

Kandyoti, D. 1988. Bargaining with patriarchy. *Gender and Society* 2, no. 3: 274–290.

Kato, E. 2004. *The tea ceremony and women's empowerment in modern Japan: Bodies and re-presenting the past.* New York: Routledge.

Kelly, W. 1990. "Regional Japan: The price of prosperity and the benefits of dependency." *Daedalus* 110, no. 1: 209–227.

———. 2002. "At the limits of new middle-class Japan: Beyond 'mainstream consciousness.' " In *Social contracts under stress: The middle classes of America, Europe and Japan at the turn of the century,* ed. O. Zunz, L. Schoppa, and N. Hiwatari, pp. 232–254. New York: Russell Sage Foundation.

Kelsky, K. 2002. *Women on the verge.* Durham, NC: Duke University Press.

Kinsella, S. 1995. "Cuties in Japan." In *Women, media and consumption in Japan,* ed. L. Skov and B. Moeran. New York: Curzon Press.

Kitamura, A. 2007. "Gokon: Political field where 'boy meets girl.' " Paper presented at Conference of Anthropology of Japan. Tokyo, November 17–18.

Kondo, D. 1990. *Crafting selves: Power, gender and discourses of identity in a Japanese workplace.* Chicago: University of Chicago Press.

LeBlanc, R. 1999. *Bicycle citizens: The political world of the Japanese housewife.* Berkeley: University of California Press.

Lebra, T. 1992. "Self in Japanese culture." In *Japanese sense of self,* ed. N. Rosenberger, pp. 105–120. Cambridge: Cambridge University Press.

Long, S. 2005. *Final days: Japanese culture and choice at the end of life.* Honolulu: University of Hawai'i Press.

Lovell, T. 2003. "Resisting with authority: Historical specificity, agency, and the performative self." *Theory, Culture and Society* 20, no. 1: 1–17.

Lukacs, G. 2010. *Scripted affects, branded selves: Television, subjectivity, and capitalism in 1990s Japan.* Durham, NC: Duke University Press.

Lunsing, W. 2006. "Quitting companies: Individual responses to changing employment patterns in early 2000s Japan." In *Perspectives on work, employment and society in Japan,* ed. P. Matanle and W. Lunsing, pp. 168–186. New York: Palgrave Macmillan.

Lyon, M., and J. Barbalet. 1994. "Society's body: Emotion and the 'somatization' of social theory." In *Embodiment and experience: The existential ground of culture and self,* ed. T. J. Csordas, pp. 48–66. Cambridge: Cambridge University Press.

Mahmood, S. 2001. "Feminist theory, embodiment and the docile agent: Some reflections on the Egyptian Islamic revival." *Cultural Anthropology* 16, no. 2: 202–236.

Mainichi Shimbun. 2006. "Shotgun wedding numbers skyrocket, ministry stats show." March 4.

Maree, C. 2004. "Same-sex partnerships in Japan: Bypasses and other alternatives." *Women's Studies* 33: 541–549.

Martin, L., H. Gutman, and P. Hutton, eds. 1988. *Technologies of self: Seminar with Michel Foucault*. Amherst: University of Massachusetts Press.

Mathews, G. 2003. "Can 'a real man' live for his family? *Ikigai* and masculinity in today's Japan." In *Men and masculinities in contemporary Japan: Dislocating the salaryman doxa,* ed. J. Roberson and N. Suzuki, pp. 109–125. New York: Routledge.

McCall, L. 2005. "The complexity of intersectionality." *Signs: A Journal of Women in Culture and Society* 30, no. 3: 1771–1800.

Melucci, A. 1989. *Nomads of the present: Social movements and individual needs in contemporary society*. Philadelphia: Temple University Press.

———.1996. *Challenging codes: Collective action in the information age*. Cambridge: Cambridge University Press.

Miura, A. 2005. "*Shohi monogatari no soshitsu to samayou 'jibunrashisa'*" (The loss of the narrative of consumption and roaming 'as self'). In *Datsu Aidenteitei beyond identity,* ed. C. Ueno. Tokyo: Keiso Shobo.

Miyazaki, H. 2010. "The temporality of no hope." In *Ethnographies of neoliberalism*, ed. C. Greenhouse, pp. 238–250. Philadelphia: University of Pennsylvania Press.

Mock, J. 2006. "The social impact of rural-urban shift: Some Akita examples." In *Wearing cultural styles in Japan: Concepts of tradition and modernity in Practice,* ed. C. Thompson and J. Traphagan, pp. 25–46. Albany: State University of New York Press.

Morrison, E. 2010. "Discipline and desire: Surveillance, feminism, performance." PhD diss., Brown University.

Muraki, N. 2007. "Alternatives and ambiguities: College women and the transformation of middle class citizenship in Japan's new economy." PhD diss., University of Illinois Urbana-Champaign.

Naikakucho (Cabinet Office). 2008. *Shojika Shakai Hakusho* (White Paper of Society with Fewer Children). Tokyo: Nikkei Insatsusha.

Nakano, L., and M. Wagatsuma. 2004. "Mothers and their unmarried daughters: An intimate look at generational change." In *Japan's changing generations: Are young people creating a new society?* ed. G. Mathews and B. White, pp. 137–153. New York: Routledge.

Ogawa, Akihiro. 2009. *The failure of civil society?: The third sector and the state in contemporary Japan*. Albany: SUNY Press.

Okano, Kaori. 1995. "Habitus and intraclass differentiation: Non-university-bound students in Japan." *International Journal of Qualitative Studies in Education* 8, no. 4: 357–369.

———. 2009 *Young women in Japan: Transitions to adulthood.* New York: Routledge.

Oksala, J. 2005. *Foucault on freedom.* Cambridge: Cambridge University Press.

Ortner, S. 2006. *Anthropology and social theory.* Durham, NC: Duke University Press.

Osawa, M. 2002. "Twelve million full-time housewives: The gender consequences of Japan's postwar social contract." In *Social contracts under stress: The middle classes of America, Europe and Japan at the turn of the century,* ed. O. Zunz, L. Schoppa, and N. Hiwatari. New York: Russell Sage Foundation.

Owens, C. 1992. *Beyond recognition: Representation, power, and culture.* Berkeley: University of California Press.

Padilla, M., J. Hirsch, M. Munoz-Laboy, R. Sember, and R. Parker, eds. 2007. *Love and globalization: Transformations of intimacy in the contemporary world.* Nashville, TN: Vanderbilt University Press.

Parker, L. 2005. "Resisting resistance and finding agency: Women and medicalized birth in Bali." In *The agency of women in Asia,* ed. L. Parker, pp. 98–132. Singapore: Marshall Cavendish.

Rattansi, A. 1995. " 'Western' racisms, ethnicities and identities in a 'postmodern' frame." In *Racism, modernity, and identity: On the western front,* ed. A. Rattansi and S. Westwood, pp. 15–77. Cambridge: Polity Press.

Rayn, Malin Noem. 2005. "A matter of free choice? Some structural and cultural influences on the decision to have or not to have children in Norway." In *Barren states: The population 'implosion' in Europe,* ed. C. Douglas, pp. 29–47. London: Berg Press.

Reader, I. 1991. *Religion in contemporary Japan.* Honolulu: University of Hawai'i Press.

Rebick, Marcus. 2005. *The Japanese employment system.* Oxford: Oxford University Press.

Roberts, G. 1994. *Staying on the line: Blue-collar women in contemporary Japan.* Honolulu: University of Hawai'i Press.

———. 2002. "Pinning hopes on angels: Reflections from an aging Japan's urban landscape." In *Family and social policy in Japan: Anthropological approaches,* ed. R. Goodman, pp. 54–91. Cambridge: Cambridge University Press.

Rosaldo, R. 1989. *Culture and truth: The remaking of social analysis.* Boston: Beacon Press.

Rosenberger, N. 1984. "Middle-aged Japanese women and the meaning of the menopausal transition." PhD diss., University of Michigan.

———. 1992. "Tree in summer, Tree in winter: Movement of self in Japan." In *Japanese sense of self,* ed. N. Rosenberger, pp. 67–92. Cambridge: Cambridge University Press.

———. 2001. *Gambling with virtue: Japanese women and the search for self in a changing nation.* Honolulu: University of Hawai'i Press.

———. 2006. "Young women making lives in northeast Japan." In *Wearing cultural styles in Japan: Concepts of tradition and modernity in practice,* ed. C. Thompson and J. Traphagan, pp. 76–95. Albany: SUNY Press.

———. 2007. "Rethinking emerging adulthood in Japan: Perspectives from long-term single women." *Child Development Perspectives* 1, no. 2: 92–95.

———. 2009. "Global food terror in Japan: Risk perception in media, nation and women." *Ecology of Food and Nutrition* 48: 4, July–August.

———. 2011. "Women in an alternative agro-food initiative: Japanese women in organic farming." Paper presented at Rural Sociological Association Conference. Boise, Idaho, July 27–31.

———. In press. " 'Making an ant's forehead of difference': Organic agriculture as an alternative lifestyle in Japan." In *Capturing contemporary Japan*, ed. S. Kawano, G. Roberts, and S. Long. Honolulu, HI: University of Hawai'i Press.

Rosenbluth, F. 2007. "The political economy of low fertility." In *The political economy of Japanese fertility,* ed. F. Rosenbluth, pp. 4–36. Stanford, CA: Stanford University Press.

Rudd, E., and L. Descartes. 2008. "Changing landscapes of work and family." In *The changing landscape of work and family in the American middle class,* ed. E. Rudd and L. Descartes, pp. 1–16. New York: Lexington Books.

Ryang, S. 2006. *Love in modern Japan: Its estrangement from self, sex and society.* New York: Routledge.

Sakai, J. 2004. *Makeinu no toboe* (The howl of the losing dog). Tokyo: Kodansha.

Sand, J. 2006. "The ambivalence of the new breed: Nostalgic consumerism in 1980s and 1990s Japan." In *The ambivalent consumer: Questioning consumption in east Asia and the West,* ed. S. Garon and P. Maclachlan, pp. 85–108. Ithaca, NY: Cornell University Press.

Shakai Jitsujo De-ta Zuroku (Data chart of societal actual conditions). 2005. http://www2.ttcn.ne.jjp/honkawa/1540.htm (accessed 7/13/11).

Shimodaira, Y. 2004. "*Serviceka, globalka wa risku kozo o dono you ni kaeta ka?* (How have change to service and global [economy] changed the risk structure?)." In *Risuku shakai o ikiru* (Living the risk society), ed. T. Toshiaki, pp. 21–24. Tokyo: Iwanami Shoten.

Shinnyoen. 2011. www.shinnyoen.org (accessed 7/6/11).

Shirahase, S. 2007. "Women's economic status and fertility: Japan in cross-national perspective." In *The political economy of Japanese fertility,* ed. F. Rosenbluth, pp. 37–59. Stanford, CA: Stanford University Press.

Sodei, T. 2005. "The status of women scientists in Japan: Gender mainstreaming in the science council of Japan." Paper presented at the 5th Conference of the Science Council of Asia. Hanoi, May 11–13.

Spielvogel, L. 2003. *Working out in Japan: Shaping the female body in Tokyo fitness clubs.* Durham, NC: Duke University Press.

Statistics Bureau, Ministry of International Affairs and Communications. 2010. Statistical Handbook of Japan. http://www.stat.go.jp/english/data/handbook/index.htm (accessed 6/12/11).

———. 2011. Statistical Handbook of Japan. http://www.stat.go.jp/english/data/handbook/index.htm (accessed 6/12/11).

Statistical Survey Department, Statistics Bureau, Ministry of Internal Affairs and Communications 2012. "Population 15 Years Old and Over by Age Group and Marital Status" [data file]. http:///english/data/nenkan/1431-02.htm (accessed 2/25/13).

Tachibanaki, T. 2006. "Inequality and poverty in Japan." *The Japanese Economic Review* 57, no. 1.

Takahashi, K. 2003. *Konna watashi ni kamisama ga oritekita* (God descended to a me like this). Tokyo: Kodansha.

Thorn, M. 2004. "Girls and women getting out of hand: The pleasure and politics of Japan's amateur comics community." In *Fanning the flames: Fans and consumer culture in contemporary Japan,* ed. W. Kelly, pp. 169–188. Albany: SUNY Press.

Tobin, J. 1992. "Japanese preschools and the pedagogy of selfhood." In *Japanese sense of self,* ed. N. Rosenberger, pp. 21–39. Cambridge: Cambridge University Press.

Touraine, A. 1995. *Critique of modernity.* Cambridge: Blackwell.

Traphagan, J. 2000. *Taming oblivion: Aging bodies and the fear of senility in Japan.* Albany: SUNY Press.

Traphagan, J., and C. Thompson. 2006. "The practice of tradition and modernity in contemporary Japan." In *Wearing cultural styles in Japan: Concepts of tradition and modernity in practice,* ed. C. Thompson and J. Traphagan, pp. 2–24. Albany: State University of New York.

Tsuge, A. 2000. "*Seishoku gijutsu to josei no 'shitai' no aida*" (Rethinking new reproductive technologies and woman's 'natural body'). *Shiso* (Thought; volume on Politics of biosphere: Life, body, social spheres) 908: 181–198. http://www.iwanami.co.jp/shiso/0908/shiso_e.html (accessed 9/3/12).

Ueno, C. 2005. "*Datsu aidenteitei*" (Beyond identity). In *Datsu aidenteitei no riron* (Theory of beyond identity), ed. C. Ueno. Tokyo: Keiso Shobo.

Ueno, C., and S. Nobuta. 2004. *Kekkon teikoku onna no wakaremichi* (The split path for women in the empire of marriage). Tokyo: Kodansha.

Uno, K. 1991. "Women and changes in household division of labor." In *Recreating Japanese women: 1600–1945,* ed. G. Bernstein, pp. 17–41. Berkeley: University of California Press.

Vygotsky, L. 1966 (1933). "Play and its role in the mental development of the child." *Psychology and Marxism Internet Archive.* http://www.marxists.org/archive/vygotsky/works/1933/play.htm (accessed 7/12/11).

Wagatsuma, H., and G. DeVos. 1984. *Heritage of endurance: Family patterns and delinquent formation in urban Japan.* Berkeley: University of California Press.

Weber, M. 1946. *Max Weber: Essays in sociology.* New York: Oxford University Press.

Williams, R. 1981. *The sociology of culture.* New York: Schocken Books.

Winant, H. 1995. "Racial formation and hegemony: Global and local developments." In *Racism, modernity, and identity: On the western front,* ed. A. Rattansi and S. Westwood, pp. 266–289. Cambridge: Polity Press.

Wolf, S. 1987. "Sanity and the metaphysics of responsibility." In *Responsibility, character, and the emotions: New essays in moral psychology*, ed. F. Scoeman, pp. 46–62. Cambridge: Cambridge University Press.

Yamada, M. 1999. *Parasaito shinguru no jidai* (The age of parasite singles). Tokyo: Chikuma Shinsho.

Yanagida, M. 1991. *Honto no jibun o motomete* (Searching for the real self). Tokyo: Geibunsha.

Yoda, T. 2000. "The rise and fall of maternal society: Gender, labor and capital in contemporary Japan." *The South Atlantic Quarterly* 99, no. 4: 865–902.

Yoder, R. 2004. *Youth deviance in Japan: Class reproduction of non-conformity*. Melbourne: Trans-Pacific Press.

Index

About the Author

Nancy Rosenberger, a professor of anthropology at Oregon State University, has been conducting research in Japan for more than three decades. Since doing her dissertation research at the University of Michigan on experiences and conceptions of menopause in Japan, she has written numerous articles and several books: *Gambling with Virtue: Japanese Women and Sense of Self in a Changing Nation*; an edited volume entitled *Japanese Sense of Self*; and *Seeking Food Rights: Nation, Inequality and Repression in Uzbekistan*. She is currently researching the alternative lifestyle of organic farmers in Japan as well as continuing the longitudinal study of Japanese women featured in this book.

Production Notes for ROSENBERGER | *Dilemmas of Adulthood*
Cover design by Julie Matsuo-Chun
Design and Composition by Publishers' Design and Production Services, Inc. with display and text type in Garamond Premier Pro
Printing and binding by Sheridan Books, Inc.
Printed on 55 lb. House White Hi-Bulk D37, 360 ppi.